icehotel

cuisine and adventure in Jukkasjärvi

text Lars Magnus Jansson and Lars Petterson images Erik Svensson and others
graphic design Puck Petterson recipies Åke Larsson Birgitta Ståål drinks Per Holmberg

Arena

Publishing House Arena in cooperation with
Publishing House Goda Sidor

Bokförlaget Goda Sidor
Box 6229
102 34 Stockholm
lm@lmjmedia.se

©2002 Publishing Houses Arena and Goda Sidor
(Lars Magnus Jansson, Lars Petterson, Puck Petterson)
Images Erik Svensson, locationpix@earthlink.net
Other photographs: see the index on page 229
Design: Puck Petterson
Production: Goda Sidor
Printed by: Fälth & Hässler, Värnamo 2002

ISBN 91-7843-181-6

We would like to extend our thanks to the staff of Icehotel for all their help and enthusiasm during the production of this book, especially Cecilia Mörck for her foresight.

contents

Icehotel	12
The Ice Church	40
Ice	48
The sculptures	56
The theater	70
The Midnight Sun	78
The wilderness	80
Lapland	104
Iron ore	122
Research	128
The Northern Lights	132
The cuisine	138
Drinks	194
Portraits	208
The staff	212
Export	216
Index	220

map

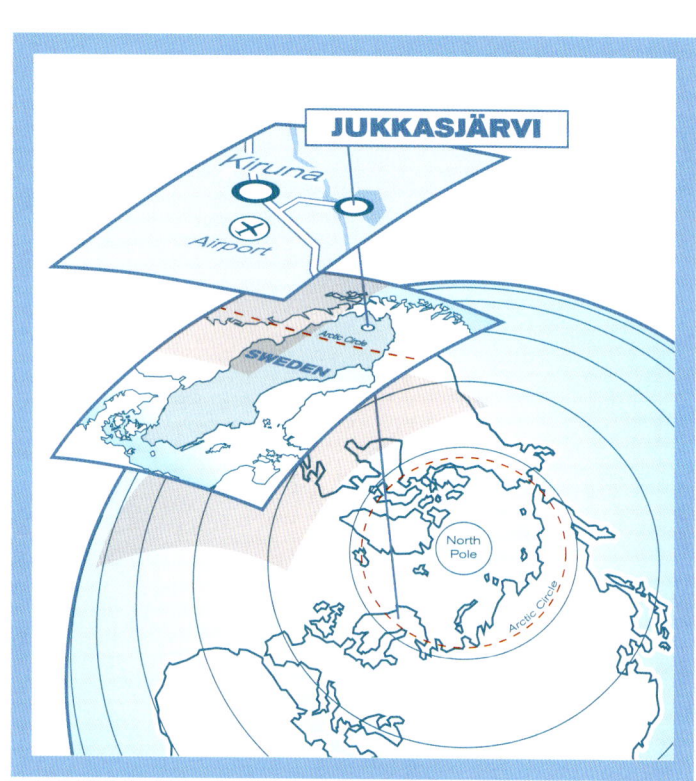

preface

Welcome to Icehotel

Does this book really need a preface?
Of course it does!
Then who's going to write it?
Yngve Bergqvist, obviously! After all, Icehotel is his brainchild.
What makes a good preface?
It should be short, so that the reader can get on with the book.
Yngve, your turn!
"Seize the day and make the most of every moment.
Live up to that motto and you'll discover that, even if we don't live for ever, almost anything is possible."
Yngve Bergqvist

Yngve Bergqvist

Yngve Bergqvist has been awarded a number of prestigious prizes for his exceptional creation. The picture shows him receiving the Royal Medal of the Eighth Grade from His majesty the King of Sweden for "... meritorious efforts as the founder and head of Icehotel in Jukkasjärvi".

ICEHOTEL

You can hear the silence

Behind the Reindeer-clad door of Icehotel, the atmosphere is nothing less than sacred. The thick outer walls, made from hard-packed snow, and the crystal-clear interior carved from perfect blue ice taken from the frozen waters of the Torne River, instill a feeling of almost audible silence.
It is spiritual.
We are in the Village of Jukkasjärvi, some 200 kilometers north of the Polar Circle. Day-trippers, wrapped up warm to keep out the biting cold, pass through the long corridors that crisscross the hotel. They look, curiously, into some of the 60 rooms and suites.
In the Absolut Ice Bar — housed in a 10 meter high, 14 meter wide dome located right at the heart of the hotel — visitors from some far-away land sip colorful drinks.
The temperature inside is a chilly -8° celsius, but it feels much warmer. Outside the thick walls, it is far, far colder — a biting -30 degrees. The contrast is dramatic in an environment where people who wear glasses find themselves constantly wiping them free of condensation.
One guest visiting Icehotel for the first time declared that it was the "... Eighth Wonder of the World!" This may have been a spontaneous, and rather enthusiastic exaggeration, but it was far from an understatement as, for most visitors to this place, Icehotel in Jukkasjärvi is an experience they will carry with them for the rest of their lives.
The world's largest igloo has a penchant for etching itself into people's memories. Like something rare and treasured.

ICEHOTEL

Let's build the world's largest igloo!
It was in February 1991 that Yngve Bergqvist, Swedish visionary and talented entrepreneur, began to realize an idea that he'd been nurturing for years.
Ever since the middle of the 1970's, Yngve had been organizing fishing and boating trips along the mighty Torne River. He'd also offered trekking, snow scooter and reindeer safaris for adventurous travelers.
But Yngve wanted more. He wanted to create a building made entirely out of snow and ice – an enormous igloo that would serve as a meeting place where people could build bridges between cultures, ideologies and local history. Where the unique landscape, and its contrasting climate, would leave an indelible mark.
When a group of Japanese artists visited Jukkasjärvi in 1989, they left behind them works of art, made from ice, that were featured in a celebrated exhibition. The following year, the French artist, Jannot Derid, decided to display some of his paintings in a cylinder-shaped igloo that was called the ARTic Hall which prompted visitors to ask if it was possible to sleep over in the 60 square meter large gallery.
And with that, the idea that was to become Icehotel was born.

The ARTic Hall may long since have melted into mere memory, but it was the starting point for what has grown into Icehotel which today covers a total area of some 4,500 square meters – that's more than 75 times larger than the original building. No less that 30,000 cubic meters of snow are used each year to build its walls, and 3,000 tons of ice are cut, transported and shaped to form pillars, interior walls, fittings and decoration.
The methods used to build the hotel, refined and developed by concrete molder, Kauko Notström, are unique. At the end of October each year, powerful snow cannon and snow blowers are used to cover metal moulds with perfectly tempered snow flakes. After that, the whole structure is left in the pre-winter cold and the flakes quickly freeze to form the solid outer walls and the roof. Once the building has stabilized, the moulds are removed, and what remains is a set of integral tunnels hidden under a snowy shroud.
From here, the challenging task of creating the hotel is handed over to a team if workers, skilled in construction methods using ice, who have gathered at this place from all over the world. Artists too are brought in to begin the painstaking process of decorating the hotel's interior.
1x2 meter large crystal clear ice blocks are taken from the cold storage warehouse, where they have been kept throughout the summer after being carved from the frozen river the previous March when the ice is at its thickest.
Using sharp tools and a careful touch, walls, pillars, beds, chairs, tables, chandeliers and a myriad of other interior fittings and fixtures are carved from the cold, blue ice.

ICEHOTEL

At the heart of the hotel lies the enormous ice dome which houses the Absolut Icebar. The dome is supported by an iron framework – the only place in the entire building where construction materials other than snow and ice are used. At 14 meters wide and 10 meters high, the dome is an impressive structure. During the summer, its metal framework is the only visible sign that it ever existed at all.

The patented technology used to build the hotel was developed by Kauko Notström, an expert in poured concrete construction. Originally, the outer walls of the hotel were made from natural snow. However, as the building grew, it became too costly to gather and transport the vast amount needed to make its walls. Today, huge snow cannon and snow blowers are used instead to produce massive piles of a special kind of artificial snow called "snis". Large construction vehicles are used to transport the snis to the building site while snow canon are used to spray snis directly onto the moulds which are part of the secret of Icehotel's structure.

Tunnel-like, they are placed in a carefully measured pattern which forms the basis of that year's hotel. Once the walls are set, the moulds are carefully removed from the finished building leaving large open spaces, work progresses, and the hotel grows in size by the day.

ICEHOTEL

The word Igloo originates from the Inuit iglu and means snow dwelling.
The Inuit have lived in the Arctic and sub-Arctic regions, which stretch from the north-west corner of Asia, all the way over the North American continent, for generations. Most Inuit now prefer to be called Eskimos. Igloos are a winter dwelling that have long since been used by Canadian Eskimos who live in the region between the Mackenzie River and the Labrador Peninsular They are also used by Eskimos who live in the Polar region of north-western Greenland.
The Igloo is a domed structure made from blocks of fine-grained snow that has been packed solid by the winds. The entrance is made up of a half-cylindrical tunnel, approximately three meters long.
Igloos are usually heated by lamps which slowly burn aromatic seal oil.

Icehotel has a number of suites, each one carrying the hallmark of a specific artist. Sculptors from all over the world are invited to Jukkasjärvi each year, where they are given the framework from which they create individual suites based on their own unique ideas. The skill and creativity of these artists guarantees that no two Ice Hotels are the same.

ICEHOTEL

One of the artists who was invited to decorate a suite at the hotel wanted to honor rock legend, Frank Zappa. The result was a rock n' roll inspired living space featuring Zappa's guitar made entirely from ice and snow, with excerpts from his work carved into the walls. There is even an ice mural of Zappa himself sitting on a toilet. The picture shows the creation of this suite. But has this rock icon ever stayed here? The question remains unanswered, for at Icehotel, discretion is paramount.

Icehotel began as an art gallery, and ever since, art has played an important part in creating the atmosphere that lies within. Icehotel's Ice Gallery is home to the works of many artists throughout the winter season.

ICEHOTEL

Pillars, inner walls, interior details and fittings are all carved from blocks of ice that have been sawn from the frozen waters of the Torne River. Sculptors from all over the world are invited to create the hotel's suites. Each year, many young adventurers are attracted to Jukkasjärvi to take part in the construction of Icehotel.

During the six-month long winter season, some 50,000 people visit this place to experience its unique ambience until finally, the warm rays of the spring sun begin to relentlessly melt the hotel, returning the ice it is made from as water back into the flowing river.

Guests sleep on reindeer-skin covered ice beds, kept warm by polar sleeping bags. Many people who stay here say they have never had such a good night's sleep in their lives.
Carol and Emilie from Washington, DC were skeptical before they spent their first night at the hotel staying in its classic Viking Suite. But come morning, they awoke happily surprised at how peaceful their night's sleep had been.

The Viking Suite is one of the most popular in the hotel and is, therefore, incorporated in various guises into its design year after year.

Some of the suites are equipped with "real!" beds. One of these is Suite One, where there is also a complete dining room set and open fire.

ICEHOTEL

30,000 cubic meters of snow are used each your to build the hotel's walls and ceilings. 3,000 tons of ice is used to create supporting structures, inner walls, sculptures and interior design details. With the arrival of spring in May, the snow and ice can no longer hold out against the warming rays of the sun, and slowly melt running back into the Torne River.

But when October turns into November, the time has come to begin construction of a new Ice Hotel. Day-by-day, week-after-week, the building takes shape. Outside, its contours look basically the same each year, but under the hard-packed, frozen snow walls there is constant change and renewal. And as the hotel grows, the nights get longer and the sun barely rises above the horizon. But the darkness doesn't stop the building process, and working days are long. Very long indeed.

Snow cannons and snow blowers create perfectly tempered snow flakes that are spread over metal moulds. After a few days, the snow crystals have frozen into solid walls and ceilings, and the moulds are removed leaving tunnels which form the inner framework in which the new hotel will take shape.

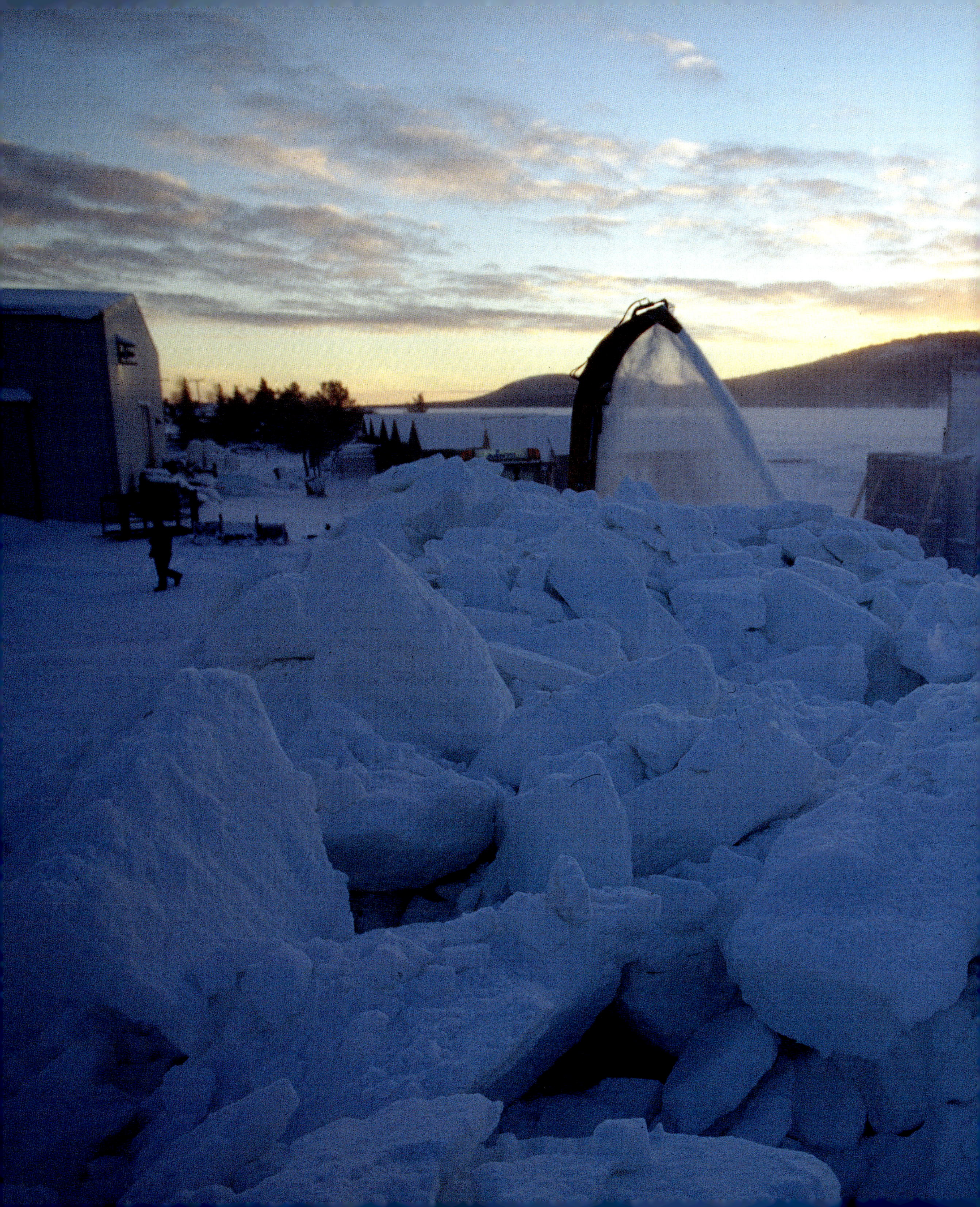

the ice church

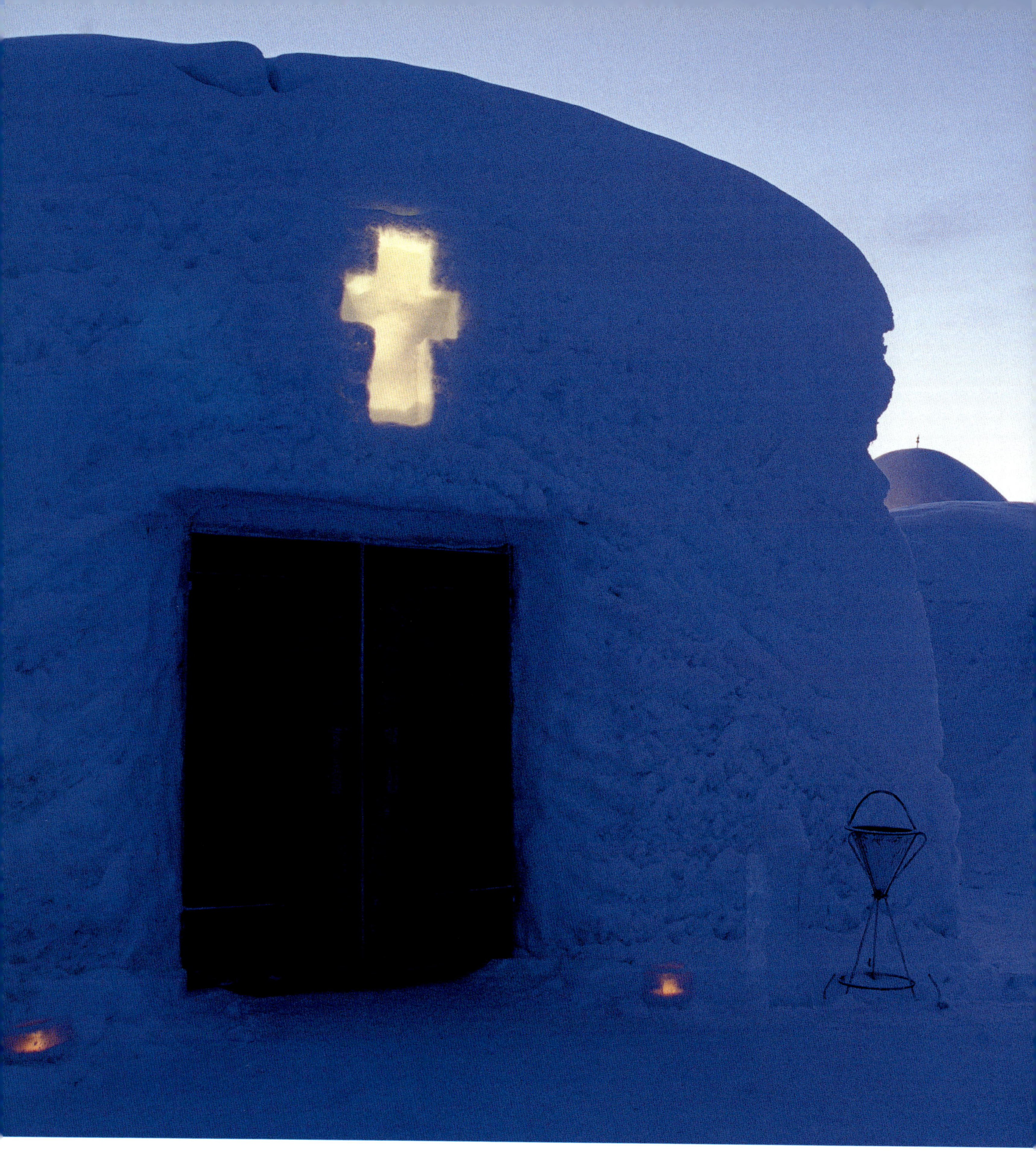

THE ICE CHURCH

A divine
conception
filled with
reverence and
communion

The very first service was held in the Jukkasjärvi Ice Church, which is built from ice and snow each winter on a plot of land adjacent to Icehotel, on March 28, 1992. And each year since then, the Ice Church has evolved until it now melts perfectly into its surroundings.
In all its frozen glory, this unique, religious monument attracts many curious visitors – parents christen their children here, and thousands of couples choose to marry before the church's frozen alter.

The Ice Church has everything that you'd normally associate with a house of God. There is an altar, a cross, a christening font, candle holders, a pulpit and church benches. The only difference is that here, they are all made from solid ice.
Its unique outer structure, peculiar acoustics, the unexpected temperature and fascinating shifts in light and color, make every visit to the Ice Church an experience filled with reverence and communion.

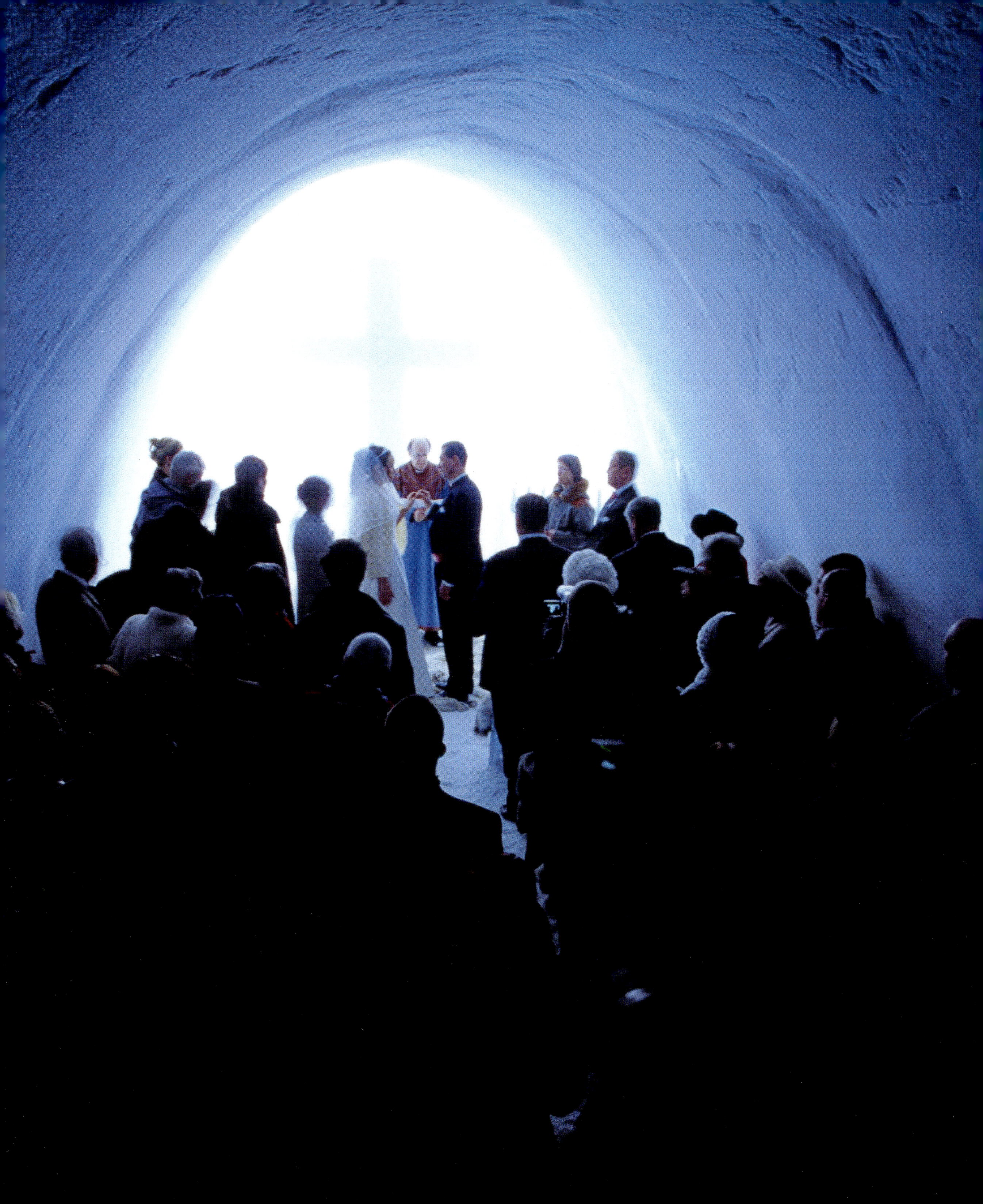

THE ICE CHURCH

When they first created the Ice Church, Arne Bergh and Åke Larsson, were inspired by the works of Bror Hjort. Hjort's original altar still resides in the wooden church in Jukkasjärvi.
Bror Hjort (1894-1964) was one of Sweden's most influential artists. With his unique style, his works are intimately bound with traditional, Swedish art.
On the altar at Jukkasjärvi's old wooden church, a relief made entirely from carved teak, reflects the drama and religious conviction that Preacher, Lars Levi Laestadius instilled in his parishioners. Laestadius was active here during the first half of the last century, and his religious movement still wealds a strong influence on churchgoers throughout northern Sweden.

The previous two-page spread shows an ice sculpture which depicts a Troll Drum. The original carving can be found in Jukkasjärvi's wooden church and was created by the Sámi artist, Lars Levi Sunna.

Icehotel **47**

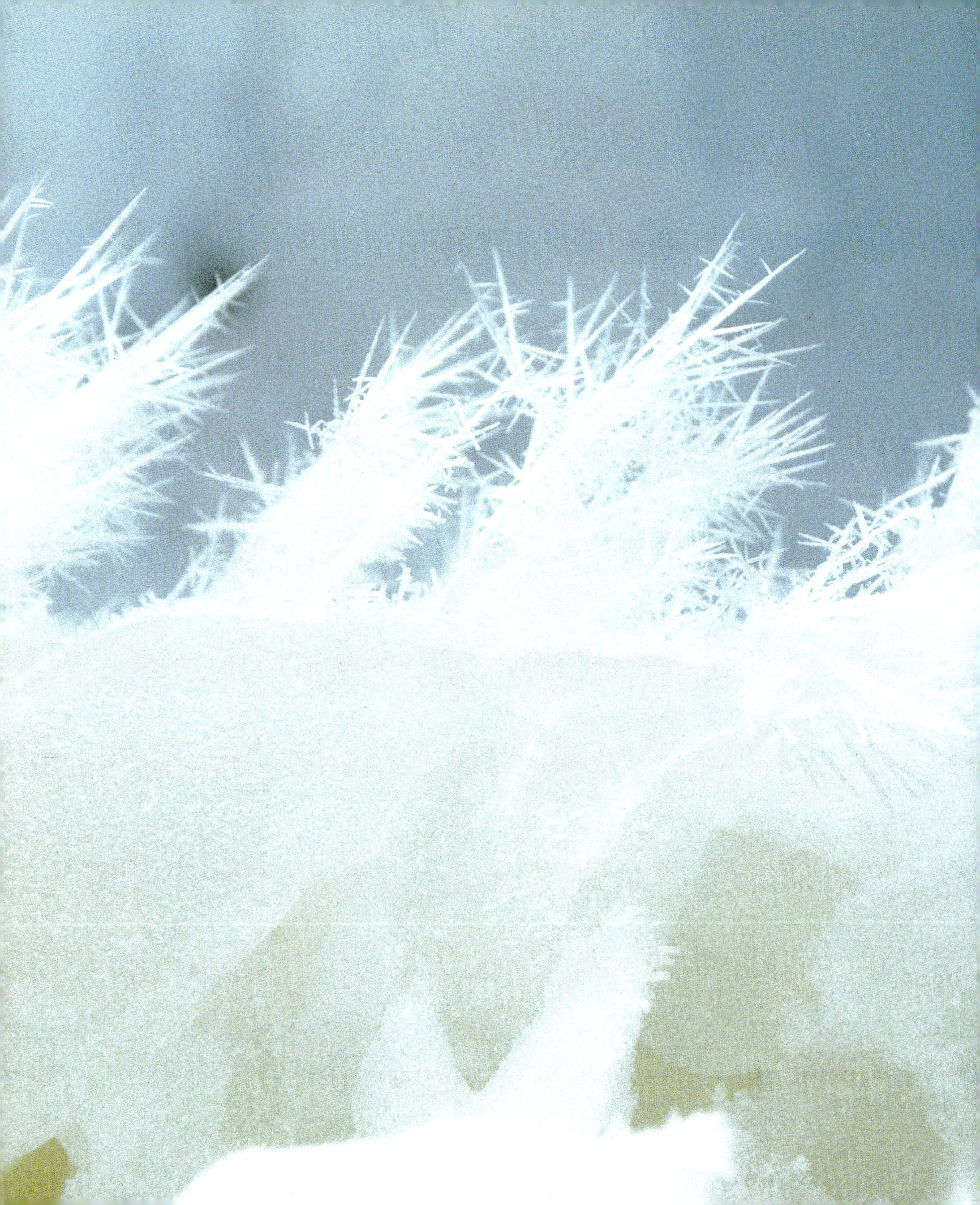

ICE

An encumbrance and a resource

The Torne River flows all the way from Torne Marshes, which lie in northern Lapland, to the south east, eventually running out into The Gulf of Bothnia through the town of Haparanda. The 510 kilometer long river is one of the few in the region that is not used to generate hydro electricity – a fact which also means that it is one of just a handful of completely untouched major rivers outside the tropics.

It is from this virgin source that the building materials that are used to construct Icehotel come. The river's clean flowing water produces ice that is crystal clear, and quite unique.
Ice begins to form here between October and November, growing down into the water with each passing day until, with the advent of spring in March or April, it can be up to 70 centimeters thick. To make the ice even thicker, workers keep part of the frozen river free from snow allowing the cold to make the ice crust to grow still further.
Once the ice has formed a layer about a meter thick, hydraulic chainsaws are used to carve out the blocks that will be used to form the hotel. Blocks that are 1 x 2 meters in size. These are stored in a large ice warehouse which is located on the bank of the Torne River until it is time to begin building the next Icehotel.

Ice can create problems for some. But in Lapland, it is a resource to be treasured. It forms roads over water, and eases passage for those who live in the bitter winter climate that is common here north of the Polar Circle. A material of contrasts, it is unique and can provide comfort and protection against the harshness of winter.
It is a natural, seemingly inexhaustible resource which, for more than a decade, has provided the building blocks for Icehotel, and provided the raw material for some very skilled and creative sculptors.
But by the end of April, the ice meets its match. The warmth of the spring sun begins relentlessly eating into its heart, its rays dissolving the solid form before returning it, once more as water back into the Torne River.

Without a trace of sentimentality, Icehotel once again recommits its soul to nature. And next year's hotel is already on the drawing board.

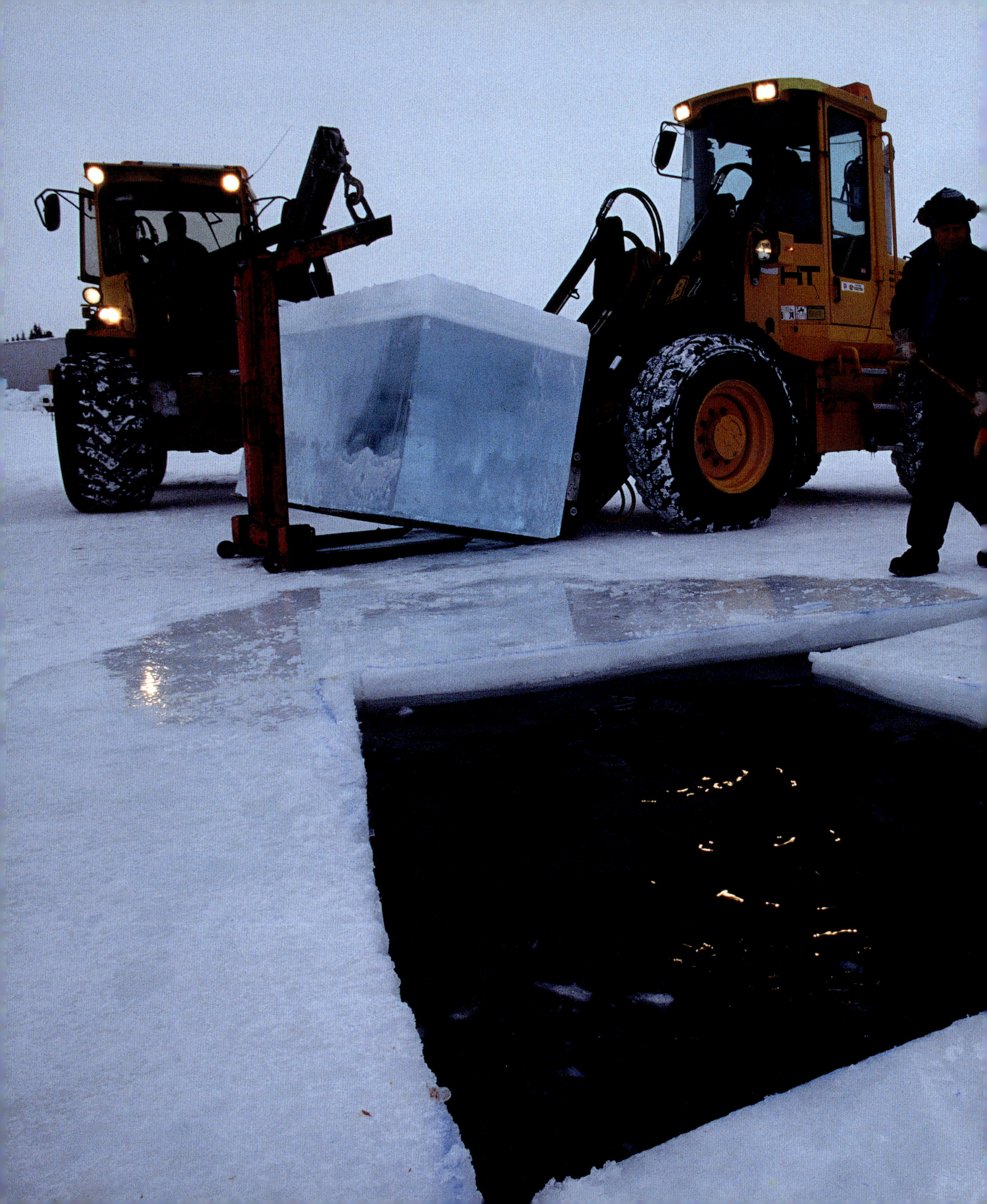
HT

ICE

Ice is a solid form of water. It is created when water, or its vapor, freezes to form a truly unique material.

There are eleven ice structures, and the only known stable form is that which is created by nature. Pure ice is transparent, and in thicker layers – such as that which occurs in the Torne River – it is truncated by a blue tone that is best seen when it is illuminated.

Ice that forms naturally often contains air bubbles which cloud its transparency. But this is something which does not occur in the ice formed from the waters of the Torne River.
In ice, water molecules take on a random pattern and disorganized structure which has fascinated scientists ever since the beginning of the 18th century. And many questions still remain. Questions about the nature of ice.
At the Norrbotten University, there is now a specific course – Arctic Engineering – which focuses on structures made from snow and ice, where researchers are using modern methods to look for the answers.

Icehotel **51**

ICE

Ice that is carved from the frozen waters of the Torne River is unique. The cold, constantly moving water, with its limited flow, means that no air bubbles are formed in the 1x2 meter blocks. This makes for crystal clear ice, completely devoid of cracks and fissures.
The freezing process takes time to complete – it is a slow and steady process – and with the almost constant darkness, no sunlight is able to dissolve the bonds which form between individual ice crystals. Unlike artificially produced ice, the ice from the Torne River is full of life and easy to work.

Using hydraulic chainsaws, the 1x2 meter large blocks of ice are cut from the frozen waters of the Torne River during March and April each year.

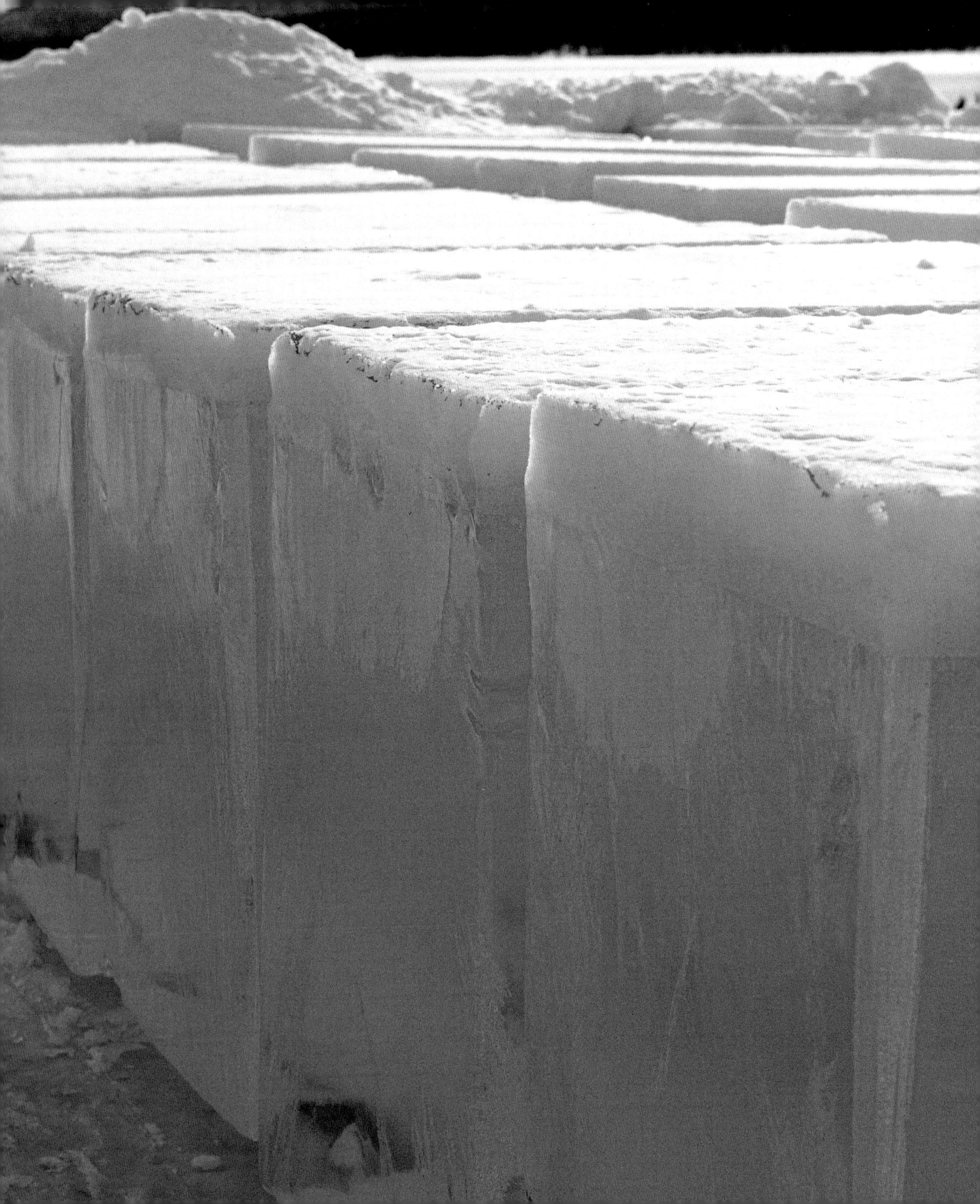

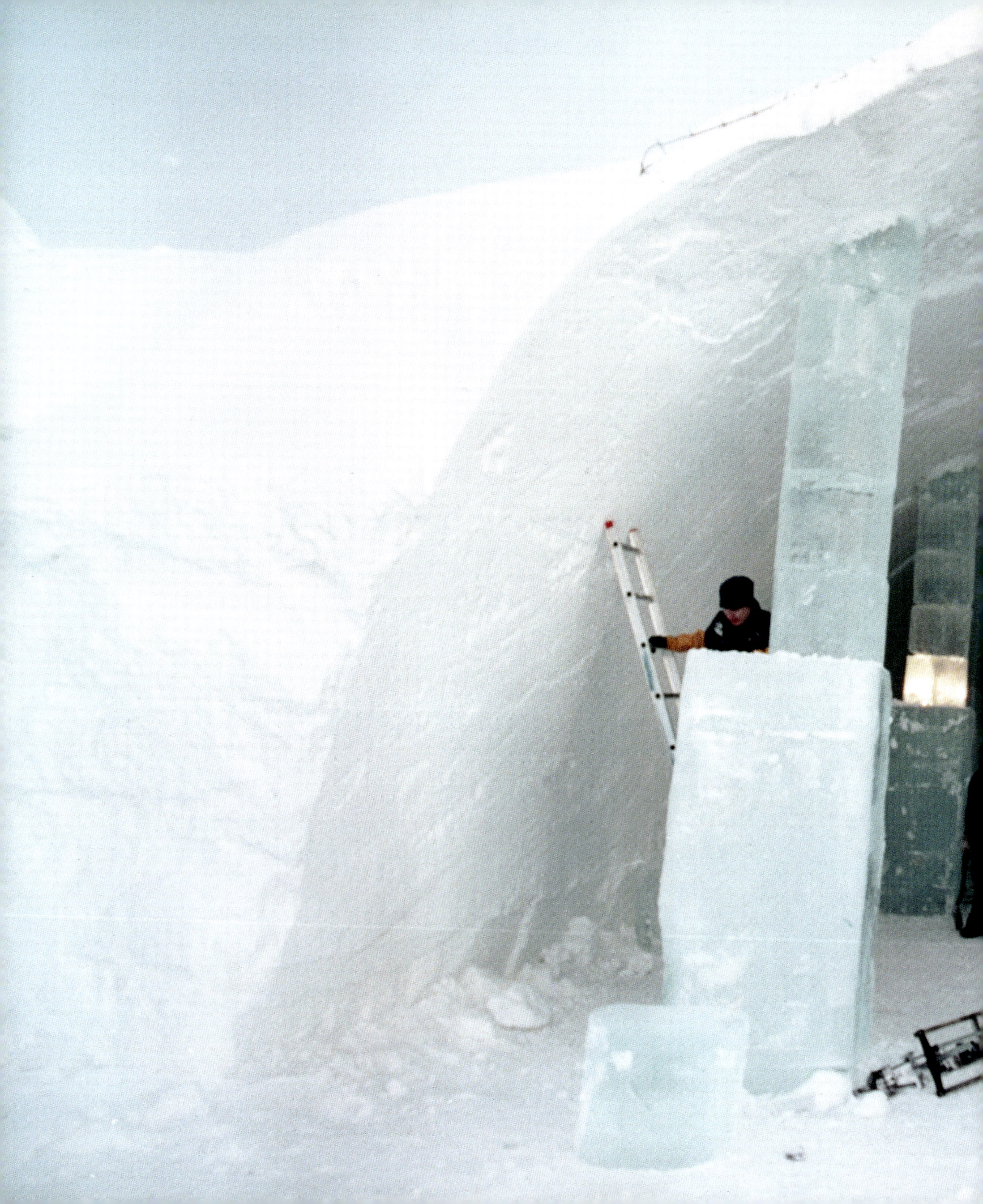

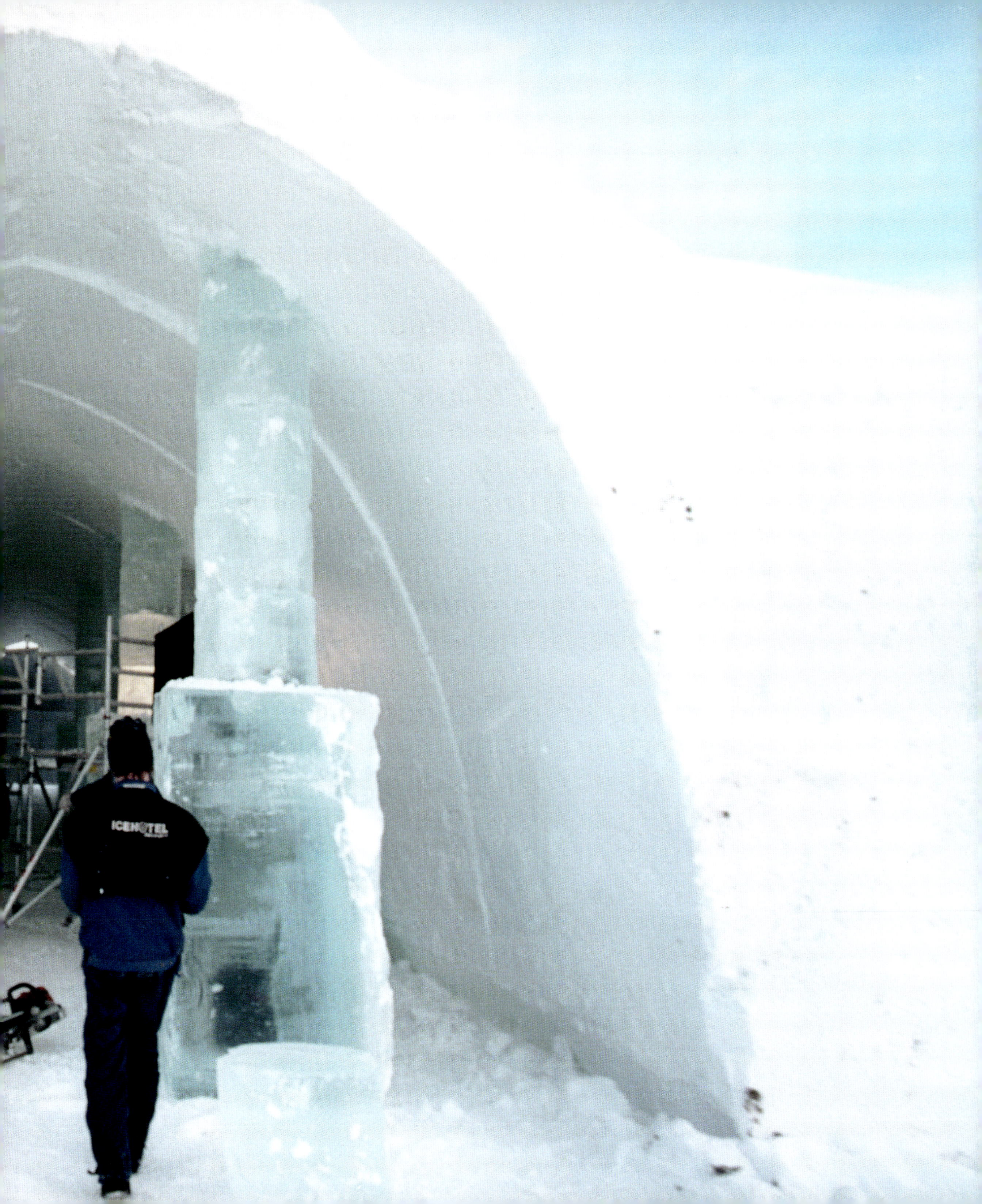
ICEHOTEL

sculptures

Throughout the ages, man has erected images of his Gods. Sculptures, works of art in granite, monuments often associated with power. The sculptor impresses, dominates and celebrates something eternal. A splendid work of art which reminds all who look upon it the reason why it was created.

Here, ice sculptures expose conflicting truths: they are ephemeral. Alive in the present – here and now. Then they are gone, melting irrevocably back into an eternal cycle. An ice sculpture belongs to that which is eternal for as long as we remember its shape and expression. Then it is gone. Perishability in a finely developed form.

SCULPTURES

The ice cried out for cold...

There is no doubt about the beauty of the material. Clear, smooth surfaces, seemingly hard, and highly polished. Immovably proud, the light fills the core of the blocks, mirroring the spectrum with a glorious sparkle. Ice has an unharnessed attitude.
In reality, ice should be completely impossible to use as a material for artists and sculptors. But reality has, as it so often does, decided to play one of its own peculiar tricks.
Ice is malleable – but only on its own terms, and sculptors from all over the world will bear witness to the fact that it can be successfully turned from a creative challenge into a product of beauty which bears an artistically high value. Two established sculptors who have worked on projects in ice at Icehotel give voice to this in unwavering agreement.

This is what Isa, a Japanese sculptor has to say:
"Uncertainty, indeed fear best describes the feeling I had when I, for the first time, allowed my hands run across the surface of an untreated ice block. The soft chill and smooth surface was instantly transformed by the heat from my hand, creating a thin layer of water. It was almost a sensual experience,".
Jean, a European designer who specializes in creating in concrete agrees:
"I normally work with granite and concrete. My methods have been developed to shape and form that kind of material with their special structures and hardness. When I first came to Jukkasjärvi, I'd seen pictures of ice sculptures, but had intentionally avoided looking at one in real life out of some kind of fear, or maybe respect.
"On my arrival, I went up to an ice block – it was perhaps a cubic meter of pure, perfectly smooth ice. I was convinced that it would be crushed when I placed my chisel against its smooth surface and struck the first blow with my mallet.

"But I was mistaken! I carved, and the ice formed itself under my tools. I was sculpting!"
And finally, Åke Larsson. Åke is an ice artist and responsible for construction of Icehotel:
"When the ice is transparent, there is something magical about the material. Ice demands unconventional solutions which make working with it that more exciting. In fact, it is an irresistible challenge."

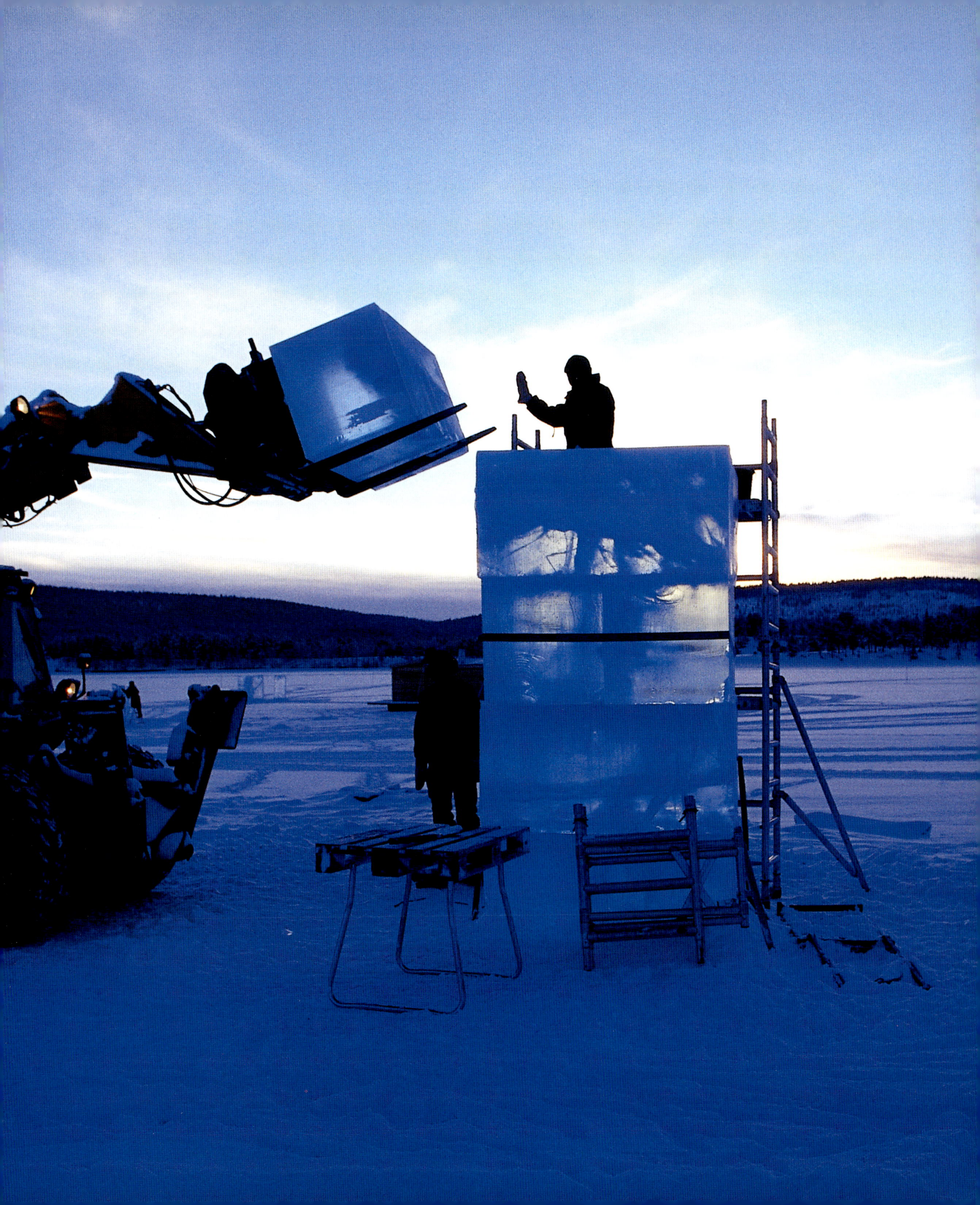

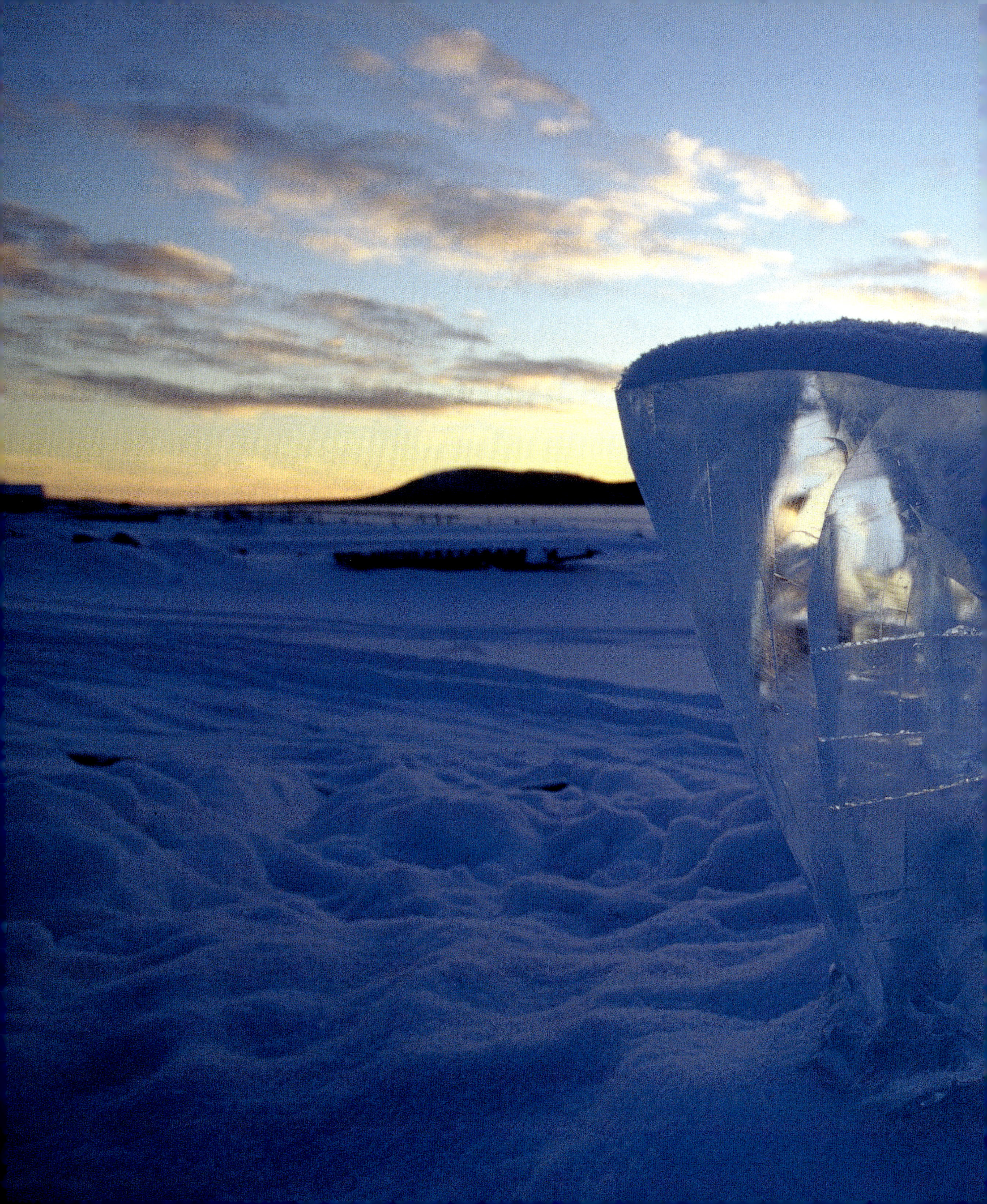

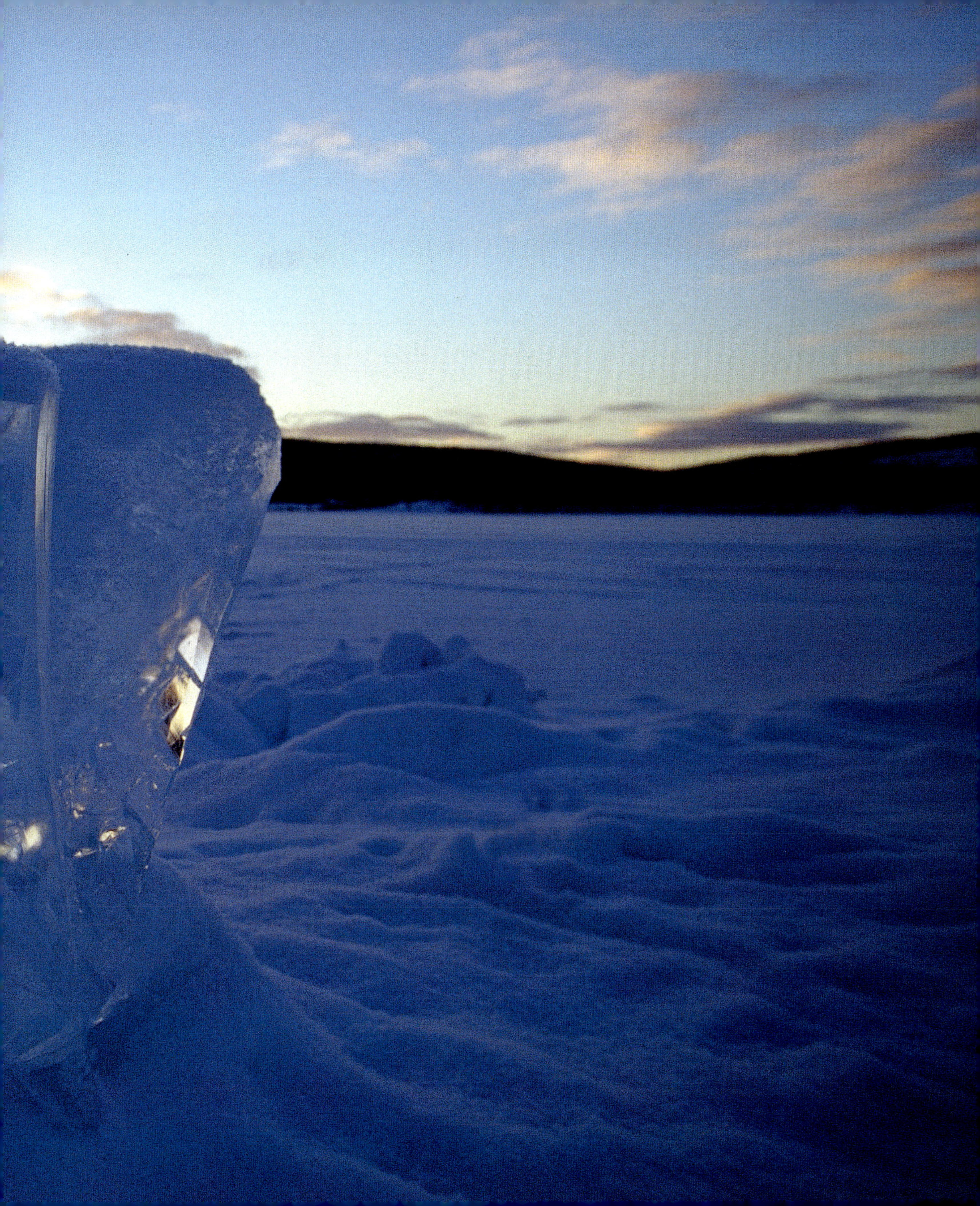

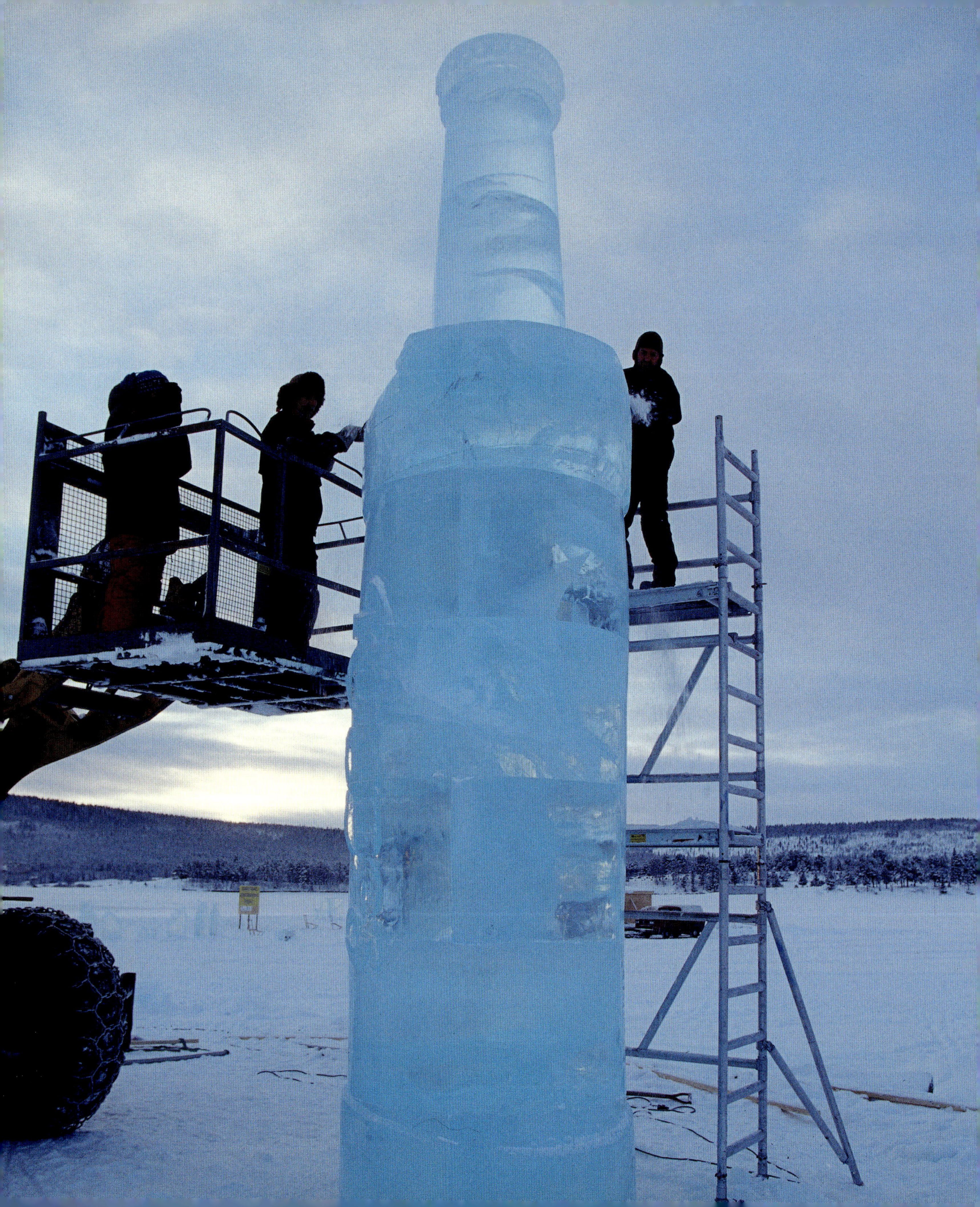

The order sheet read: "The world's largest beer bottle made from ice." The customer was a Norwegian brewery which was poised to launch a new brand of beer in the market and was looking to mark the occasion with some headline-catching PR. Not unsurprisingly, the company turned to Icehotel in Jukkasjärvi and, under the watchful eye and careful hand of Arne Bergh, its artistic leader, 1x2 meter ice blocks were stacked, one on top of the other, out on the frozen surface of the Torne river. The foundations of the gigantic bottle were laid.

Using a chain saw and ice chisels, frozen blocks of water were shaped and rounded into the bottle that the customer had ordered.

"Nothing is impossible when you work with ice," says Arne Bergh from his perch high up on the scaffolding. "The only thing that limits you is your own imagination. And what cannot be made by hand can always be created on a computer which controls advanced cutting equipment. But there is nothing like human creativity."

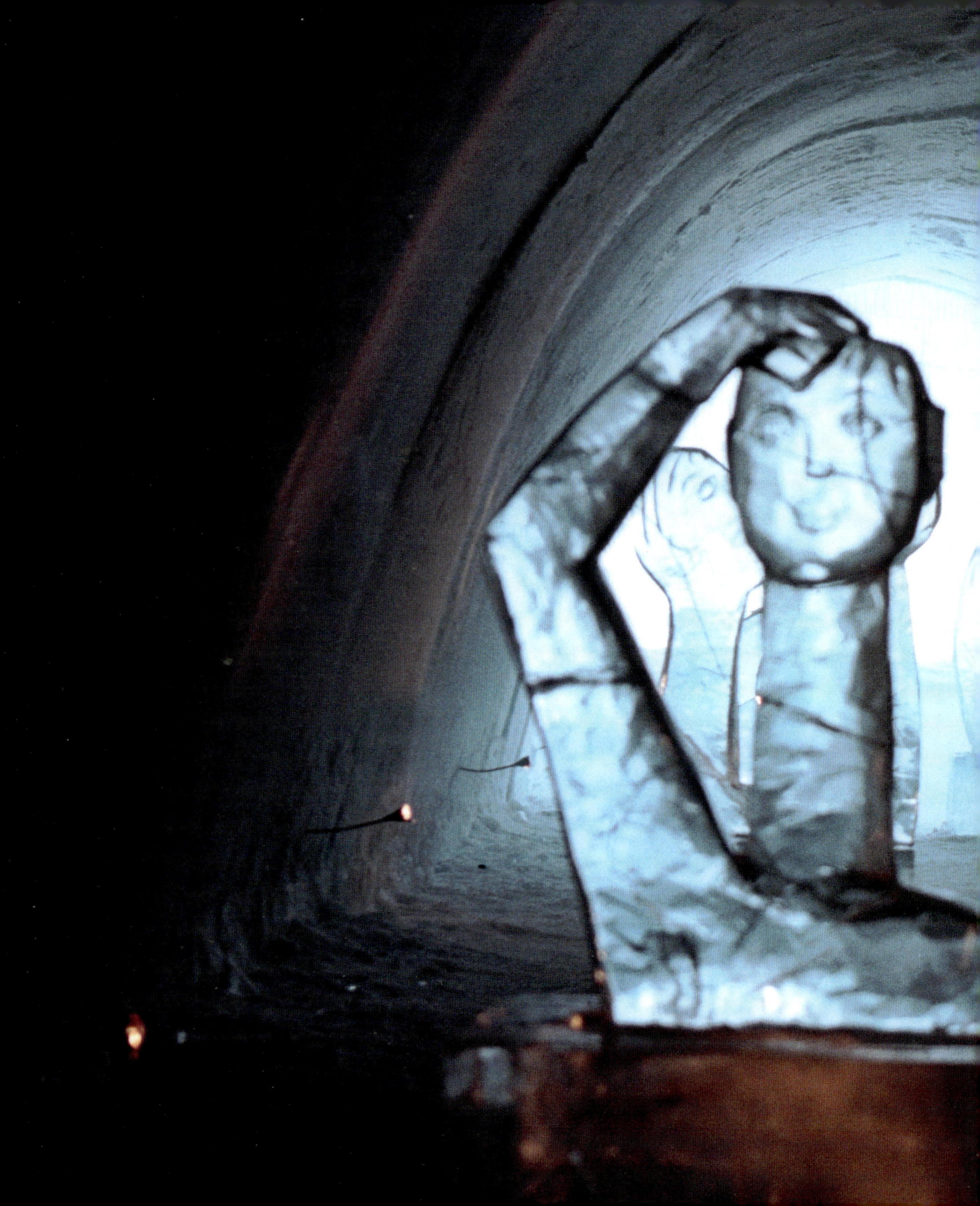

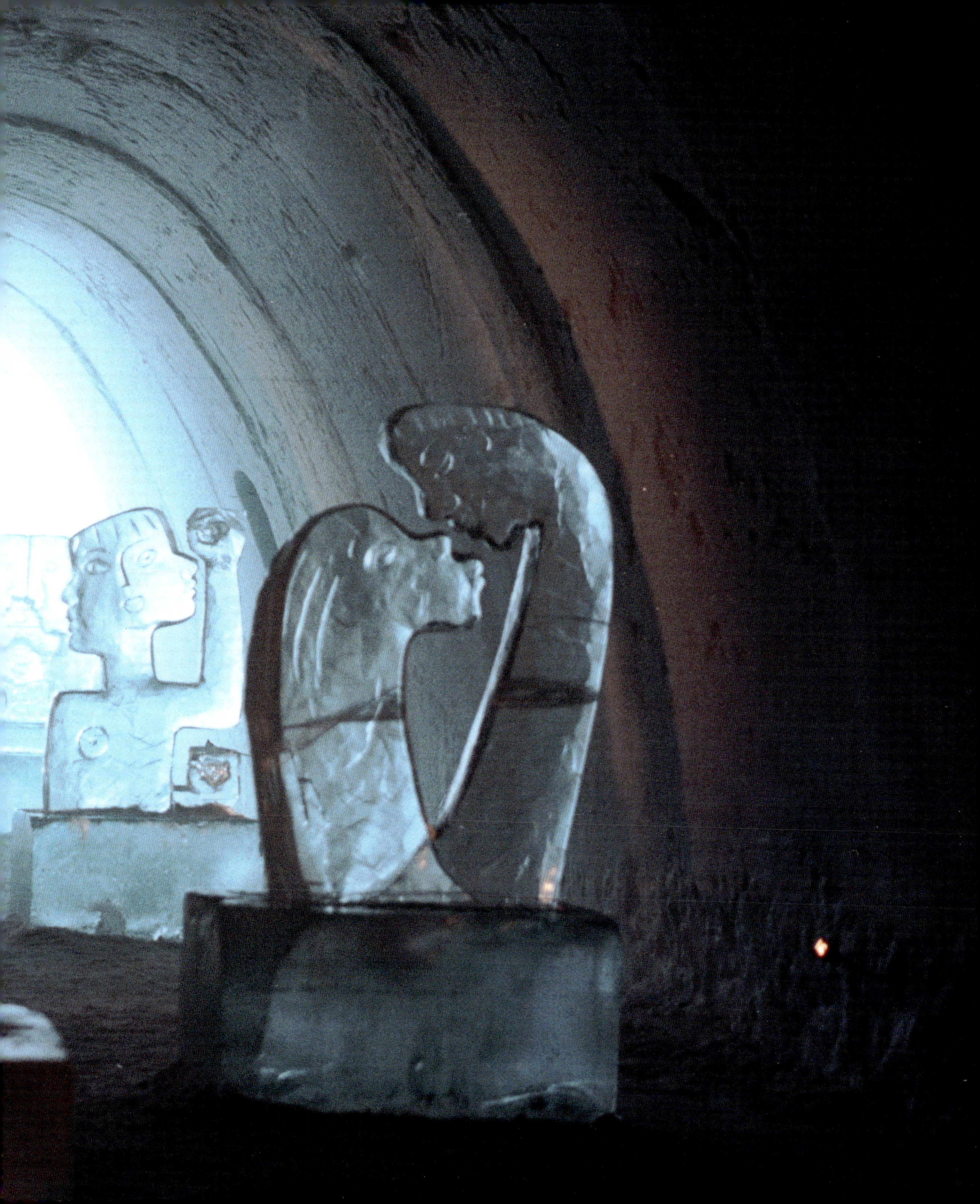

THE SCULPTURES

Artist and ice architect, Åke Larsson's visions for Icehotel have no boundaries. As there is basically no research into how buildings should be made out of snow and ice, there is, therefore, no literature from which to seek information – a luxury which other builders enjoy.
Each idea has to be thoroughly tested before it can be applied in practice. Despite the fact that responsibility for construction take up most of Åke Larsson's working day, he still finds time to sculpt and, each year, is artistically responsible for one of Icehotel's most exclusive suites.

One of the most striking suites in the hotel is built upon the theme, Kalevala, the hero's tale that has become something of a Finnish national epos. Kalevala was first composed around 1830 as a collection of popular songs and dates from various eras, not least from the middle ages.

68 Icehotel

Kalevala

the theatre

THE THEATRE

From concept to success

The Ice Globe Theatre is nothing less than a creative adventure, and a unique source of inspiration. And this is its journey from concept to success.

One day in November, 2001, Rolf Degerlund was speaking at a conference about the Swedish experience industry. Mr Degerlund is an experienced, professional actor with a career that includes some 13 years as the head of the Norrbotten Theatre in Luleå.

Now it wasn't the main body of his speech that had an impact, it was his closing remark that was significant: "I have a dream," he said. "I aim to be the world's first manager of an ice theatre."

As it turned out, he was speaking at the right forum for in the audience sat none other than the man who originally conceived Icehotel, Yngve Bergqvist.

Two weeks later, they met in Jukkasjärvi.

Rolf speaks of The Globe Theatre in London, of his dream and his concept: A copy of The Globe. In ice. In Jukkasjärvi. With Shakespeare's Hamlet performed on stage in the language of the Laps – Sámi.

"Ok," agrees Yngve. "When do you want the theatre completed?"

A project team was assigned, and work progressed at full speed in a cooperation with the Norwegian National Sámi Theatre, the Beaivvas Sámi Teater in Kautokeino.

Plans for an icy copy of The Globe Theatre as it might have looked during William Shakespeare's time were drawn up and building work commenced.

The first theater stood ready in January, 2002. A unique, beautiful creation made from ice, with a large stage and room for an audience of 500.

On January 23 that same year, the Sámi version of Hamlet had its world premier. The following day, another first takes place at the theatre. This time it's a production called Jasat – the Sámi word for snow flakes. Jasat is a jojk (like yodeling) and dance perform-

The Ice Globe Theatre is the result a dream that Rolf Degerlund once had. Through shear tenacity, Rolf became the world's first ice theatre manager in an undertaking that is no less than a creative adventure.

Icehotel 73

THE THEATRE

ICE GLOBE THEATRE

ance which is played out under the flickering Northern Lights, and is a co-production between the Beaivvas Sámi Theater and the Swedish Sámi Theater in Kiruna. During the spring, Hamlet is performed 30 times. Jasat is staged a total of 34 times. Twice a week, the Ice Globe Theatre is also used as an arts stage for productions which have been specially written for the venue by invited performers.

On April 6, when The Ice Globe Theatre had melted, and the frozen water that made up its structure returned once more to the Torne River, a total of 74 performances had been played on its unique stage.

But it doesn't stop there. Ultimately, the plan is to develop the Ice Globe Theatre into a large, internationally renowned stage where dance, theatre, fashion, cinema, music, variety and ice dance performances will be held on a stage where art cross-germinates to create an experience that mesmerizes performers and audiences alike.

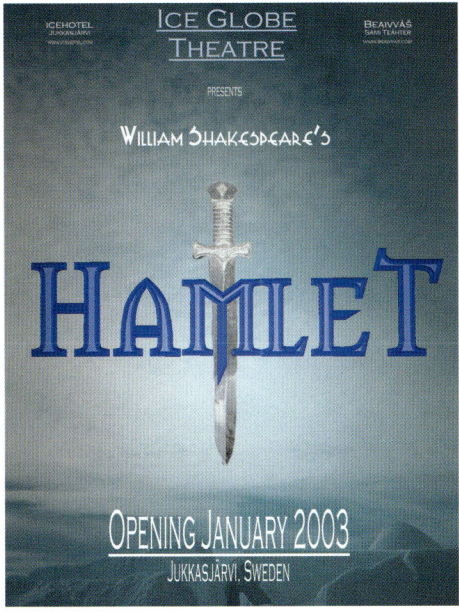

In its heyday between 1599 and 1644, The Globe Theatre was London's largest renaissance stage and it was here that many of Shakespeare's plays were performed. A new Globe Theatre, reconstructed on the very same site as the original, was officially opened in 1996.
William Shakespeare (1564-1616), has been said by many to be the world's foremost dramatist, and is part of the Globe Theatre's heritage as an actor, writer and cicerone. Hamlet was (probably) written and performed for the first time in 1601. Shakespeare in ice was created by Mats Indsted.

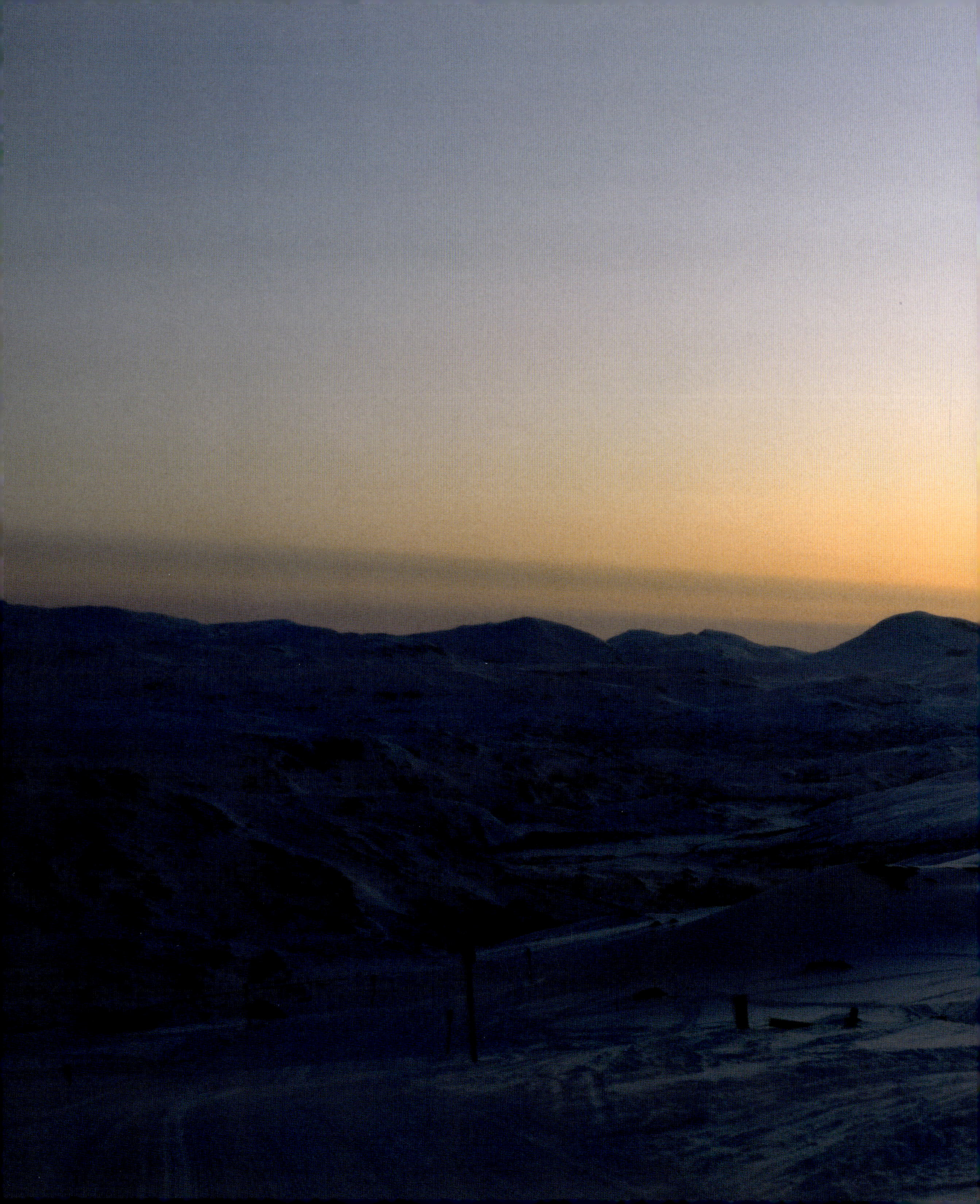

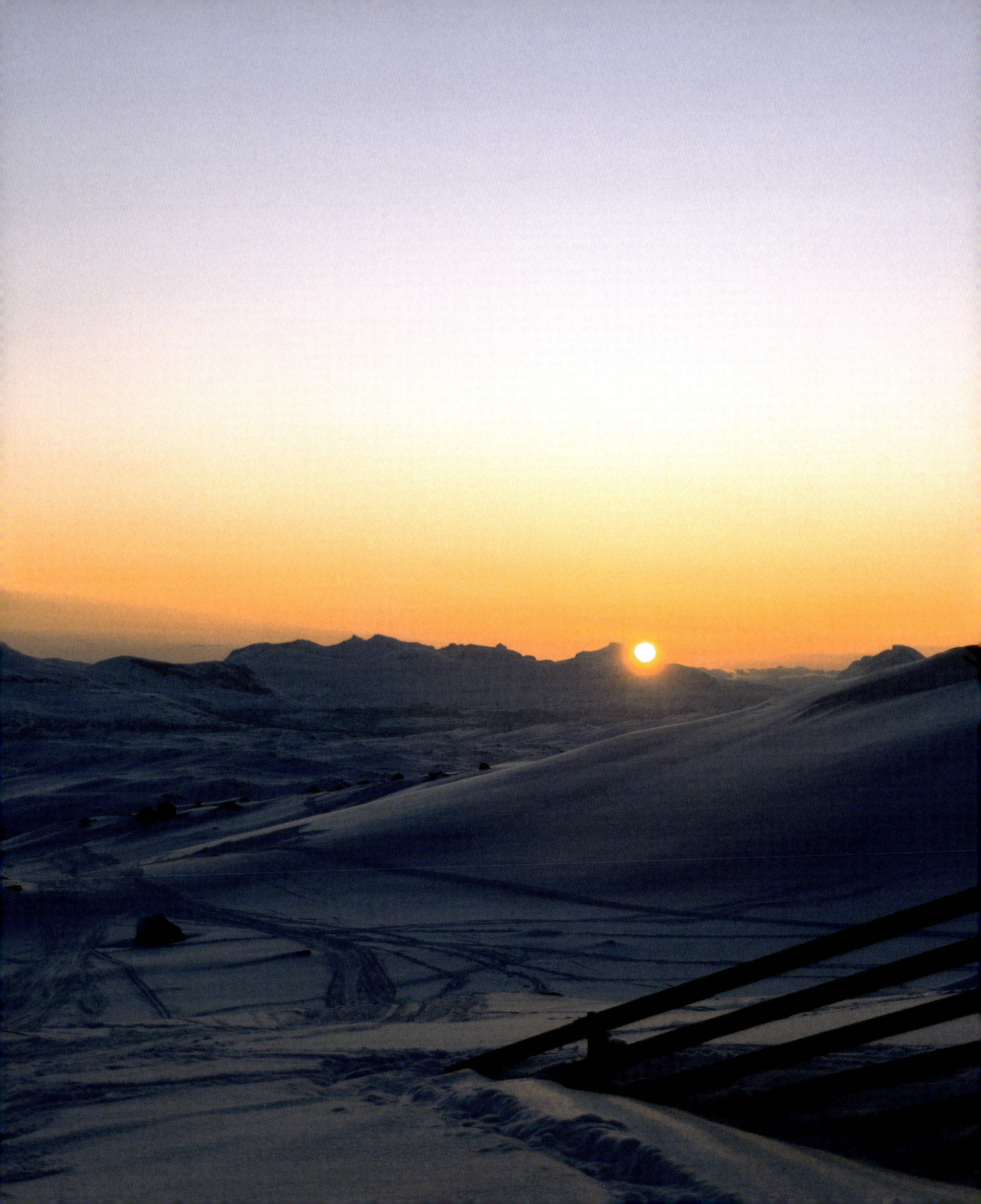

THE MIDNIGHT SUN

A bewitching light

Midnight sun is a term used in places where the sun never dips below the horizon in summer. This is true of the region above the Polar Circle. The north and south Polar Circles define theoretical boundaries (latitude ±66.6°) where you can, at least some time during the year, experience the midnight sun. The closer to the poles you get, the longer the period of midnight sun. At the Poles themselves, the midnight sun lasts for six months at a time.

"The midnight sun never sets..."
When American singer-songwriter, Quincy Jones, first put those famous words to music some 30 years ago, rumor of the exotic north had already spread far and wide. A sun that never set. A constant light. A strange, bewitching ambience.

In fact, long before Jones and his harmonious description of the Nordic summer nights ever hit the record stores, the eternal light had attracted many far-away travelers to the region. In the 50's and 60's, what came to be known as the "Dollar train" rumbled relentlessly through Sweden. A large mural of the midnight sun painted on the locomotive bore witness to where its passengers were headed. American tourists who arrived on luxury liners at the Port of Gothenburg sought to experience the sun that never set. North of the Polar Circle was where the light could be found. And it was here they were headed.

But in this region of contrasts, it's hardly surprising that the midnight sun is nowhere to be found during what is the high season for Icehotel. Instead, it is replaced by cold darkness, for during the winter months, daylight here lasts for just a few hours at a time.
The short days are a strange mixture of dawn and dusk. Indeed, during part of January, the sun never even makes it up above the horizon.

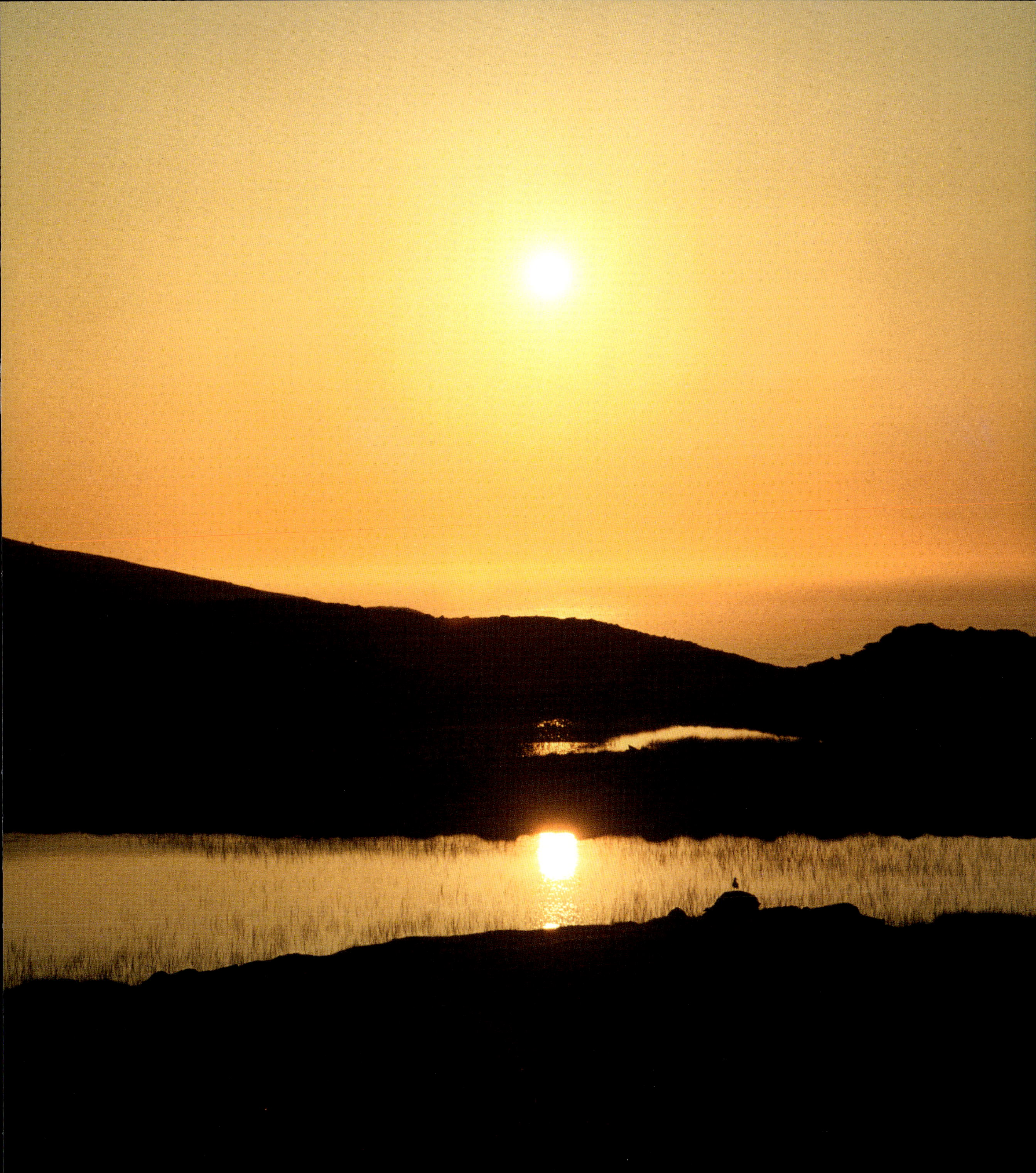

the wilderness

THE WILDERNESS

A sensitive balance

Icehotel lies beside the Torne River in the small village of Jukkasjärvi some 200 kilometers north of the Polar circle. Jukkasjärvi is part of the district of Kiruna which was once the world's largest town covering an area about half the size of Belgium.

Kiruna is Sámi for Grouse, and it is here that Lapland is undergoing its most dramatic transformation.
The region was originally populated by people who traveled up the Torne River from the south attracted by the wilds of the forests and the abundance of fish in its pristine waters. In 1631, Jukkasjärvi officially received its first settlers.
Icehotel lies in one of Europe's last true wilderness. Surrounded by forests, fells and water, it is a magnificent environment in which to experience adventure, and live at one with nature. It's also the perfect place for a moment's humble reflection over the sensitive, creative interaction that can occur between man and a reality so wild that it will never be tamed.
Jukkasjärvi, with its little more than one thousand inhabitants, has much thanks to Icehotel, become a place of pilgrimage for tourists. More than 50,000 people from all corners of the world visit this place each year looking to experience a few days of unrivaled adventure.
Most arrive by air at Kiruna Airport, and some of these travel the last few kilometers by dog-drawn sleds to their final destination, Jukkasjärvi.

Many of Icehotel's visitors choose to discover the land up here on reindeer or snow scooter safaris led by young Sámi. Others take husky-drawn sleds which carry guests along the banks of the Torne River, over the mosses and through the forests.
In winter, a classic, wood-fired sauna waits for visitors out on the frozen surface of the Torne River where they can cool off in the icy waters below entering through a hole cut through the ice.
The beautiful Ice Church provides those who wish with the opportunity to sooth their souls.

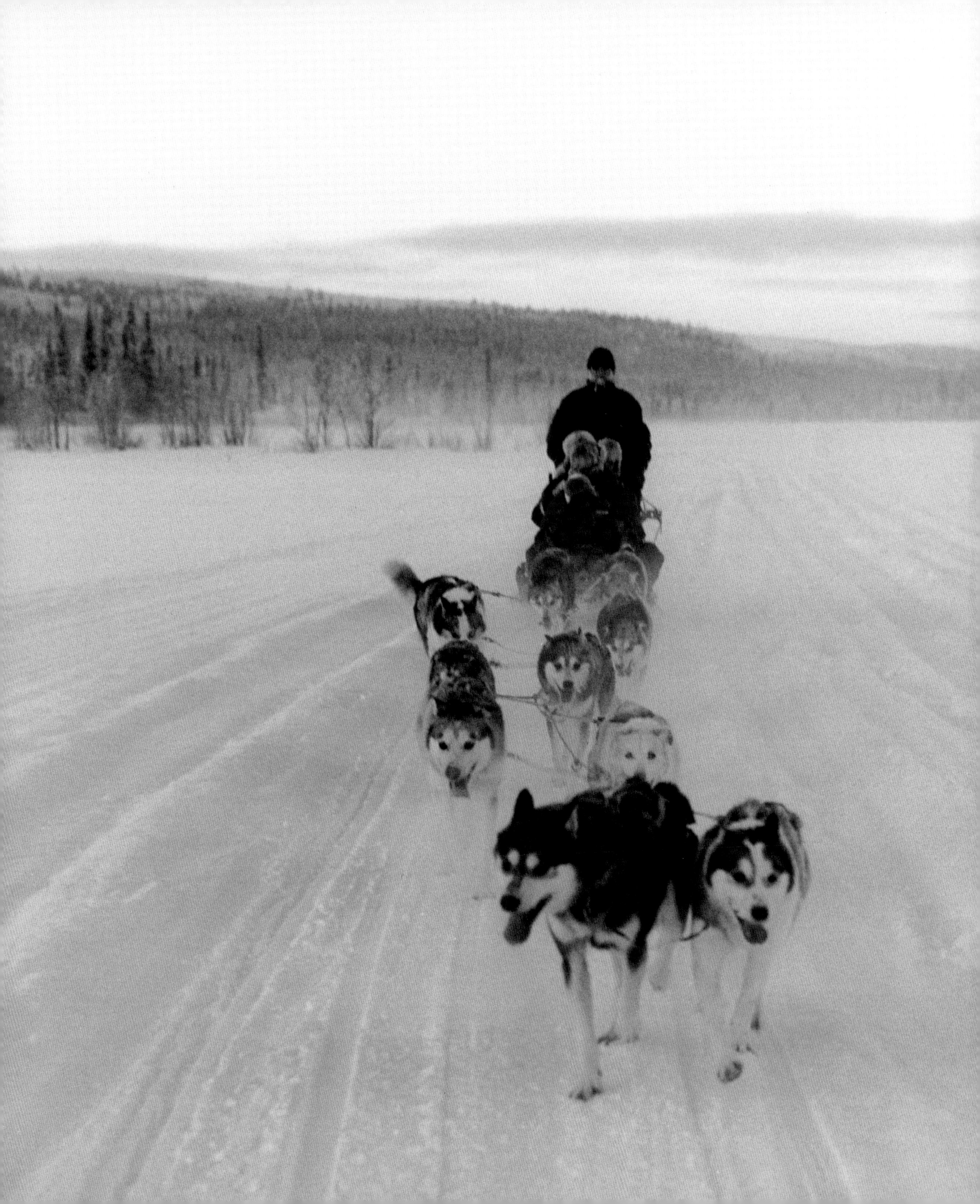

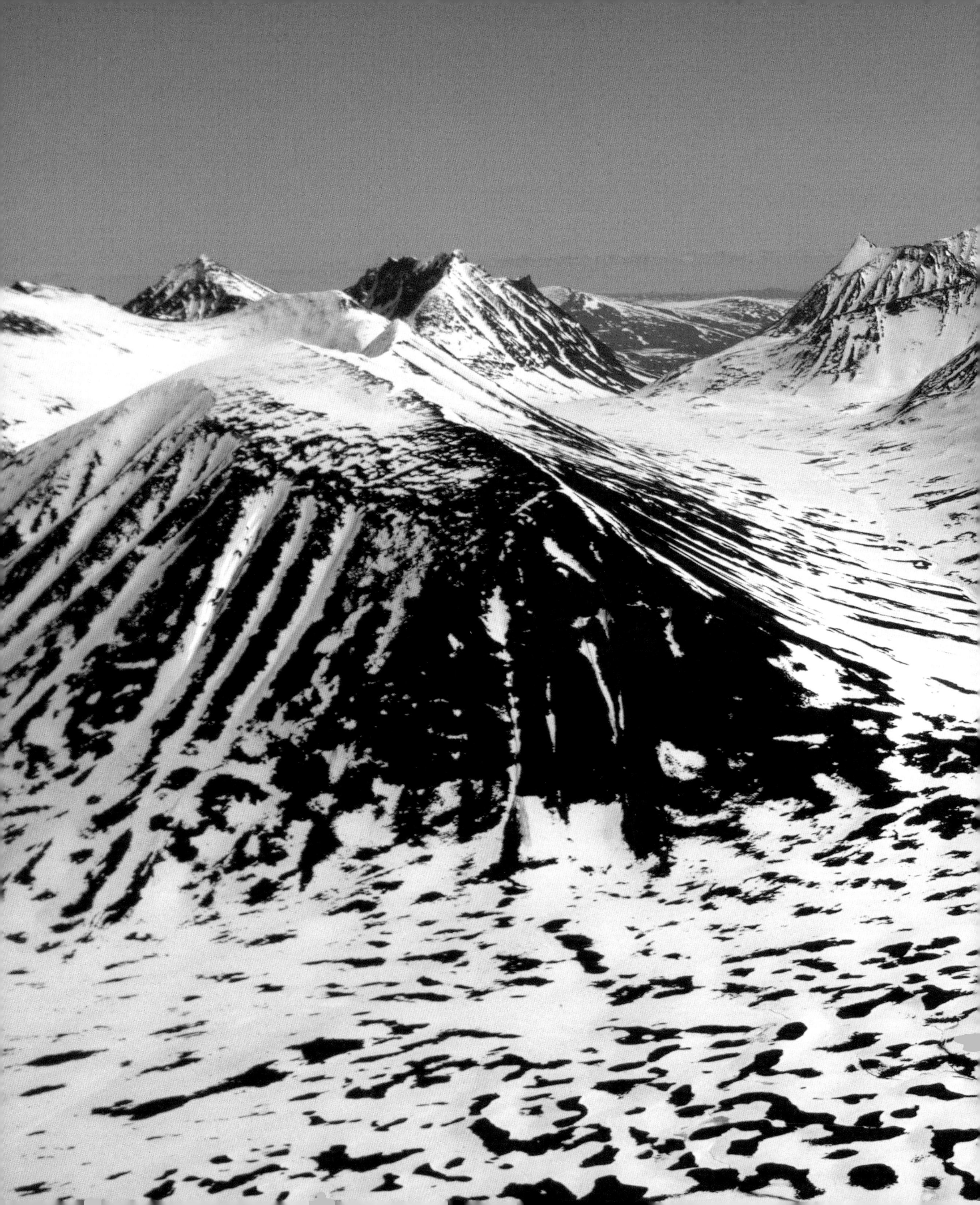

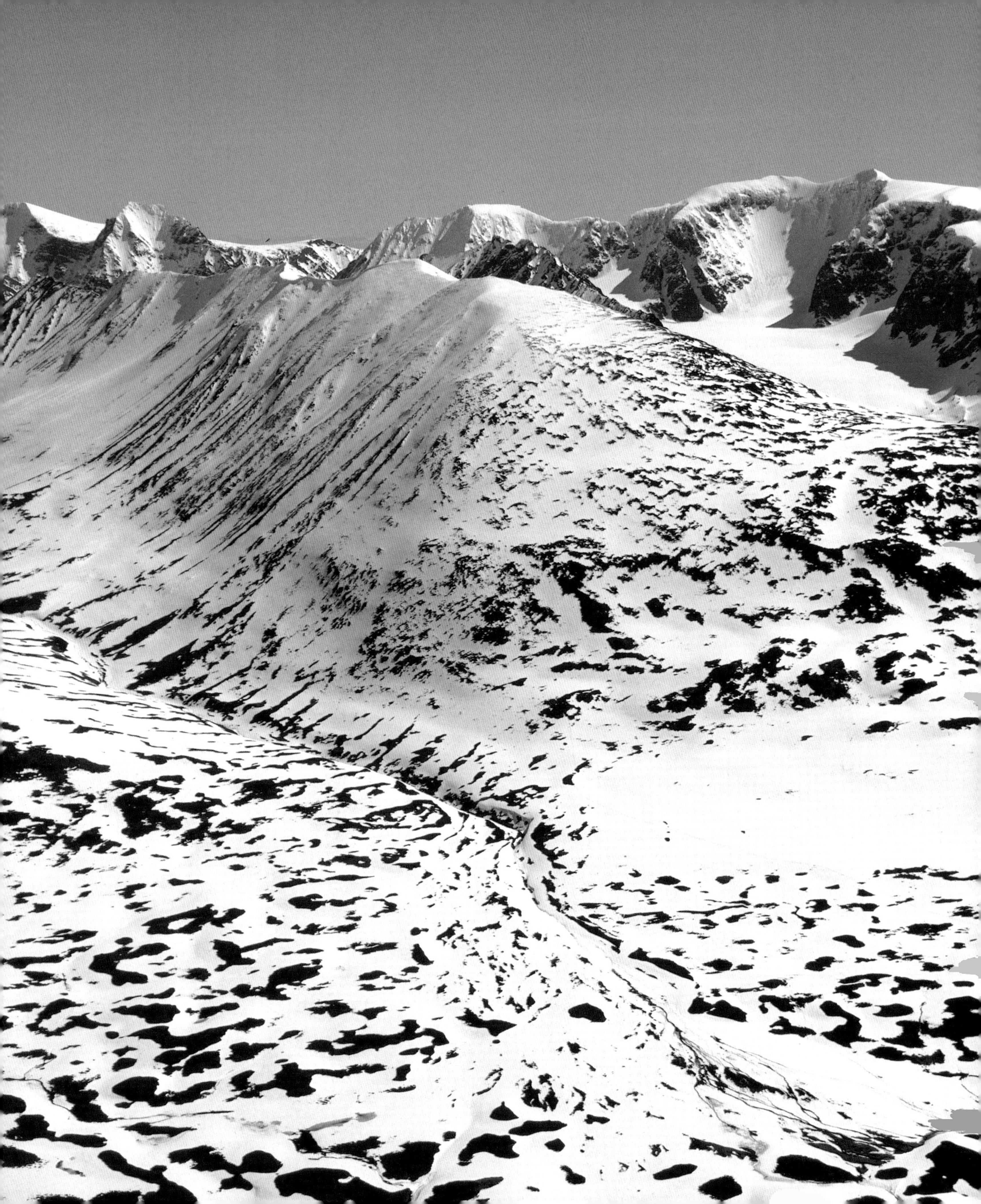

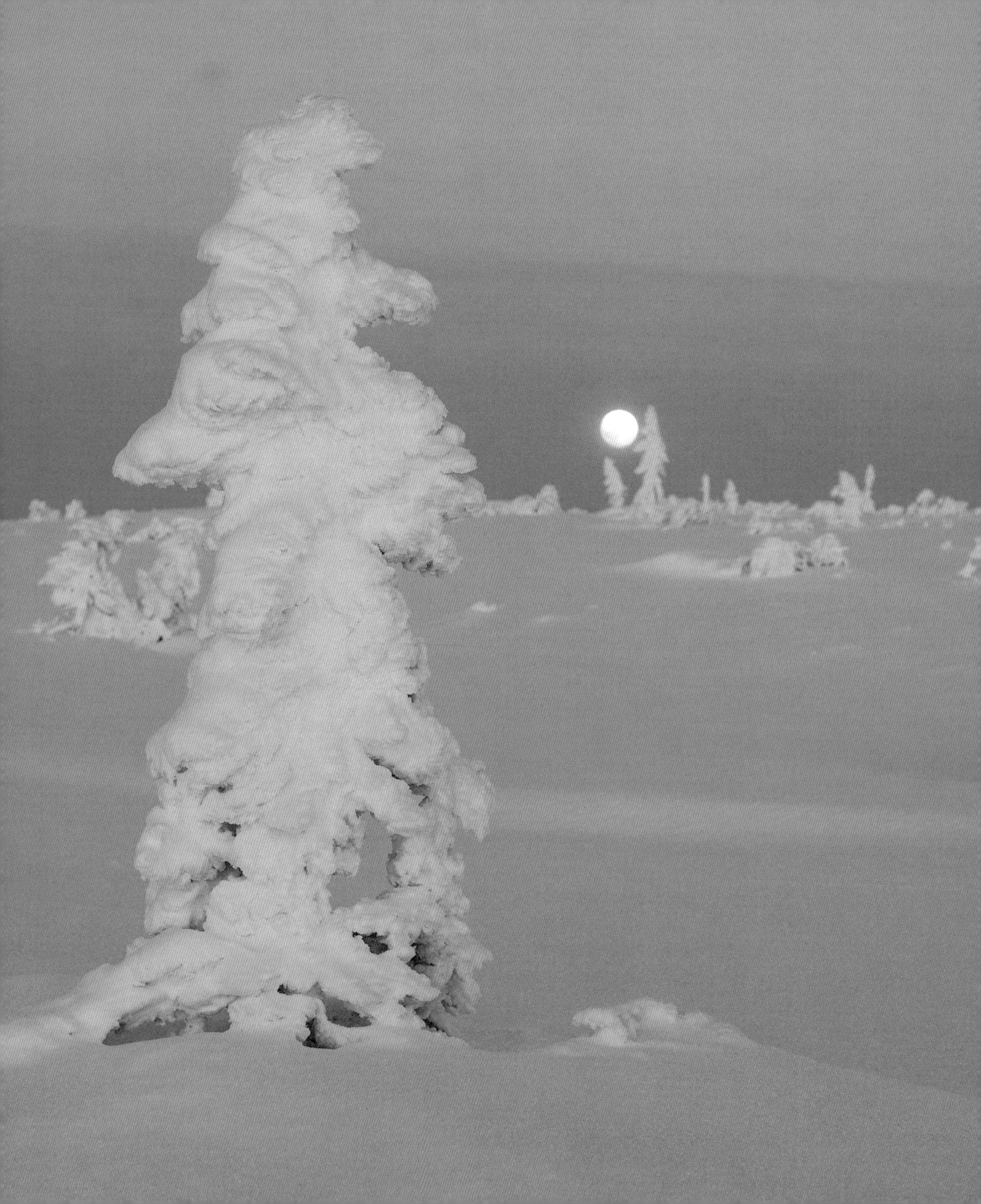

When Icehotel opens for the season a few weeks into December, it's early winter in Jukkasjärvi. The snow has already formed a thick layer on the ground, not melting until the spring even though the temperature can change with dramatic shifts. By the end of December, full winter has arrived and it won't release its grip until February. There is lots of snow, and it is cold with temperatures as low as −40°C. The sun only barely rises above the horizon and daylight hours are few.

Come March and April, and the sun climbs higher, the light slowly returns and the days get warmer. For many, it's the best season of the year. It's also when ice that will be stored and used for next season's hotel is sawn from the still frozen waters of the Torne River.
Icehotel begins to melt at the end of April and by May the sun has begun to slowly and relentlessly eat its way into its heart. Soon, it's time to close the hotel for the summer, but the ice of the Torne River is stubborn refusing to completely melt until the beginning of June when the Midnight Sun brings with it 24-hour daylight.

THE WILDERNESS

A little less than a third of the people who visit Icehotel stay for at least one night. Many of them choose to stay in one of the chalets, or in the permanent hotel building which lays adjacent to Icehotel. But wherever they decide to spend the night, it is the spacious reception area of Icehotel that forms a natural meeting place and is the focal point of their stay. Approximately 50,000 people visit Jukkasjärvi and Icehotel each year. Many people come here from places on earth where the land is never touched by snow or ice. They stay, wrapped up in the overalls and thick boots provided by the hotel no matter what the season, or how low the temperature may get.

Icehotel **89**

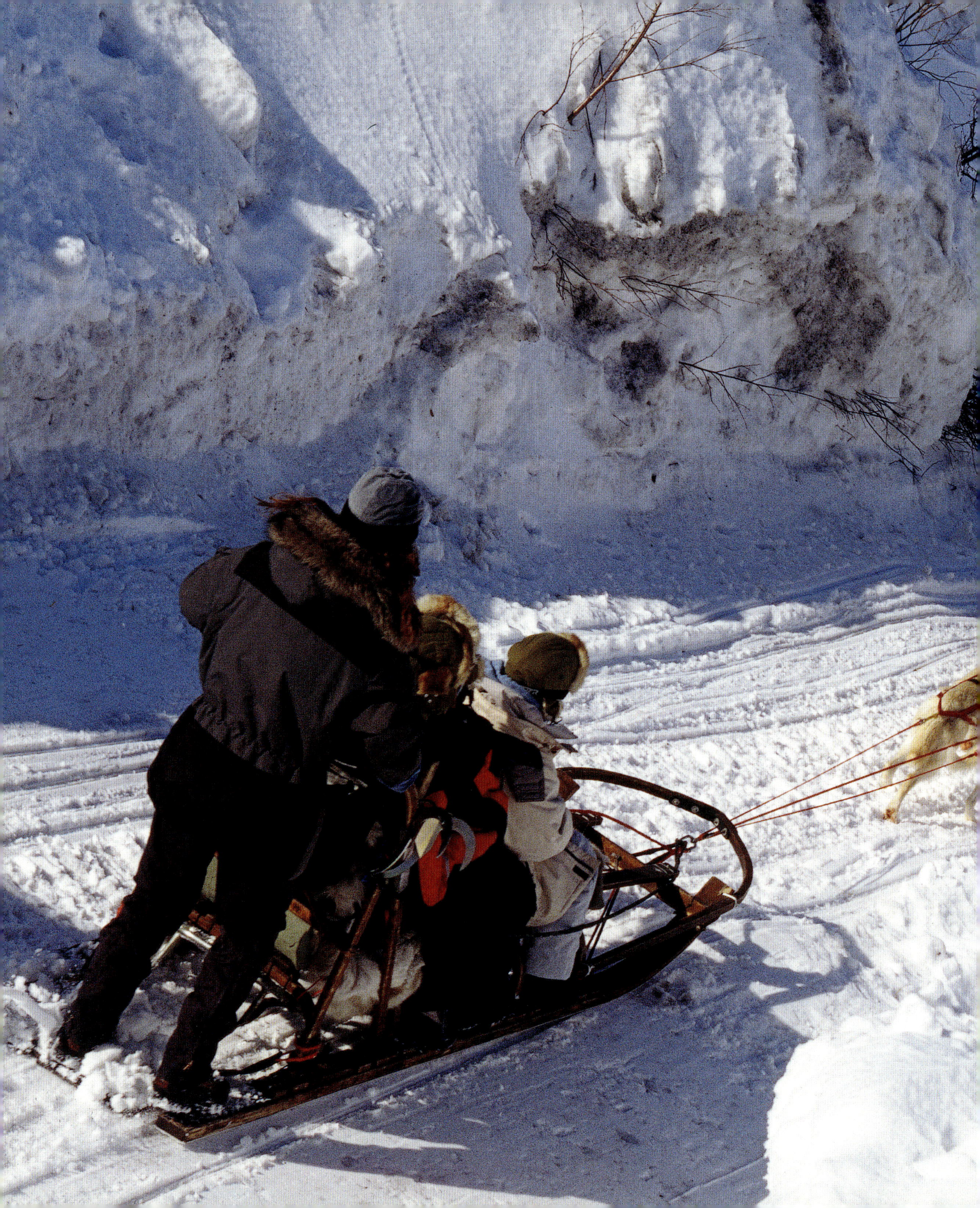

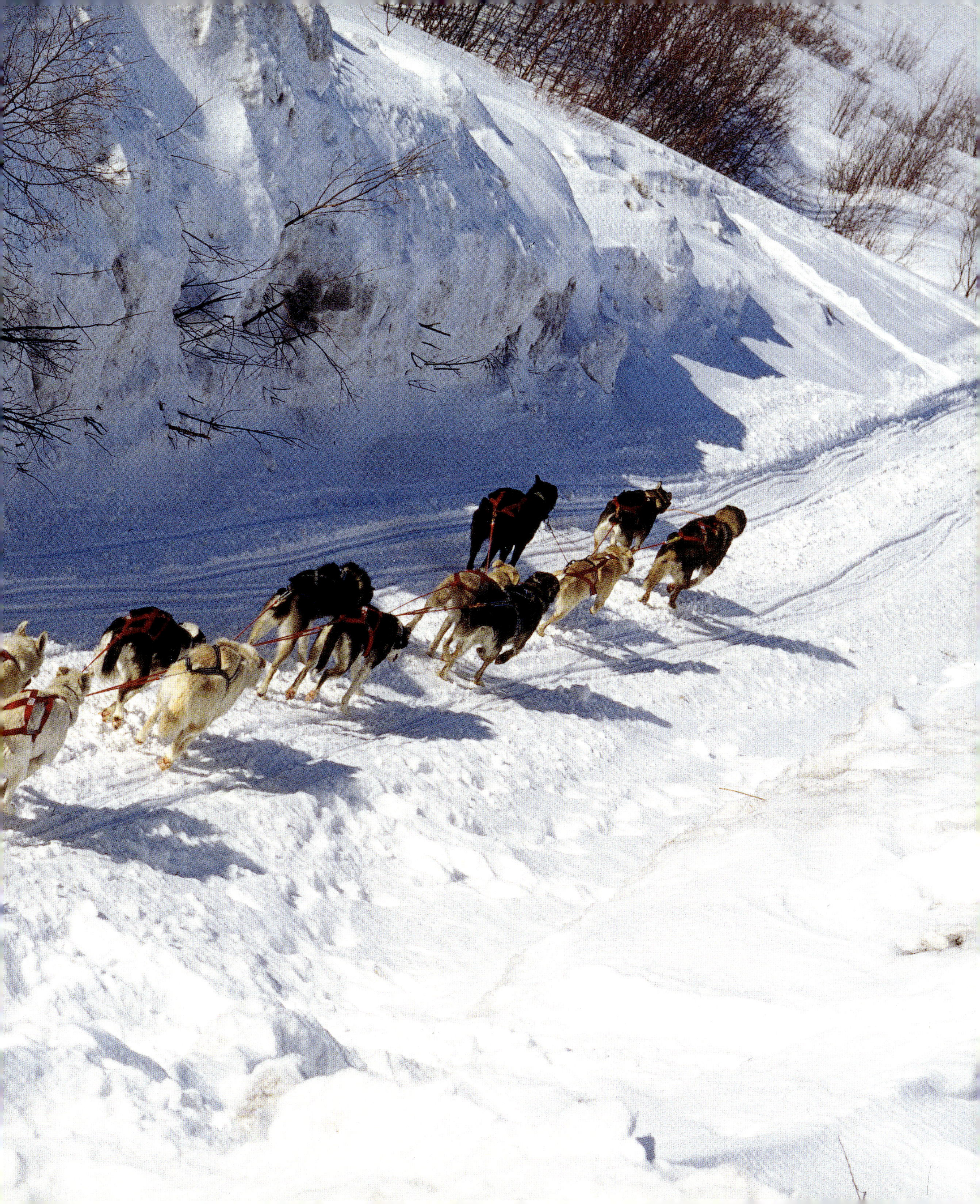

A hot bath in a large, wooden tub out on the frozen waters of the Torne River is an invigorating experience and for many, the sauna is an irresistible attraction during their stay in Jukkasjärvi.

Sauna is the term used to describe a steam bath with a temperature of close to 100°C, produced by an open oven which contains hot stones that are intermittently doused with water to produce steam.

The sauna at Icehotel — which is built out on the frozen waters of the Torne River — is a true sauna.

Taking a dip in the ice cold waters of the river is the perfect way to end a sauna. For this reason, there is always a hole in the ice big enough for those who want to try this invigorating experience.

There are many ways to move around the area surrounding Icehotel. By sleds drawn by castrated male reindeer that have been especially chosen for their docile nature (härkar), or by a foot-propelled contraption called a "spark", which is one of the most common ways to get around a winter-shrouded Jukkasjärvi.

THE WILDERNESS

Icehotel **95**

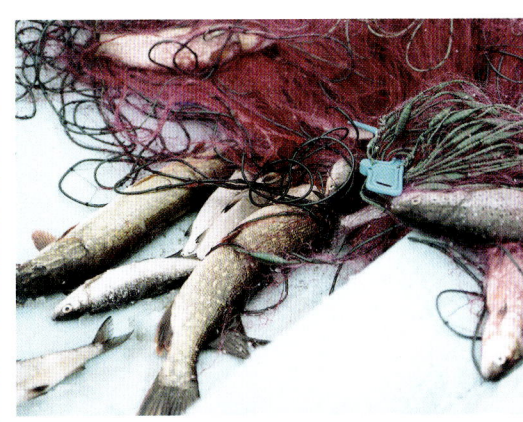

THE WILDERNESS

Icehotel nurtures the culture of the Sámi. A great many of the activities offered to visitors provide them with a clear insight of the terms under which the reindeer-tending Sámi people lived, and still live to this day.
A meal of dried reindeer meat consumed in a traditional Lap Kåta, or tent, after a trip in a reindeer-drawn sled is just one example of how visitors can experience Sámi life. Axe throwing is a way to test strength and aim.

Huskies have had a huge influence on the nomadic people of the North. Even the Polar explorers of the 1880's and into the early part of the 19th century relied heavily on huskies to get around. Today, these canine power-packs take part in contests where teams of between 3 and 20 dogs compete pulling sleds over courses marked out in the snow. In Jukkasjärvi, there are many opportunities to try out what it is like to ride in a dog-drawn sled.

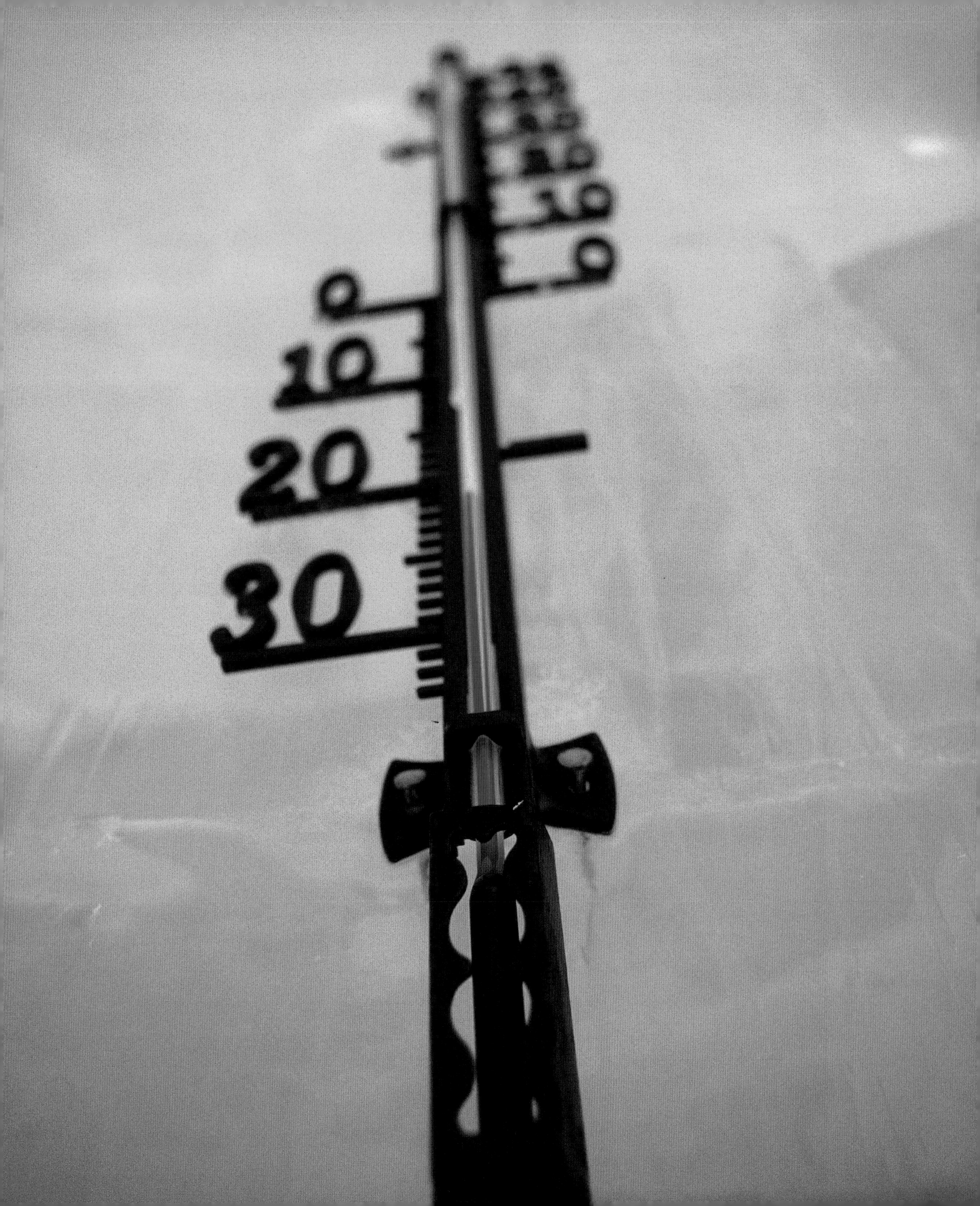
0
10
20
30

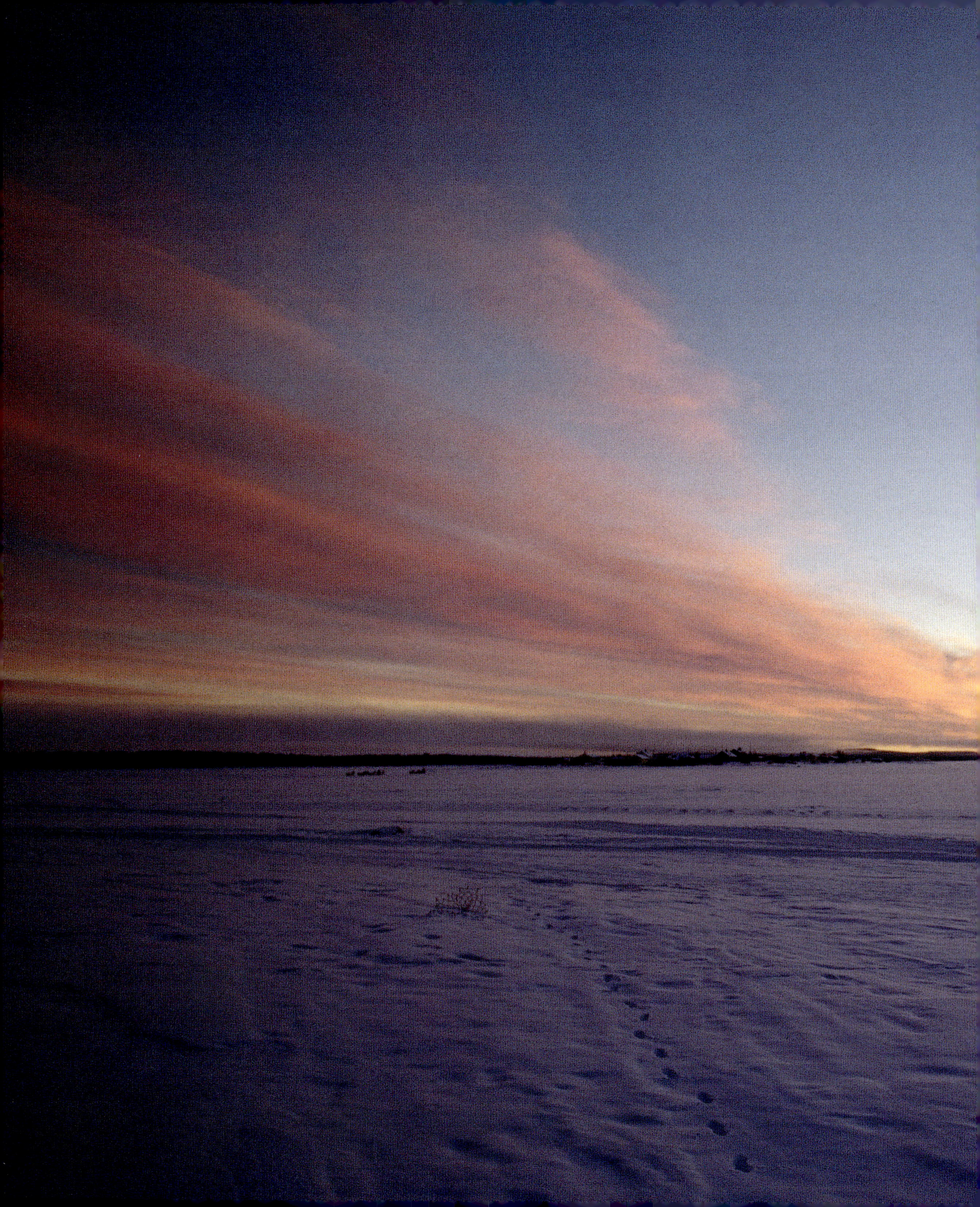

THE WILDERNESS

Guests at the hotel are offered the chance to take part in many different activities which reflect some very old Sámi traditions and a way of life which, for most visitors, is strange, exiting and exotic.
Lap is the old word for Sámi, and Lapland is the largest district in Sweden taking up around a quarter of its entire land surface. The gateway to this place lies in a mountain pass just south of the town of Abisko. The northern Polar circle crosses Lapland at about the same latitude as Jokkmokk.

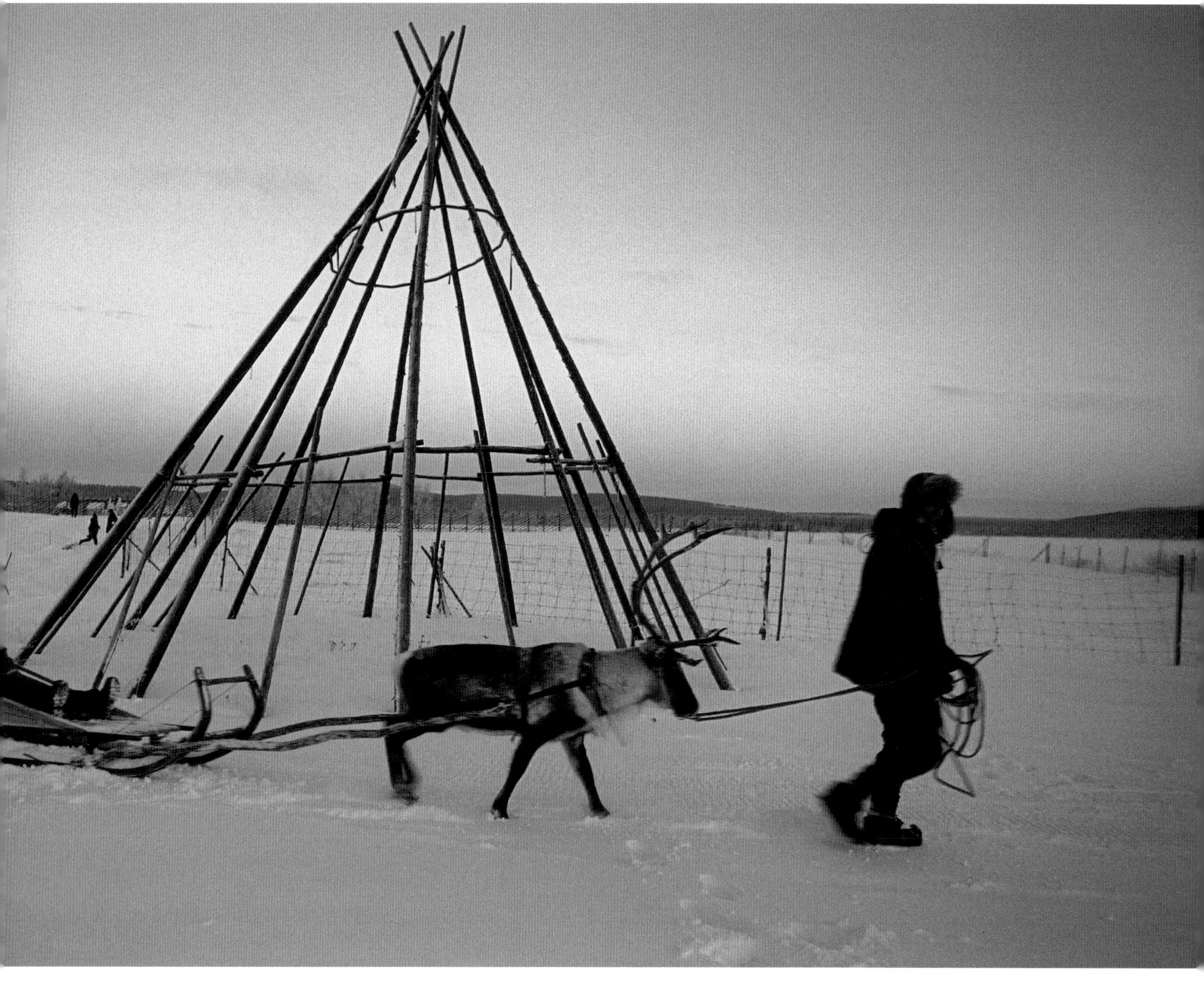

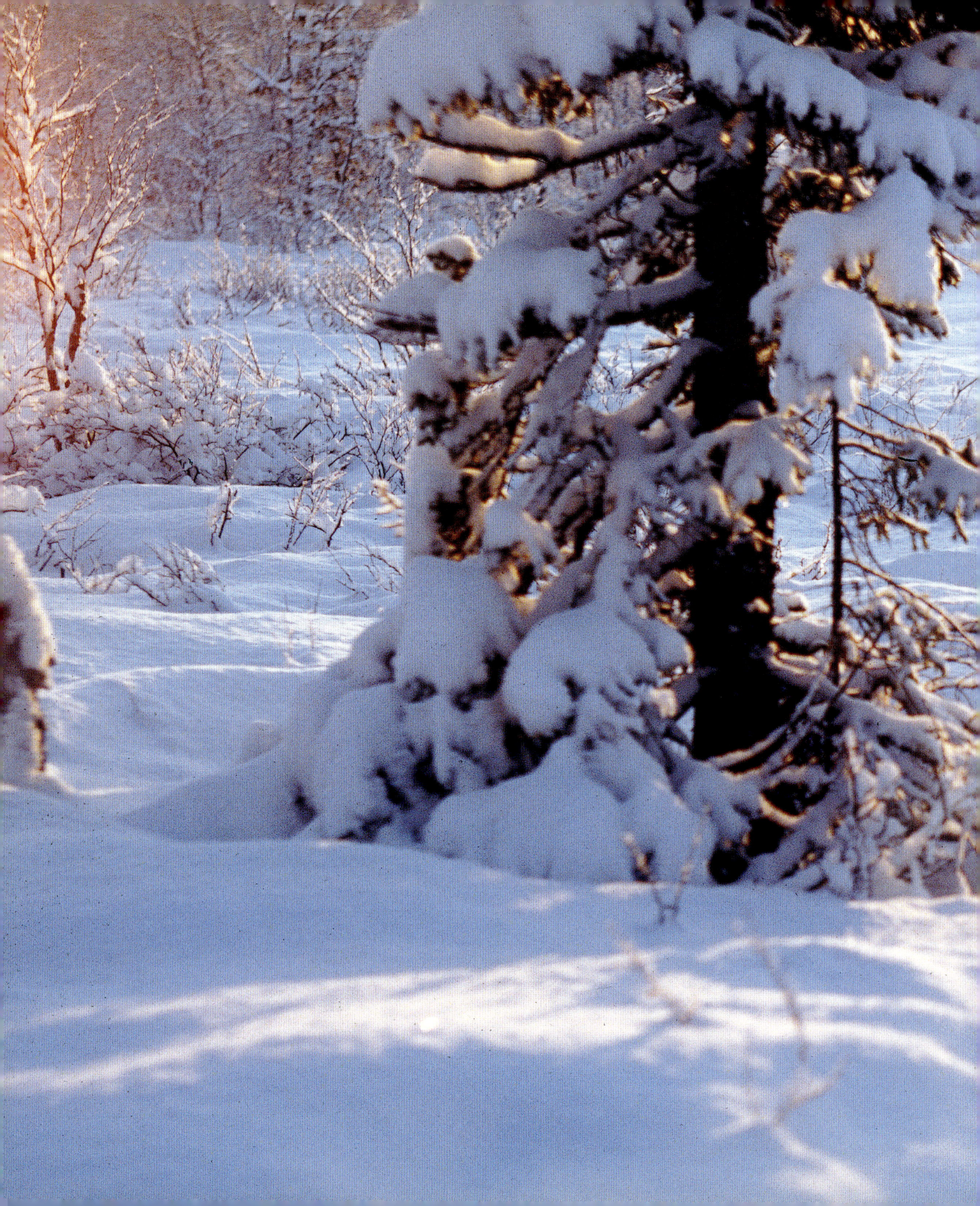

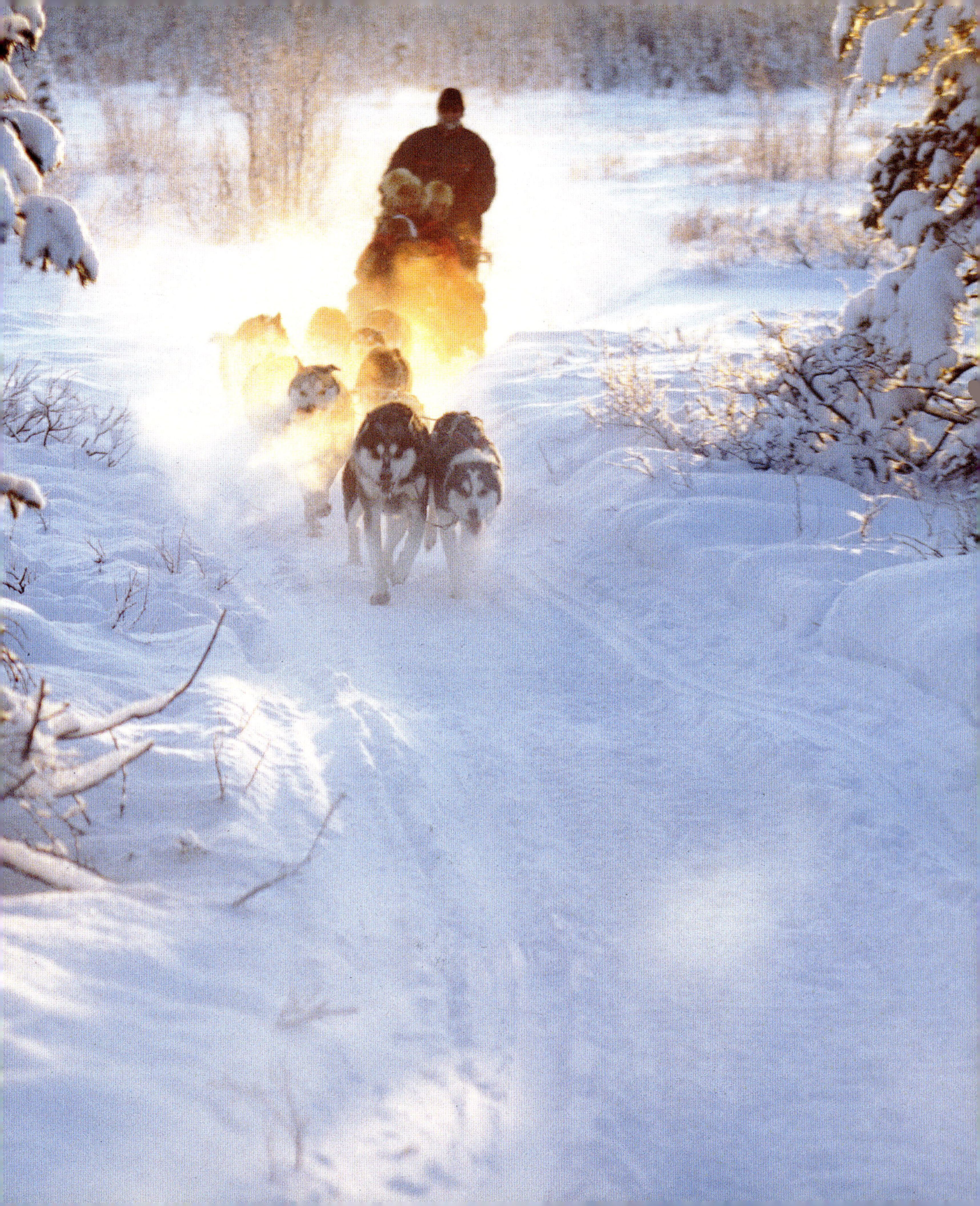

lapland

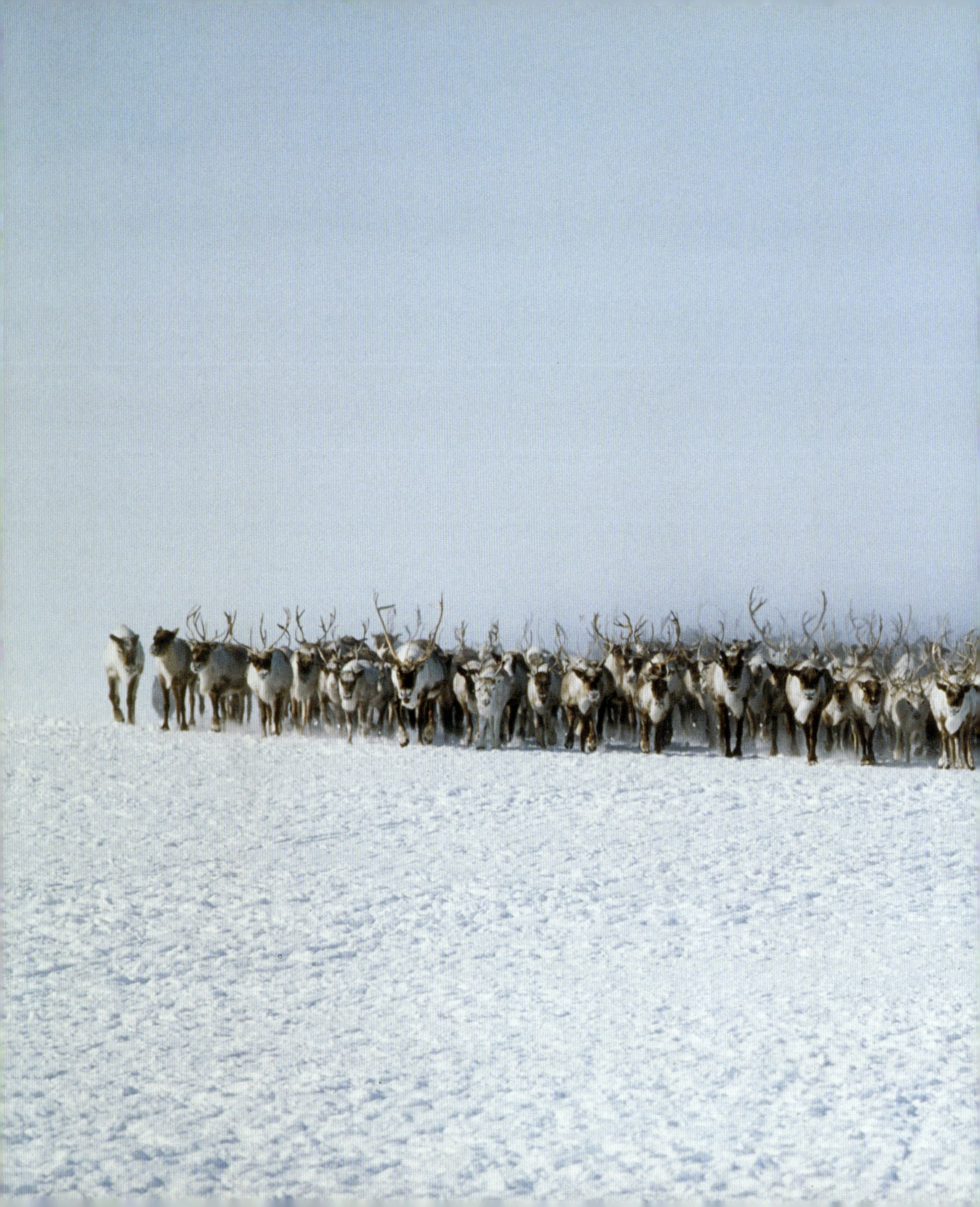

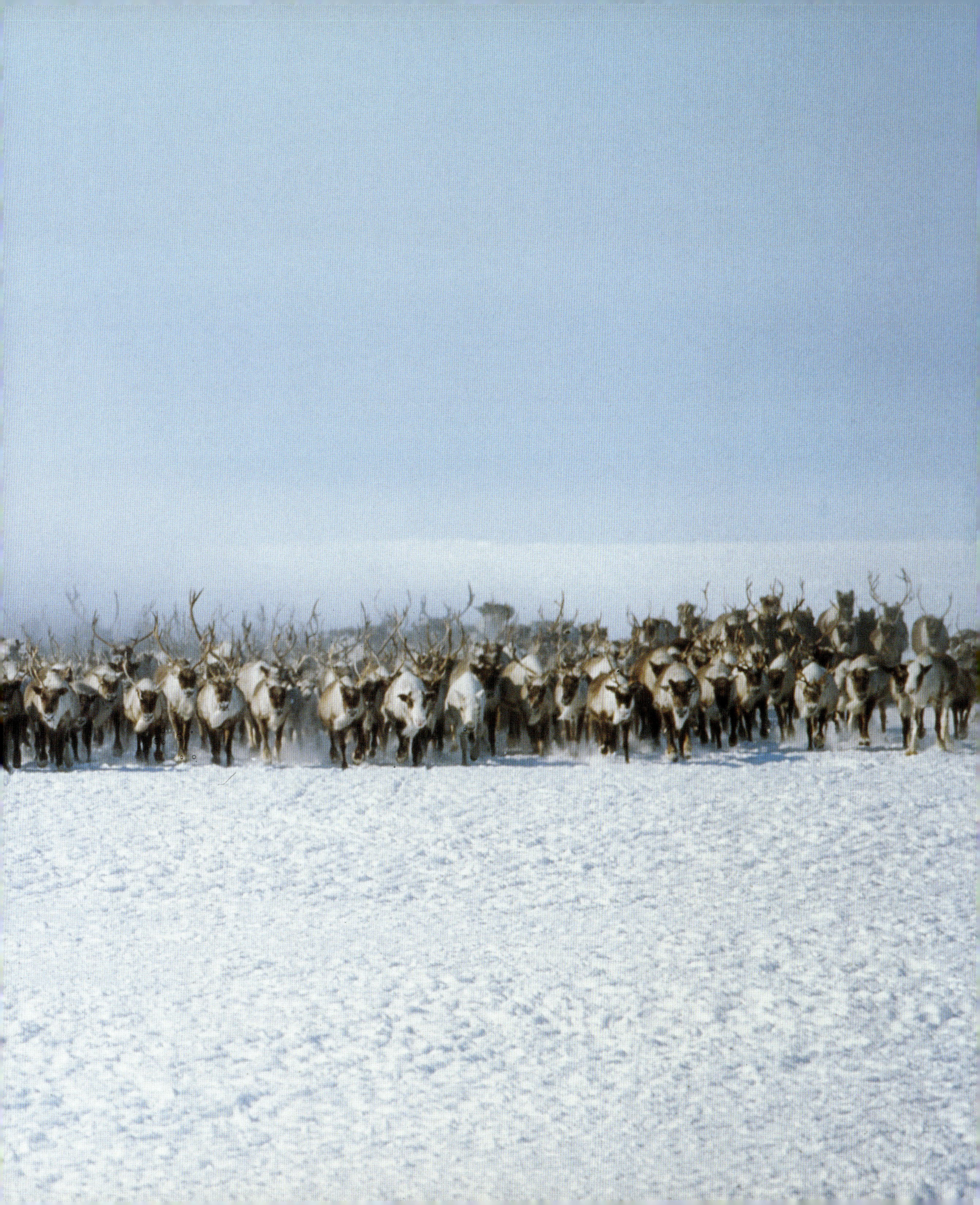

LAPLAND

The people of the sun and wind

Icehotel in Jukkasjärvi is situated in a district called Lapland, where today, visitors from far and wide can experience, first hand, the Sámi culture which plays a central role in the life of Icehotel.
The Sámi – often called the people of the sun and wind – number around 70,000in total and are spread throughout a vast tract that stretches from Norway in the west, through Sweden and Finland and on into the cold expanses of north-eastern Russia. The region that they call home is known as Sápmi or Sámeednam, and the Sámi consider it to be their land even if nationalist movements in the four countries across which it lies frequently disagree.
The Sámi make up just a few of the estimated 300 million people who collectively form a group known as minority peoples, and even if they are not subject to the kind of oppression suffered by their peers in other countries, they have still been exposed to centuries of abuse from those who have sought to take their land, and its unique heritage, away from them.

A scientific battle is constantly brewing, fueled by the question of the true origin of the Sámi, and if they really were the first people to travel along the coasts to the north when the ice age relinquished its grip on the region some 9,000 years ago. Irrefutably, archeological finds support this theory and items made from a special kind of clay, mixed with asbestos that was traditionally used by the Sámi people, have been found throughout the region that makes up the present-day Sápmi. The earliest finds have been dated to around 1,500 years before the birth of Christ while similar items from around 300 A.D have also been recovered.
Up until the 15th century, the Sámi people were primarily hunter/gatherers. Their hunting skills were especially important providing them with food and clothing. During the 15th century, however, they began to tame the large herds of reindeer that roamed the wilderness of the fells, following them throughout the year as they moved about in search of food. With this, the Sámi became nomads, but with the advent of industrialism in Sweden in the 18th century, this nomadic lifestyle gradually began to disappear. Factories, roads and railways, all left their mark. So too did the invention of hydro-electric power which led to the exploitation of the rivers of northern Sweden. All too quickly, the old ways of the Sámi were changed for ever.

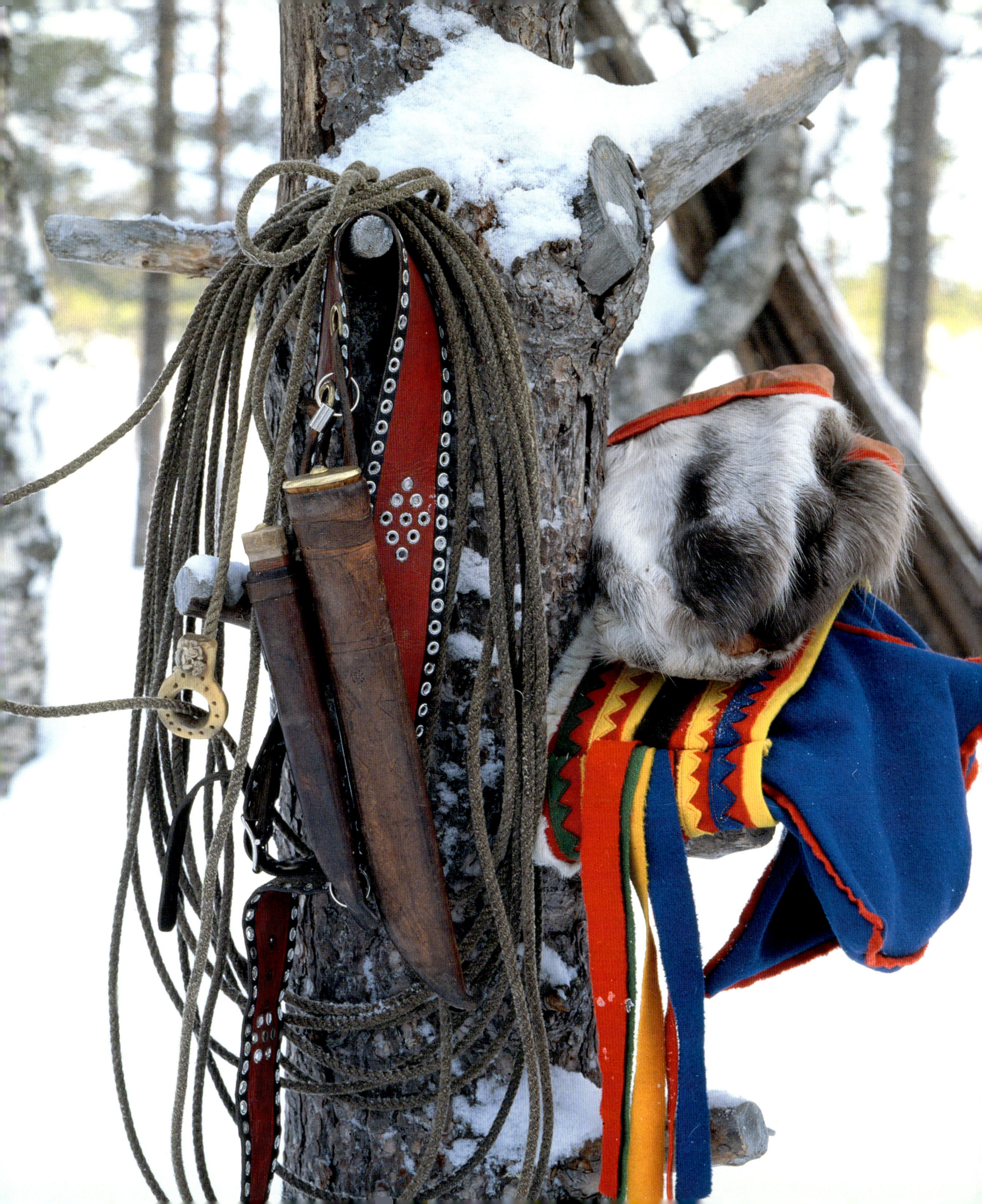

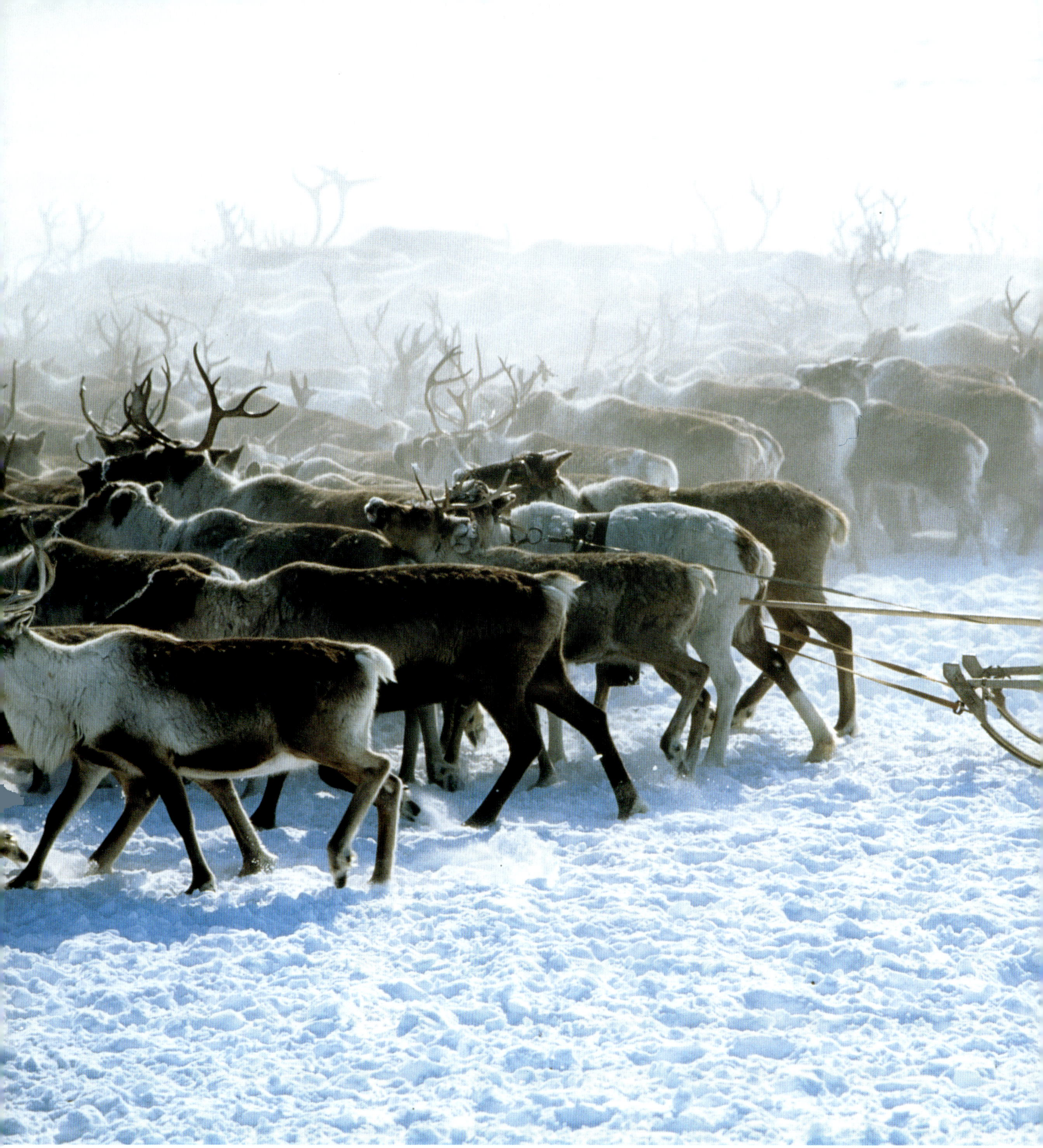

Approximately 2,500 Swedish Sámi still make their living tending the herds of reindeer that roam the vast tract that is Lapland. It's a job that has changed dramatically over the years as the trappings of modern life, like snow scooters, are introduced. But, as yet, the old ways of moving across this barren land still survive.

LAPLAND

Today, there are approximately 17,500 Sámi in Sweden – most of them have long since integrated into Swedish society. However, some 2,500 still live according to the traditional ways, surviving off the land and tending their reindeer on the fells.
But it's not a profitable enterprise: fodder for their animals is no longer free, and even the reindeer are finding it hard to seek out food. Today, the Sámi are squeezed between a rock and a hard place, their lives controlled by powerful interests.

Close by Icehotel, companies offer guests rides in real husky-drawn sleds. The animal of choice up here is the Siberian Husky which is the strongest and fastest of all the Husky breeds. Siberian Huskies, can go for long periods without food, and withstand extreme cold.

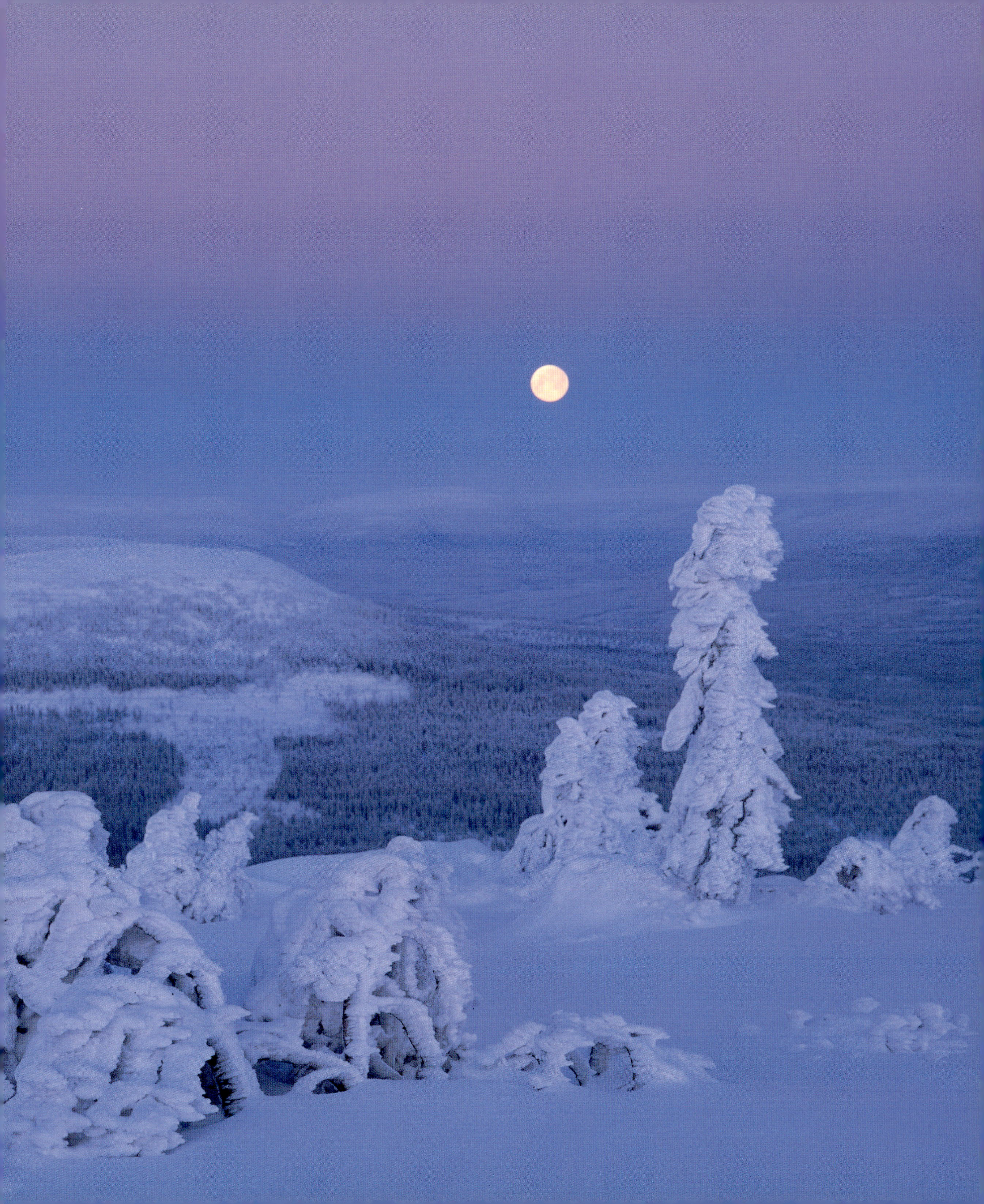

LAPLAND

The Sámi people traditionally relied on the snow to get around. Where there were no roads, the coming of winter opened up the land.

In the fells, winter is still a time for transporting goods and people. However, in this modern age, reindeer and sleds have been replaced by scooters and trailers. Snow Scooter Safaris are very popular among visitors to Icehotel.

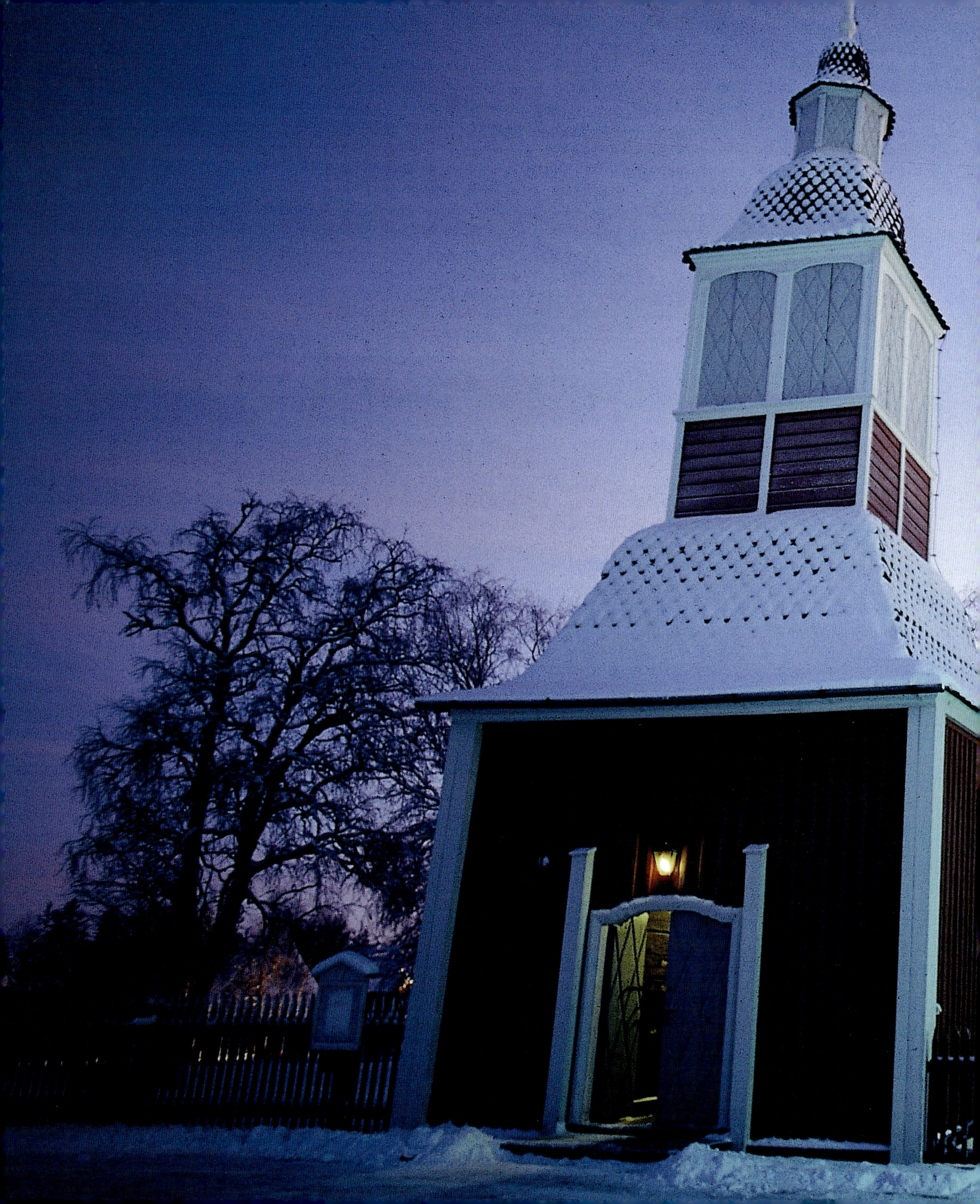

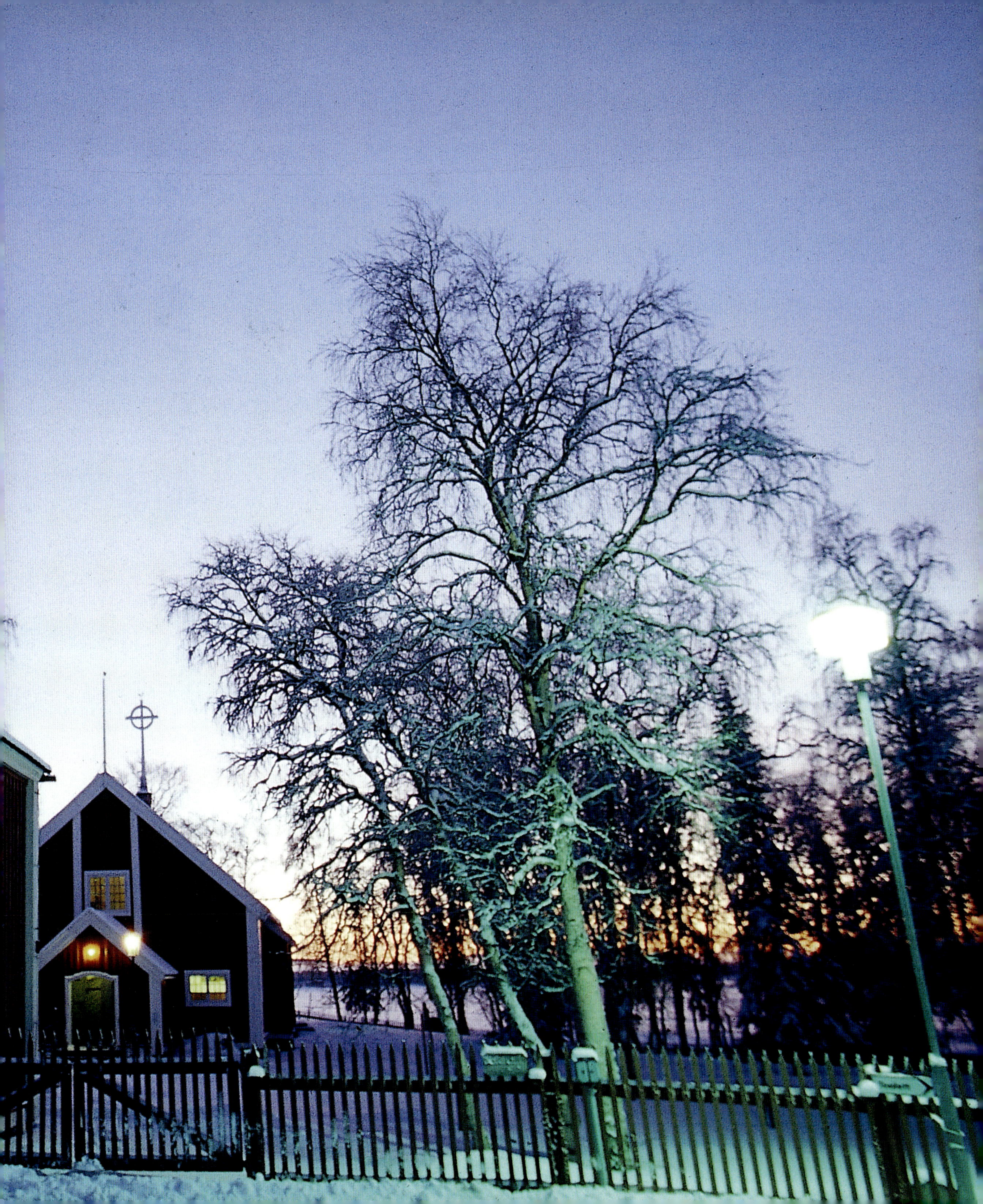

JUKKASJÄRVI CHURCH

Timeless symbolism

The village of Jukkasjärvi, with its little more than 1,000 inhabitants, may at first glance appear to be located at the end of the world. Cold and darkness hold the place in an iron grip for most of the year.

But even before Icehotel first put the village on the international tourist map, many people already traveled to Jukkasjärvi to see for themselves the old wooden church – located between the end of the road and the Torne River.

The church building is unique, and with its timbered block pillars, it is the only one of its kind in the world today.

Its colorful altar also arouses considerable attention. Made by Swedish art professor Bror Hjort, it has been lovingly carved from solid teak, and depicts images of the Laestadian Revival within the Swedish church – a period which meant, and still means, a great deal for the life of the area.

The altar, which has both symbolic and timeless value, got its name from Lars Levi Laestadius, a priest who came to Karesuando in 1845. Originally built in 1958, it was a gift from the mining company LKAB to the people of the area.

Jukkasjärvi church was built in 1608, and in its original form, was a small wooden chapel. It was rebuilt in 1726 at which time it was enlarged to its present dimensions of 9.5 x 17.5 meters. The church was clad with wooden siding and painted red in 1747. Bror Hjort's altar has a classic, three-sided design.

Icehotel 119

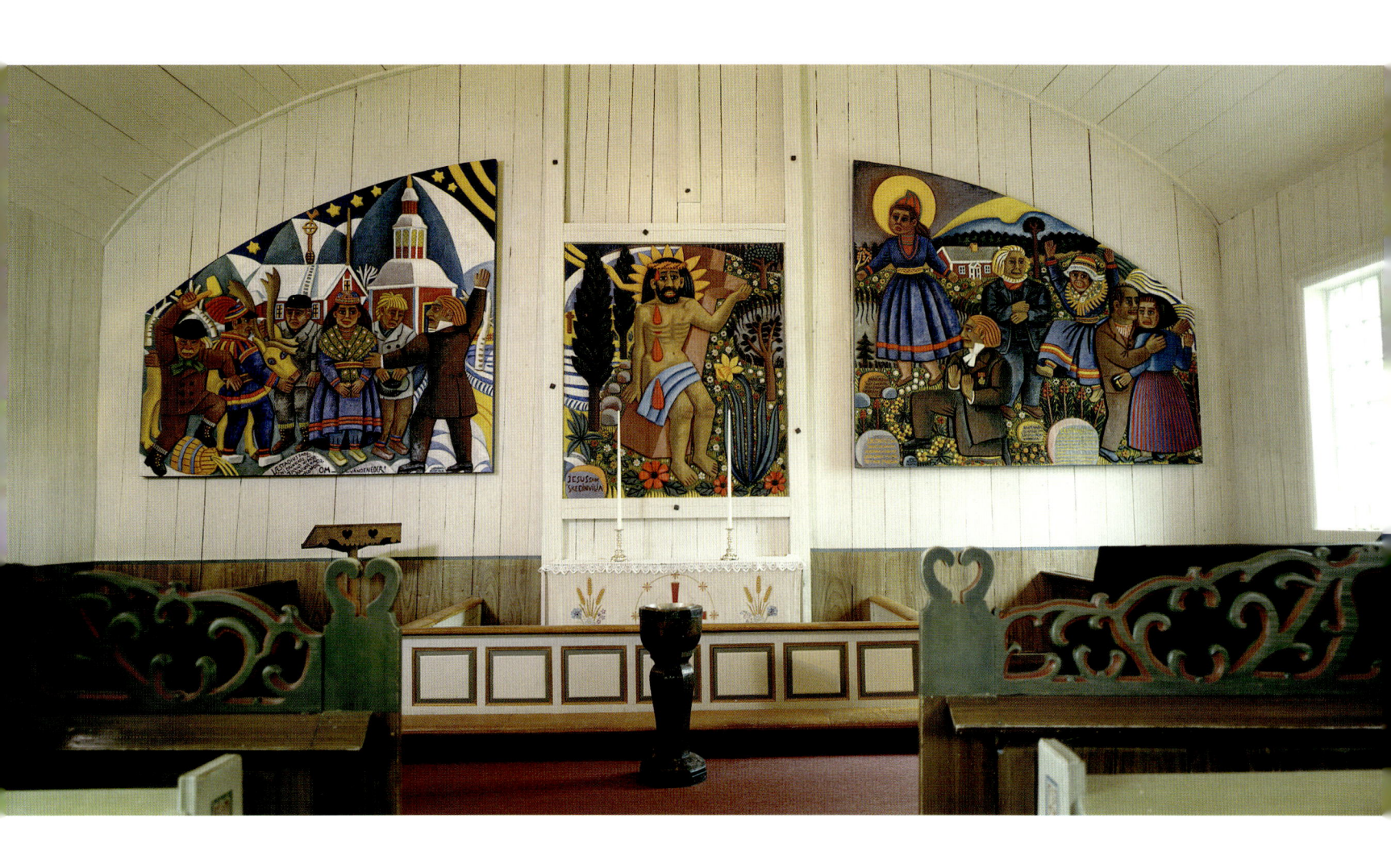

The view from Nuulla

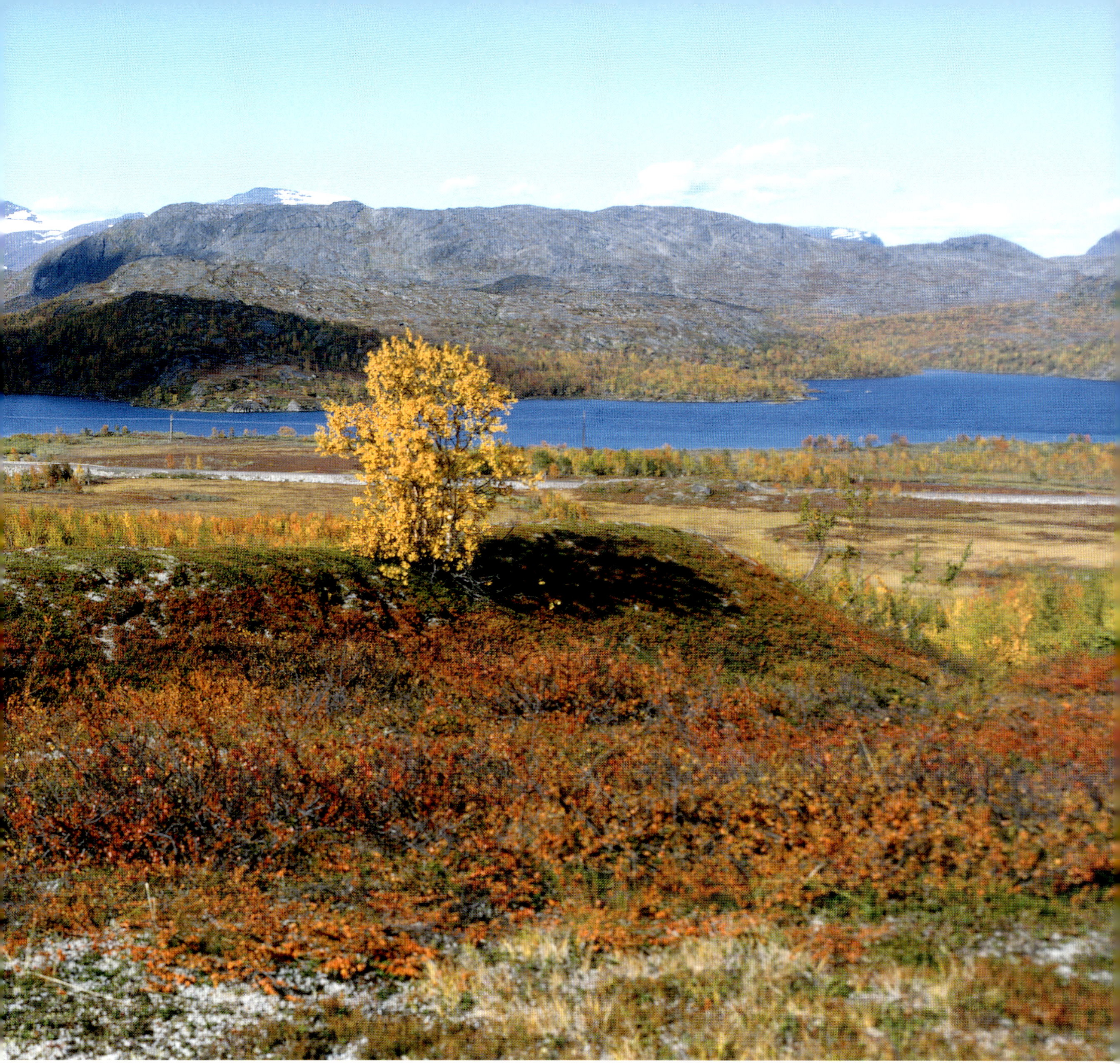

iron ore

IRON ORE

Future in steel

The backbone of Kiruna has, is, and always will be, steel and, even today, the iron mines of the region still form the cornerstone of a special kind of society.

It all began on a small scale 300 years ago when writer Samuel Olsson Mört traveled across the wilderness to see for himself the newly discovered copper field at Sjangeli. On the way, he stopped at Jukkasjärvi where he heard about the iron-rich mountains which lay close by. Before continuing on, he penned a report.

But it wasn't until 1736 that these strange formations were properly investigated by the County Mayor of Västerbotten, Gabriel Gyllengrip, who formed an expedition to study the area in more detail. With him, he took surveyor Esaias Hackzell who drew up maps of the finds, and even christened the mountains – Friedrichs Berg (Kiirunavaara) and Berget Ulrika Eleonora (Luossavaara).

In 1890, the Luossavaara-Kiirunavaara Aktiebolag was formed. Better known as LKAB and in 1903 the final stretch of the Malmbanan railway line was completed.

Iron ore mining in Kiruna has gone through many different phases during the past 100 years –from financial highs to political and economic depressions spurred by events far beyond Sweden's borders.

The largest underground mine in the world has always been a lifeline for the people of Kiruna, and LKAB's decision to invest in the venture, coupled with the company's firm belief in the future, has colored the entire district.

In 1990, the first blast into a new main level at LKAB's mine was made. Huge investments were required if the company was to continue to recover the iron ore that still remained in the ground under Kiirunavaara even after the turn of the century. Production at Luosavaara was discontinued in 1974 at a time when large parts of the world were struggling through a major recession.

LKAB's decision was aggressive.

Today, the company can continue to produce ore from the mine even after 2015, which is when the new main level is planed for completion. And Kiruna can breathe a sigh of relief.

IRON ORE

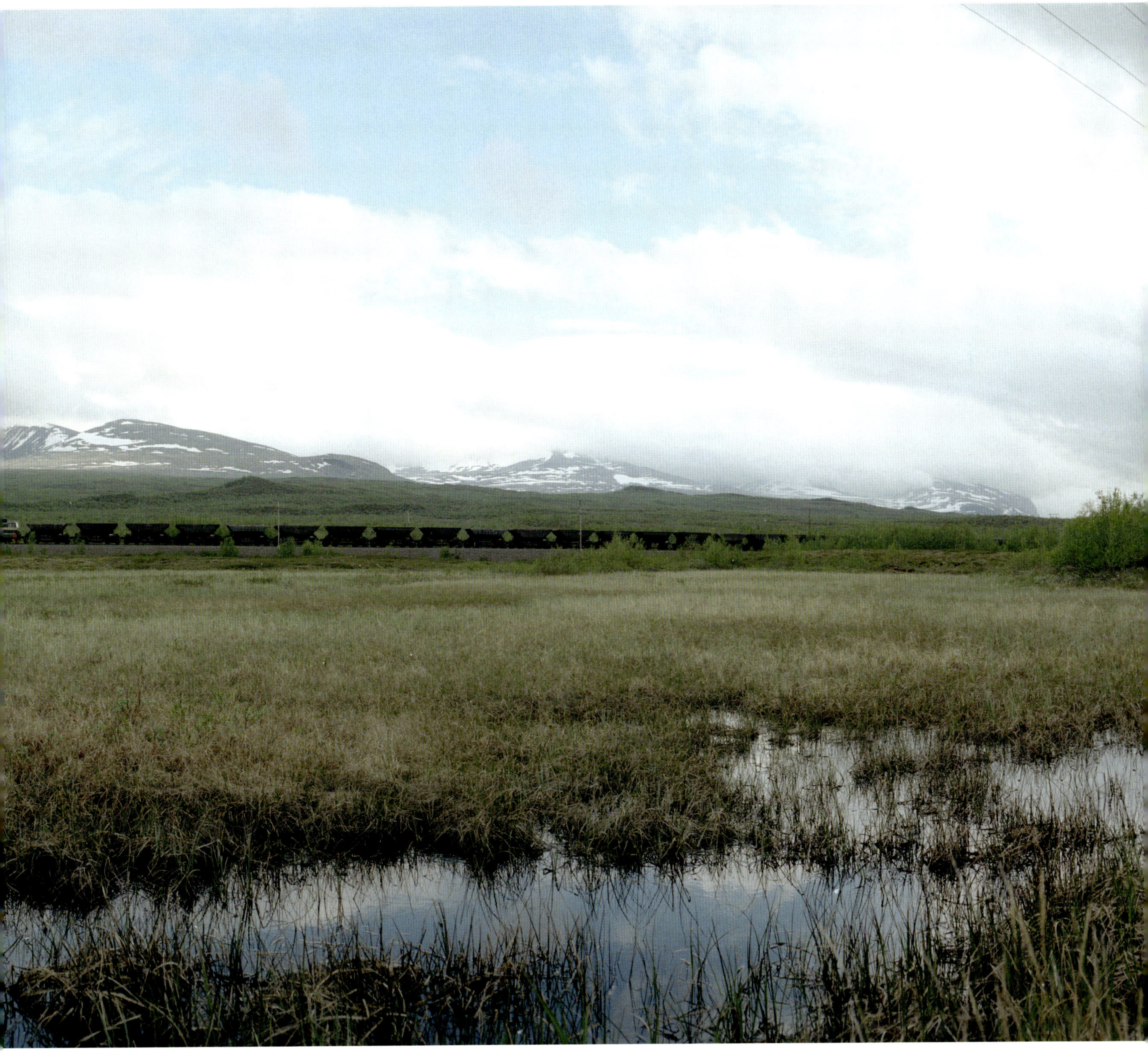

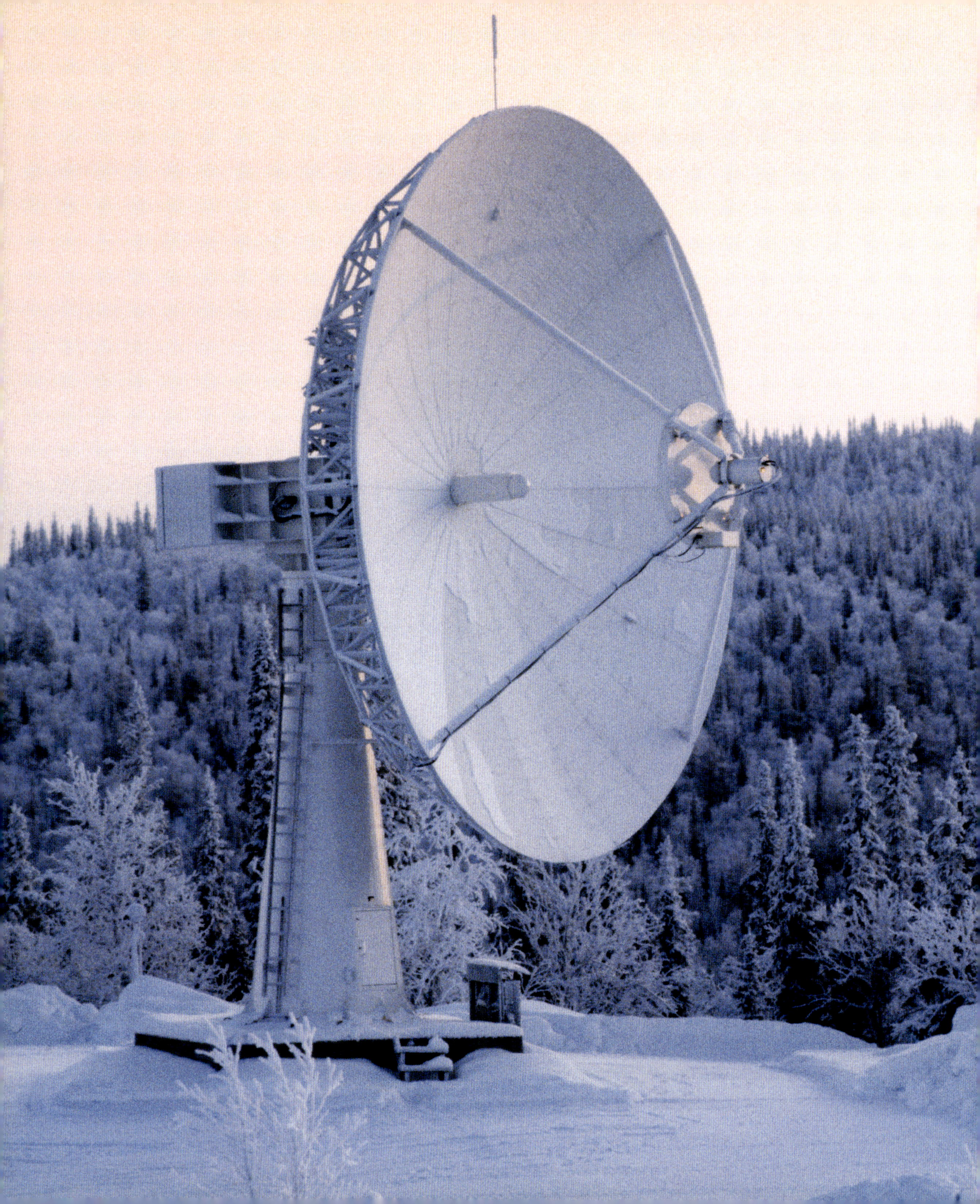

An aerial string of pearls

For the past four decades, advanced scientific research has been carried out in Kiruna. About 40 kilometers from the center of town lies Esrange, a 120 kilometer long, 75 kilometer wide site from where rockets are fired into space. Satellites that are launched from here are used to conduct all kinds of extra terrestrial research – from measuring the height of waves, to determining wind speeds, and how air currents move around our world. And of course, they gaze down upon the aerie Northern Lights which frequently pulsate across the skies above the town.

Satellite-borne systems are also developed here. These are used for research into weightless, or close-to-weightless, environments. Communications satellites too are launched from Esrange, while strategic information is gathered from orbiting intelligence platforms and used to market systems which monitor sea conditions and ensure environmental control.
The history of research in Kiruna goes back a long way. As early as the end of the 18th century in fact when geologist, Fredrik Svenonius, came upon the place while looking for a suitable site on which to establish a laboratory.
He found it on the Kiruna Fells, and in 1902, the Stockholm-based Sällskapet för Naturvetenskap (Natural History Society) purchased an engineer's house in Katterjåkk where scientists toiled to understand the enigma that is the Northern Lights. They also studied the climate of this special area, the forces which lay behind the formation of the fells, the changes that have occurred there over the years, and the source of biological life in this inhospitable, sub-Arctic environment.
This was the beginning of a scientific endeavor which, a century later, has formed a vital cornerstone of the business life of Kiruna.

The first Swedish satellite – Viking – was launched into space on February 22nd, 1986. As a cost-cutting measure, it was sent up as a piggy-back payload together with the French satellite, Spot 1, and was launched from the ESA Range at Kourou in French Guyana. During its first orbit around the earth, it was possible to track Viking from Esrange as it made observations that had never before been seen.
One of its many discoveries was the occurrence of "hot spots" – a pearl necklace like phenomenon which line the edge of the Northern Lights. The discovery roused considerable international interest and served to put Swedish space-based research firmly on the scientific map.

The historical launch of Viking was celebrated with a Snow Festival that was held in Kiruna which, since then, has become an annual event.

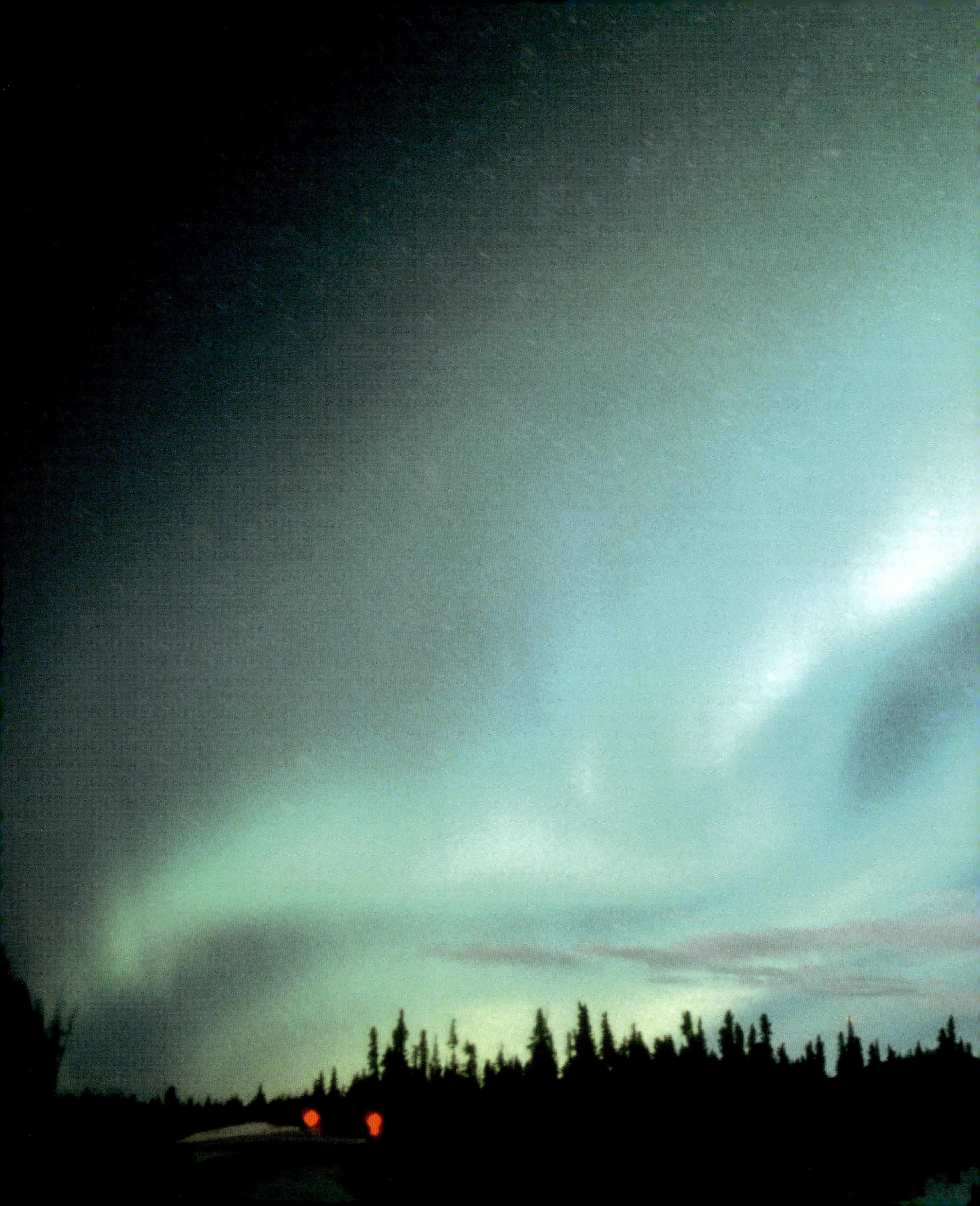

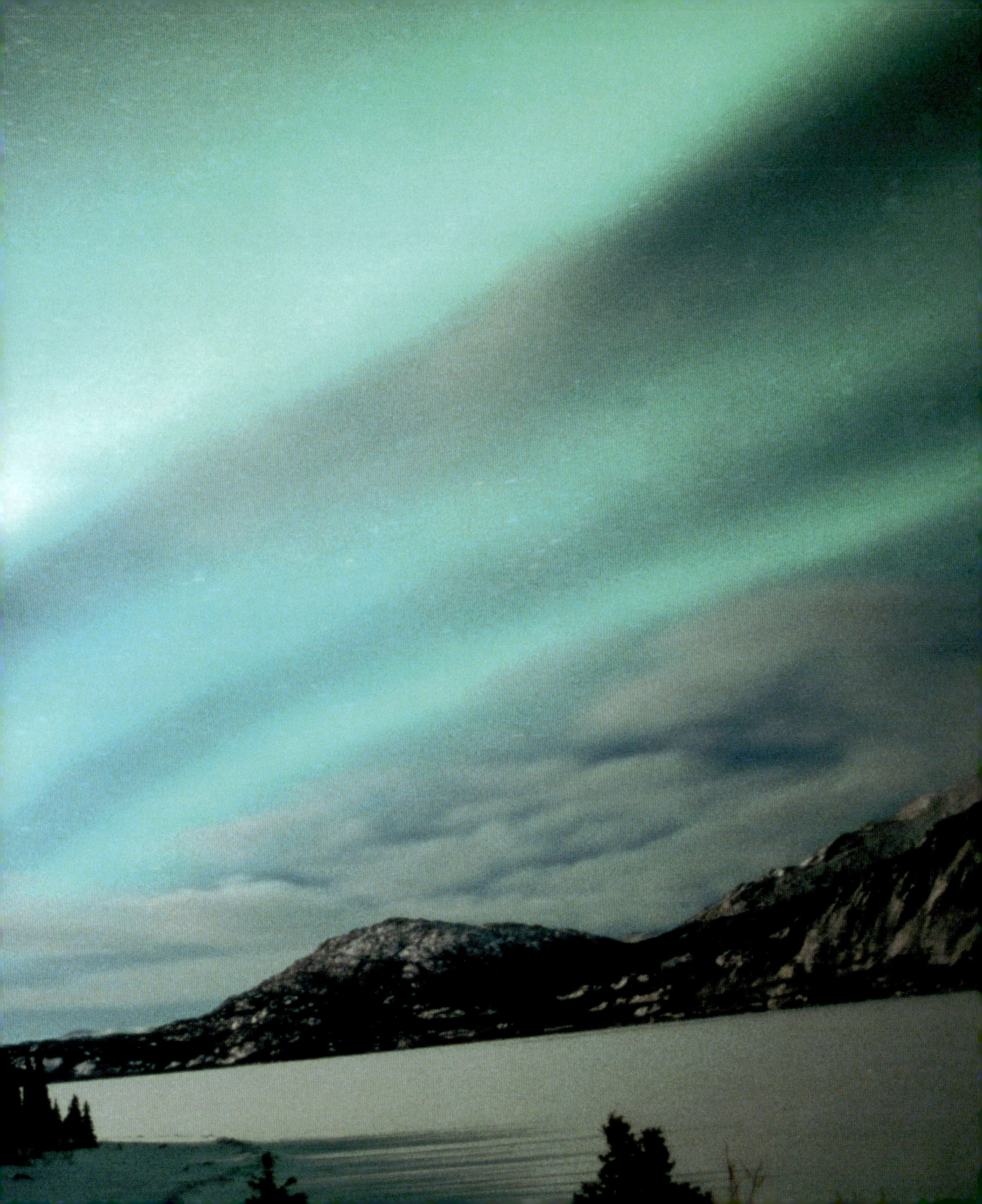

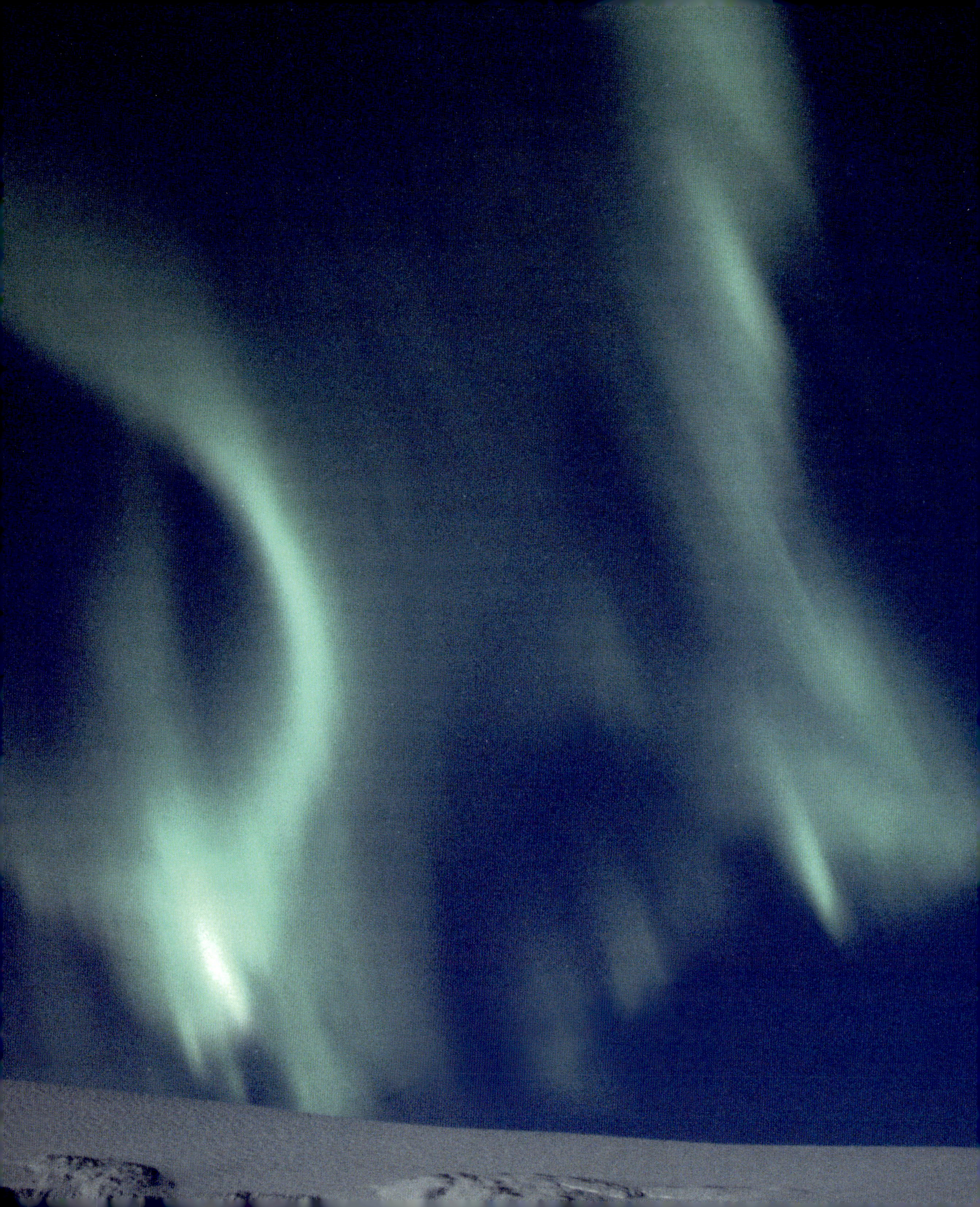

THE NORTHERN LIGHTS

A bewitching light

It is a breathtaking display. Suddenly the hue of the night sky changes from green-white or grey-blue to a deep, deep red. It's a striking palette of color that is called the Northern or Southern Lights depending upon which of the Poles you see it from. In Jukkasjärvi, 200 km north of the Polar Circle, the Northern Lights are an everyday occurrence. But, despite this, they never fail to fascinate those who witness their dramatic pulsations across the sky.

Not unsurprisingly, the Northern Lights have enthralled scientists for generations, and many have tried to explain this ghostly phenomenon. The Institute for Space Physics (IRF) in Kiruna, has even gone so far as to develop a range of new equipment with which they can measure the low-energy electrons and positive ions which make up at least some of the material that creates the Northern Lights.

By drastically reducing the size of research satellites, the institute has been able to launch more instruments into space at the same time, thereby enlarging the footprint that they cover. Now, it is possible to study the Northern lights in ways which were impossible to achieve just a few years ago, and the Astrid satellites, which were launched in 1995, have made a major contribution. All three satellites have been named after children's book writer, Astrid Lindgren's famous characters, Pippi, Emil and Mio. But even if we, theoretically speaking, know what causes the Northern Lights to pulsate through the atmosphere, there are still many questions that need answering before we fully understand their nature.

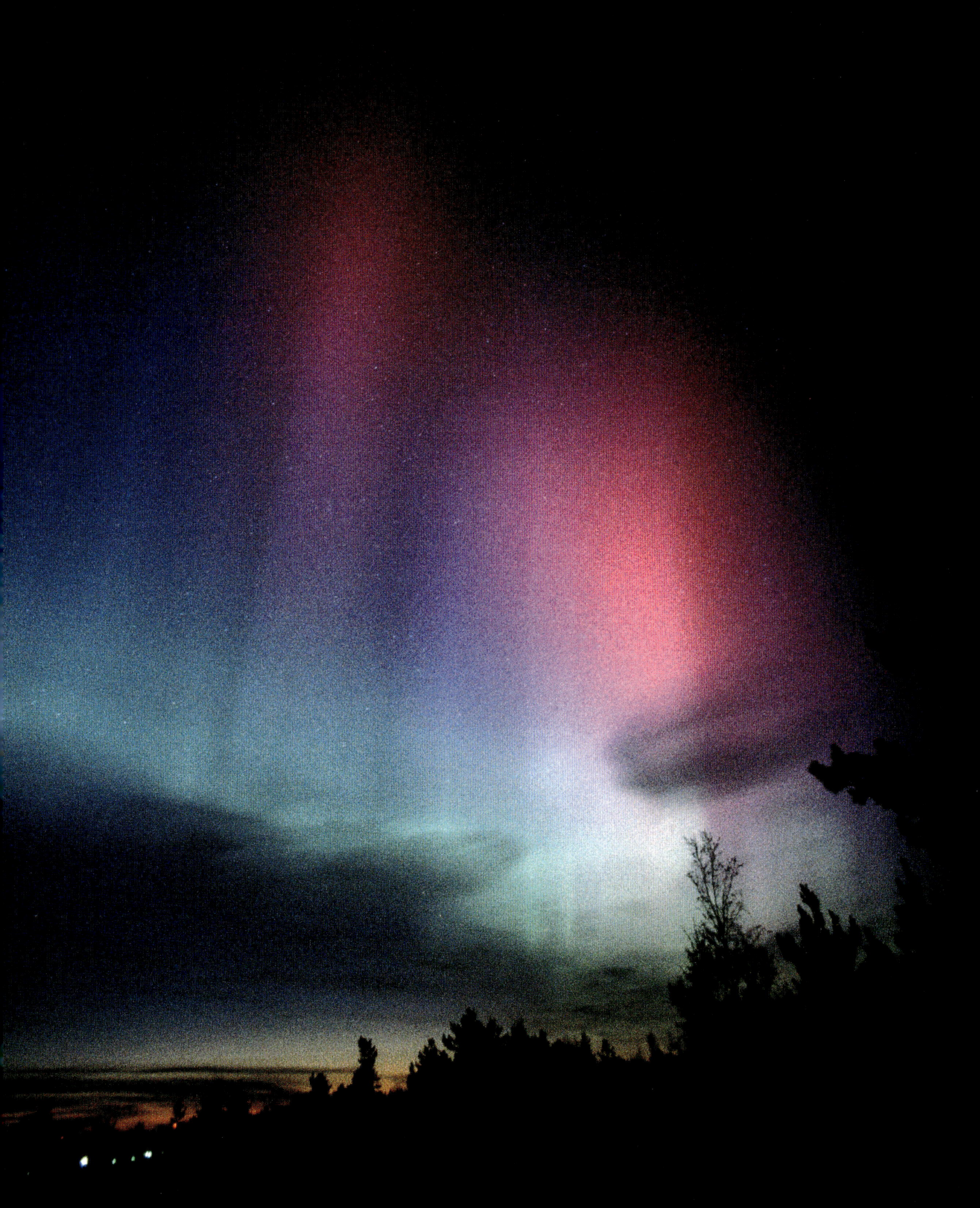

The Northern Lights appear as two luminous belts, more than 2,000 kilometers in radius, which circle the earth's magnetic poles. Their eerie, pulsating light is the result of electrical discharges in the atmosphere which occur at a height of between 100 km, and up to 1,000 km. Some discharges have even been recorded at higher altitudes.

The energy of a single discharge can amount to more than one million megawatts. Charged by the solar winds, they are controlled by the earth's magnetic field which works in tandem with the atoms and molecules which go to make up our atmosphere. The solar wind comprises charged particles of which some are thrown out by the solar flares which erupt from the sun's surface. When the Northern Lights are particularly strong, it's not uncommon that magnetic storms and disruptions in radio communications occur on earth.

ICEHOTEL

Autumn in Katterjåkk

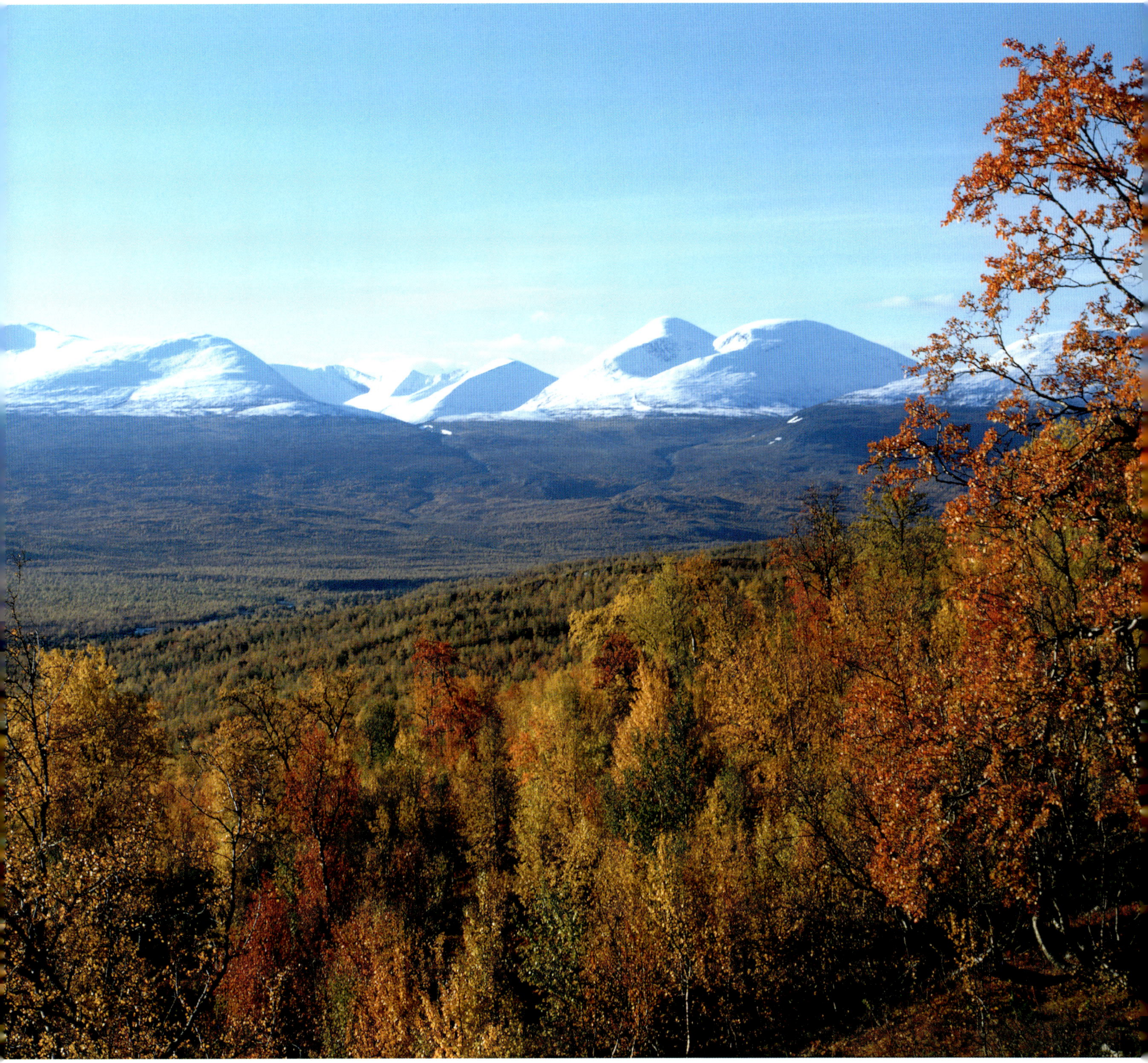

cuisine

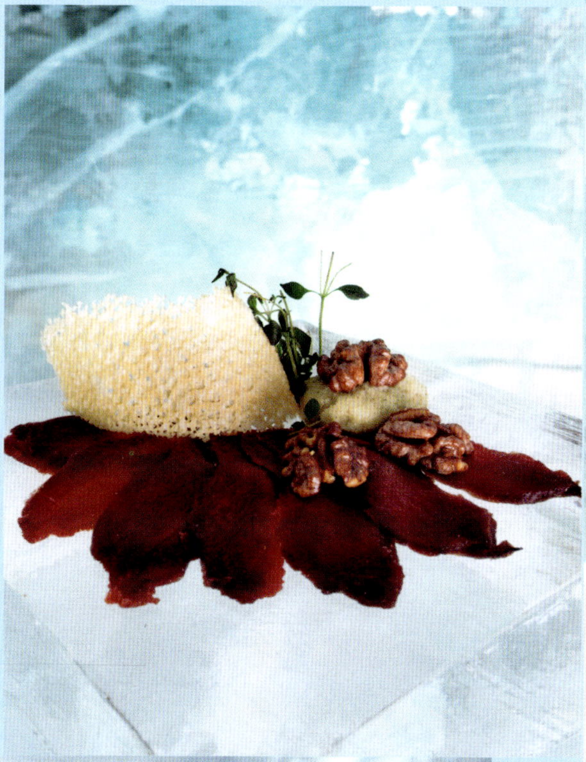
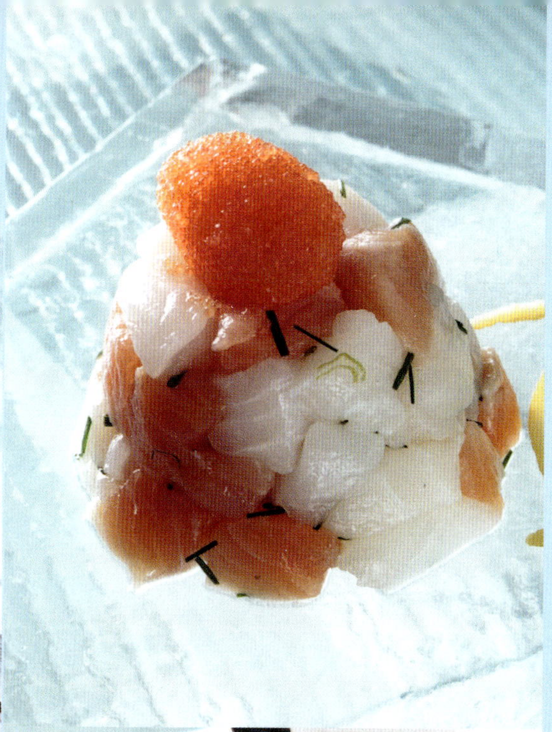
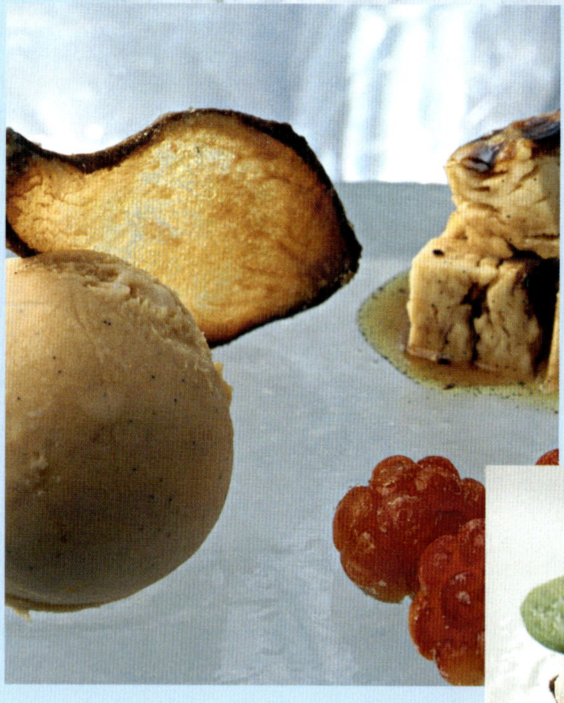
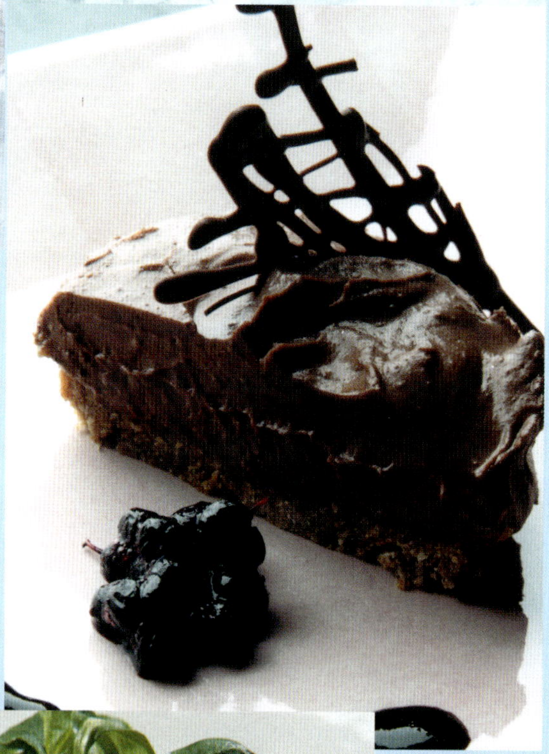
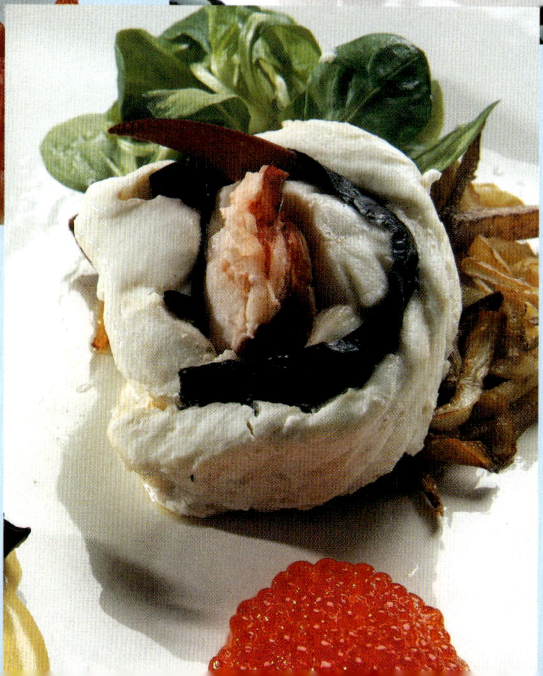

CUISINE

Exotic ingredients are an everyday thing

Nordic gastronomy is said to lack the distinctive, regional flavor that is typical of countries like France and Italy which are renowned for their culinary heritage. But in the region which lies to the north of the Polar Circle, things are different. Life here is tainted by the wilds. The summer sun never sets, the winters hold the land in almost constant darkness, and covers it in a blanket of snow. Where the marshes, mosses, fells and vast forests form a region much explored, but little understood.
In this environment, culinary tradition has evolved from the harsh reality of a landscape where need and abundance fight a never-ending battle.

In the far north, the pantry is full of ingredients that people of the south of the Polar circle would regard as exclusive. Venison, ptarmigan and wood grouse taken from the animals which live wild on the moors and in the forests. Alpine char, grayling and whiting which thrive in the pure, crystal clear waters of the region's rivers and lakes. Or cloudberries, artic bramble and lingon, carefully picked from the moss, forests and grasslands that line the fells. Beard lichen that hangs from the trees, the special shii-take mushroom which grows in abundance in the world's largest mine...
The list of Laplander delicacies is almost endless.

Reindeer have always been the giants of Lapland, and a source of food that defies all others.
Nothing goes to waste. Even the tough hooves are eaten, turned into a special dish called pölsa. Up here, the art of freezing food was developed long before mechanical refrigeration was ever invented. Back then, the ice box was right outside people's doors.
Even today, the art of using all that nature provides is not lost. Reindeer still make up one of the mainstays of the Sámi diet where everything is used: the neck, legs, blood, intestines and stomach – anything that can be eaten is eaten. Souvas, smoked venison, reindeer tongue and mince meat are just a few of the many delicacies you'll find here.
Apart from the reindeer, other common ingredients are whiting and salmon. The fine art of pickling has been lovingly refined in Lapland and, like salting, is a prime way to preserve fish and meats.
The only grain used in the bread that is made here is barley which thrives in the harsh climate of the region and is the staple ingredient of the traditional soft, thin bread and black pudding that is common here.
The mosses and lands which remain after the forests have been harvested provide the perfect growing environment for cloudberries and arctic bramble – an ideal way to finish a meal.
Today, cross-over cuisine has reached into places far north of the Polar circle and few people who venture here are surprised to find venison being prepared in a traditional Chinese wok. Venison hamburgers are also common, adding a strangely exotic touch to fast-foods. Wasabi, the green Japanese horseradish, mixed with stewed apple heightens, the flavor of venison. Sashimi made from fresh whiting, grayling and alpine char, or thinly sliced venison loin.
Nothing is impossible.

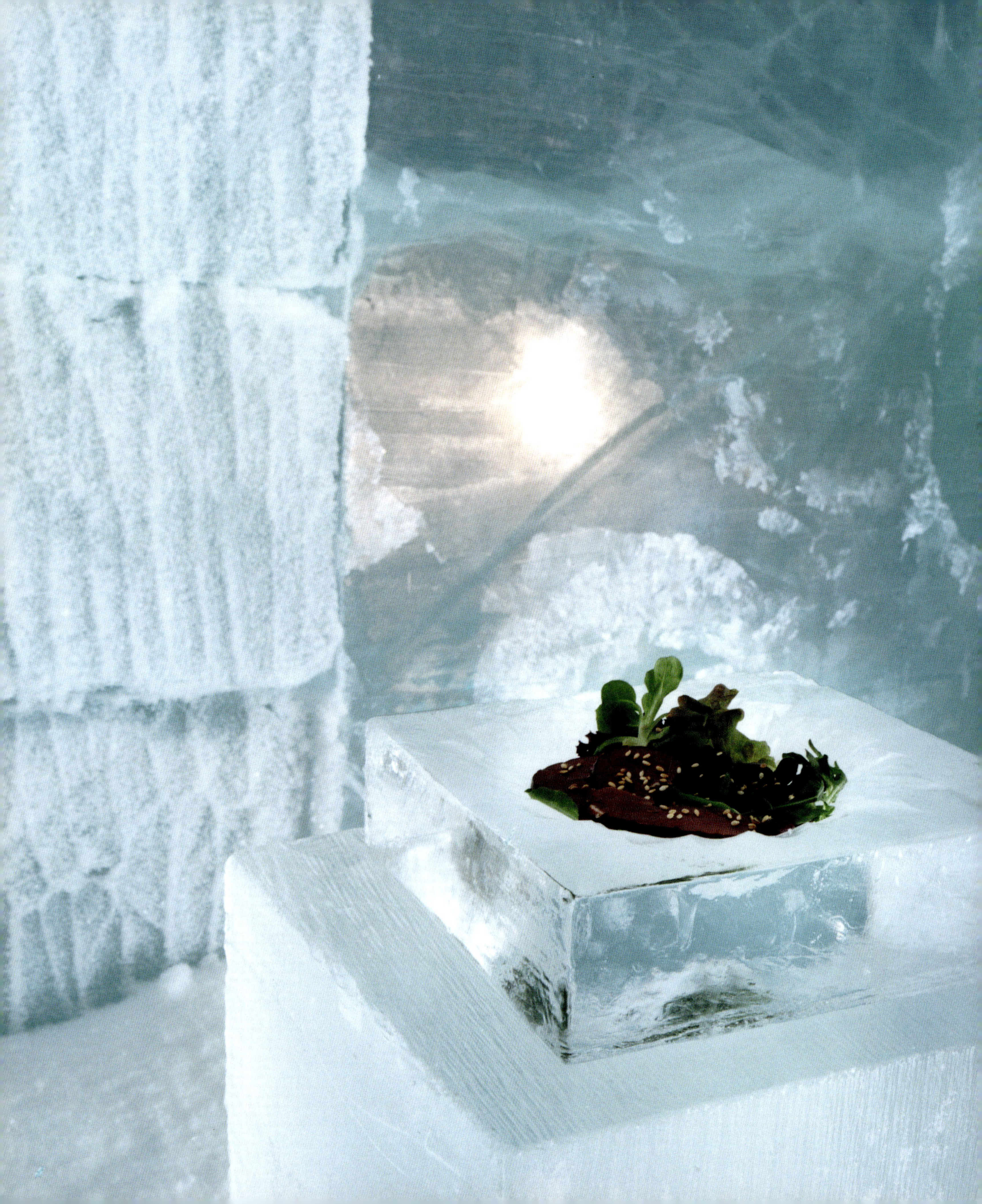

CUISINE

Salad garnished with reindeer heart

During the summer, venison is smoked in kåtor, the traditional tent dwellings of the Sámi people. Lightly salted meats hang to cure before they are placed above the gently rising smoke of glowing fires.
Meat looses a lot of its weight when it is dried and smoked which is an advantage if it is to be consumed on long journeys across the wilderness. Smoked meat was a vital part of the Sámi diet, and is still very common throughout the region.
One special delicacy is smoked reindeer heart.
This dish is a salad that is garnished with lightly smoked reindeer heart, ruccola, kidney beans and roasted sesame seeds.

Sesame seeds are first roasted in a dry, hot pan before being mixed with the ruccola and red kidney beans. To this, add thin slices of lightly smoked reindeer heart.

INGREDIENTS

Smoked reindeer heart, sesame seeds, ruccola and kidney beans.
Alternatively: A variation of salads can be added to the dish, but the three main ingredients are irreplaceable.

CUISINE

Sushinori with a thin omelet and cognac marinated whiting

Icehotel has introduced a kind of cuisine to Jukkasjärvi which has obviously been influenced by the Japanese kitchen. The fish found in the Torne River and in the clear, blue waters of the local lakes, make them ideally suited to be eaten raw – just like the finest sushi and sashimi. And this is the basis of a crossover dish which features Japanese nori – thin sheets of dried seaweed – that are used as the mantle that holds the thin omelet and cognac marinated whiting together.

First, marinate the whiting in the cognac. Lightly fry the gossamer thin omelet, and then place the whiting inside before rolling it up. Shape the Nori sheets around this mixture, and then slice the whiting filed omelet into bite-sized pieces.

INGREDIENTS

Cognac, thin slices of whiting, egg and nori.
Alternatively: the whiting can be replaced by other fish from the salmon family.

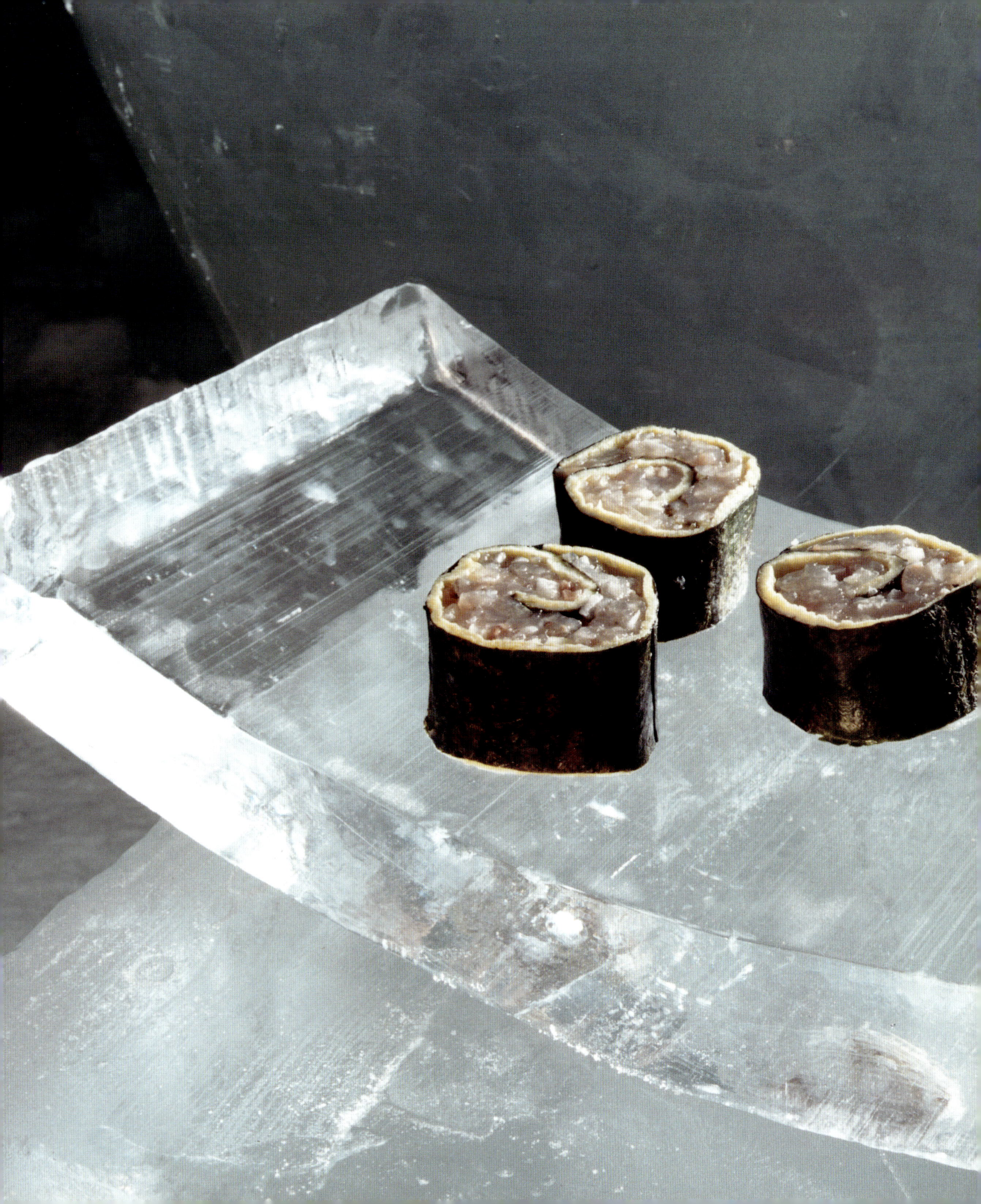

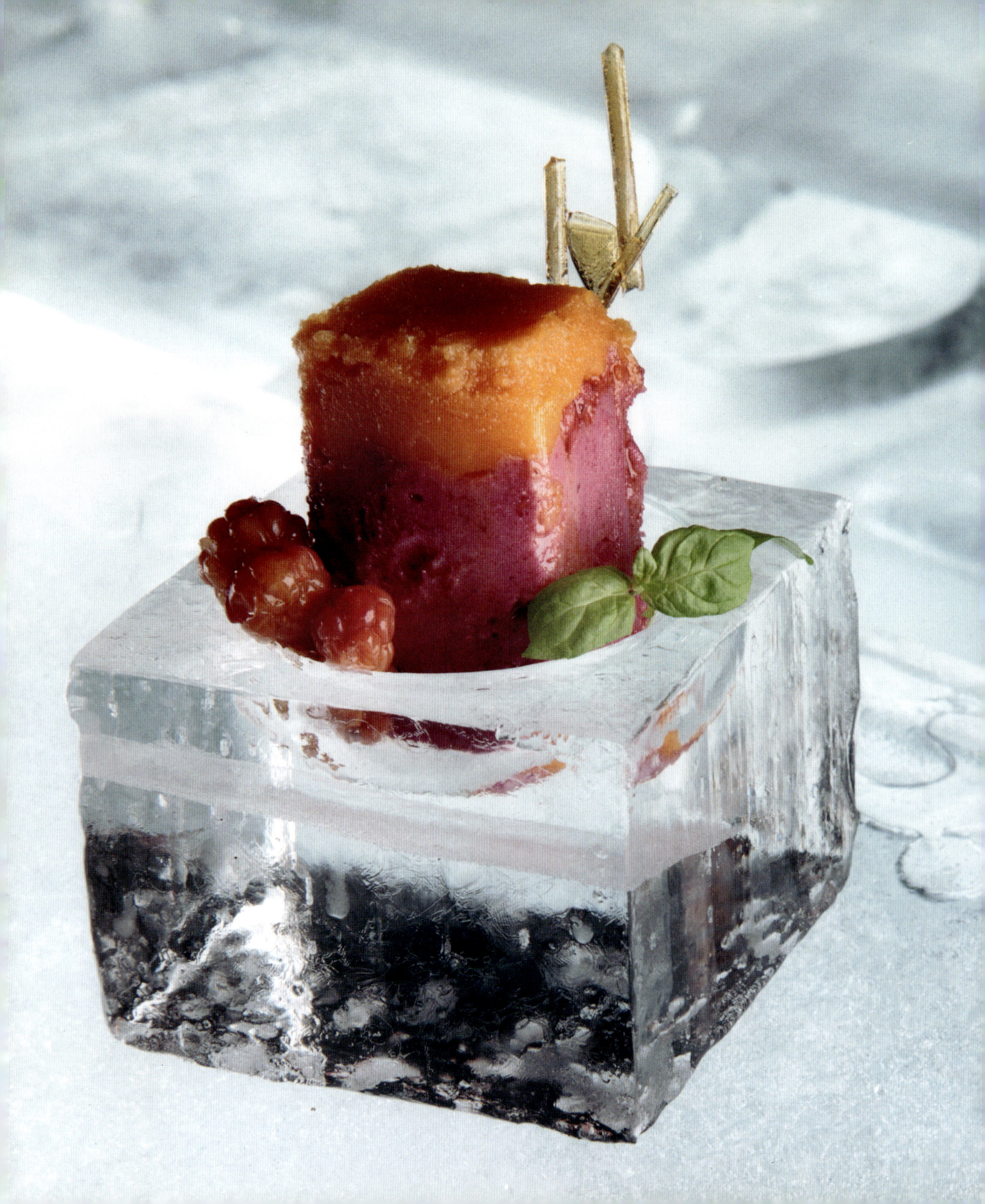

Arctic bramble and cloudberry sorbet

The renowned Swedish botanist, Carl von Linné, once called the arctic bramble a "queen among berries". It is a berry which is hard to pick, growing as it does on short thickets which grow along ditches, and in the vegetation that lines streams and rivers.
Arctic bramble looks a lot like wild strawberry, tastes like raspberry and can easily be confused with the blackberry.
Here we have made a sorbet from arctic bramble and then shaped it into a "pillar" together with the cloudberry sorbet. It is an unbeatable desert made from two of nature's finest gifts.

INGREDIENTS

sugar, water, arctic bramble and cloudberries.

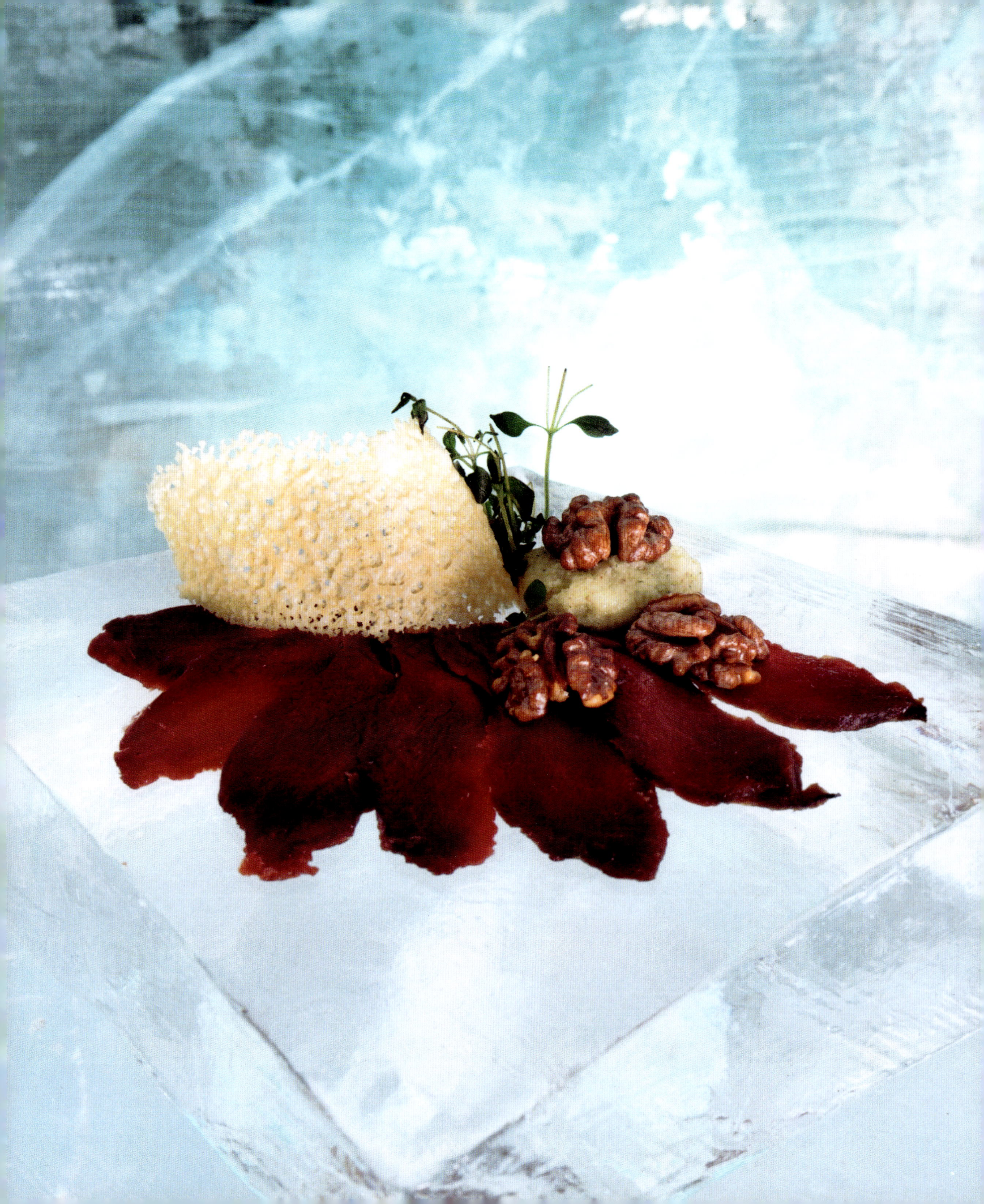

Carpaccio from elk fillet

The Swedes call the elk the King of the forest. With his majestic crown and distinctive walk, it makes light work of forests, fields and moors.
It's elk season in Sweden during the late autumn and early winter, and more than 100,000 animals are shot each year. Most of their prime meat is packed off directly into the hunters' own freezers. Just a fraction is sold on for sale to the public. Generally speaking, elk meat is prepared in much the same way as you would beef. However, the unmistakable flavor bears witness to it's origin from the wild. The fact that elk live off what they can forage from nature makes for a lean meat with a superb flavor. No wonder it is the perfect cut for our Carpaccio dish.

Wrap the fillet in foil and leave in the freezer for a while so that it is easier to slice. Use a sharp knife or machine to cut thin slices. Serve with a pesto made from Västerbotten cheese and walnuts. Make a thin flan from a slice of the cheese in a frying pan.

INGREDIENTS

Fillet of elk, pesto made from Västerbotten cheese, walnuts
Alternatively: fillet of beef and another kind of musty, hard cheese.

CUISINE

Lobster filled flounder nori

Flounder, which thrives along the Norwegian coast of the northern Atlantic, is a flat fish which can grow up to 3 meters long and weigh as much as 300 kilograms. Its firm, white meat with a defined texture and distinctive flavor, makes it ideal for a wide range of dishes. Celebrating its shear size, our recipe combines this special fish with the meat of the Atlantic lobster and the delicate taste of trout roe.

Our first nori roll is made from Japanese seaweed mixed with small pieces of lobster meat. This is then wrapped in a 1 cm thick piece of sliced flounder which is steamed over boiling water.
Our sauce is made by melting a little demerara sugar in some white wine, adding a few aniseeds and some thin slices of lemon peel. To give the sauce a really fluffy texture, gently fold egg yolks into the mixture while the saucepan stands over a steam bath.
Top off with a measure of trout roe.

INGREDIENTS

Nori (Japanese seaweed), lobster, flounder, demerara sugar, dry white wine, aniseeds, thinly sliced lemon peel, egg yolks and trout roe.
Alternatively: the flounder can be replaced with any aromatic flatfish.

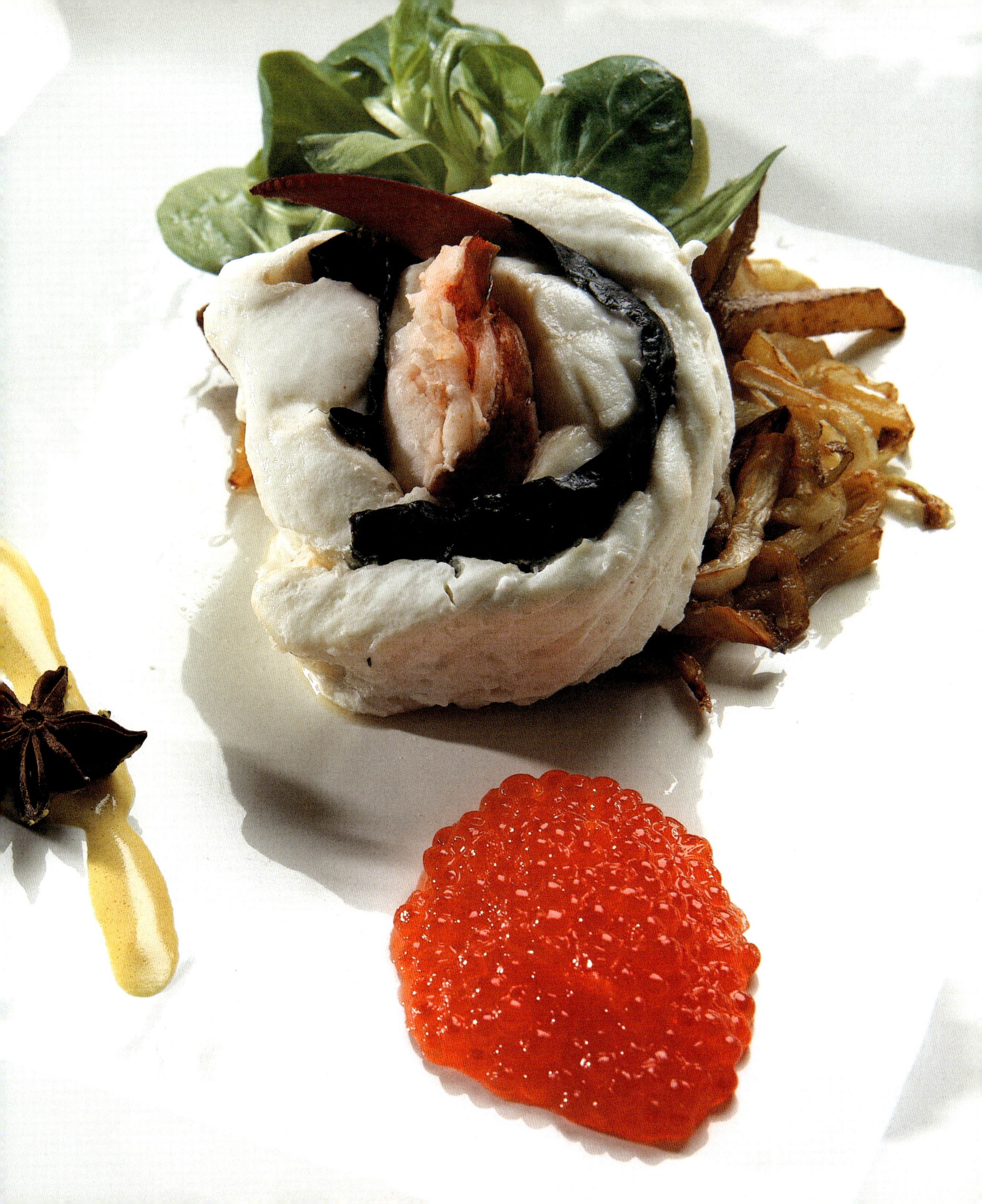

Reindeer – the mainstay of the Sámi pantry

Reindeer have almost always dictated the way in which the life of the Sámi people has taken its course, and reindeer meat has always been at the heart of Sámi cuisine.

Then, as now, the animals are slaughtered in September. Some of the meat is salted and lays untouched until April when it is hung in the warm spring winds to dry. Even today, it is possible to see south-facing walls lined with reindeer meat drying in the sun in the Sámi villages of the region. During the summer, the meat is smoked.

The Sámi people have always used everything that comes from the reindeer, and everything apart from the skin can be eaten. The head was used to make broth, the hooves were boiled to make a traditional dish called pölsa. The brain was removed and boiled in salt water before being chopped into small pieces. The intestines were used for making sausages, as was the stomach. The kidneys were eaten and the surrounding fat was used to make blood sausage and black pudding. Even the marrow bone was considered a delicacy. Today, reindeer meat still reflects pure quality and the finer cuts, such as filets, are served at the finest Swedish tables.

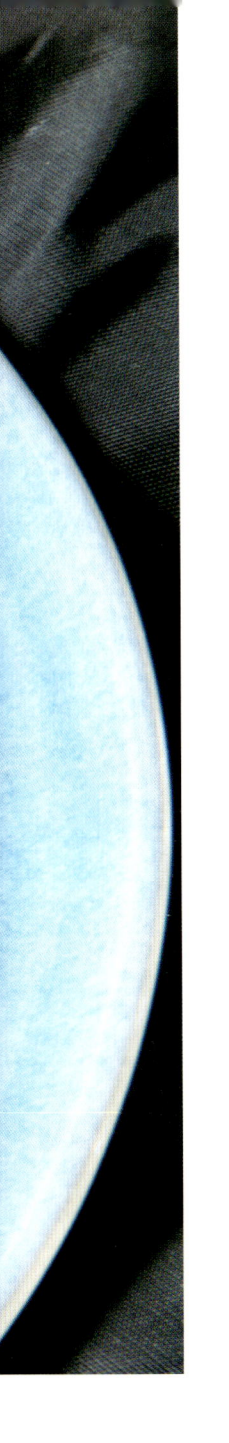

Fillet of young reindeer venison with shii-take mushrooms

The fillet of young reindeer venison should not be cooked for longer than it takes for the meat to turn pink. Inside, it should still almost be raw. The best tasting and most tender results come from meat that has been heated to no more than 58°C.
Free the fillet from fat and sinus, then fry slowly in butter. Let it rest for a moment before carving and serving which is best done together with various kinds of sliced potatoes that have been oven roasted at 250° C. The potato slices should be lightly basted with a mixture of olive oil and herbs, such as thyme and chervil.
Add shii-take mushrooms taken from the Kiruna mine that have been sauteed in butter and serve with a fresh, green salad.

INGREDIENTS

Fillet of young reindeer venison, shii-take mushrooms, various kinds of potato and herbs including thyme and chervil. Green salad.
Alternatively: the fillet of young reindeer venison can be exchanged for fillet of venison from the fallow or row deer.
Naturally, the shii-take mushrooms taken from the Kiruna mine can be replaced with Asian shii-take.

CUISINE

Chocolate cheesecake with port wine marinated blueberries

Blueberries are a valued ingredient in many Swedish desserts. However, they are mostly found in preserves and juices. This forest-growing berry has also been turned into a nutritious soup which is served each year to the thousands of skiers who take part in a cross-country race that is held between Sälen and Mora in Dalarna – a race that's called Wasaloppet.
Blueberry soup stands are erected along the 90 kilometer course where this tasty brew is served to the participants to keep out the cold, and give them much needed energy.
Blueberries taste especially good when served together with dark chocolate, for example, in a chocolate cheesecake. Concentrated blueberry juice and port wine add further flavor which, for most Swedes, reminds them of childhoods spent at cottages in the forests.

Dark chocolate is melted and carefully mixed with lightly whipped cream and cottage cheese. While the chocolate cheesecake sets, heat sugar-based syrup, concentrated blueberry juice and port wine in a saucepan to make a thick sauce. Remove from the stove and allow to cool before carefully adding fresh blueberries and serving with the chocolate cheesecake.

INGREDIENTS

Dark chocolate, cream and cottage cheese, sugar, concentrated blueberry juice, port wine and fresh raspberries.

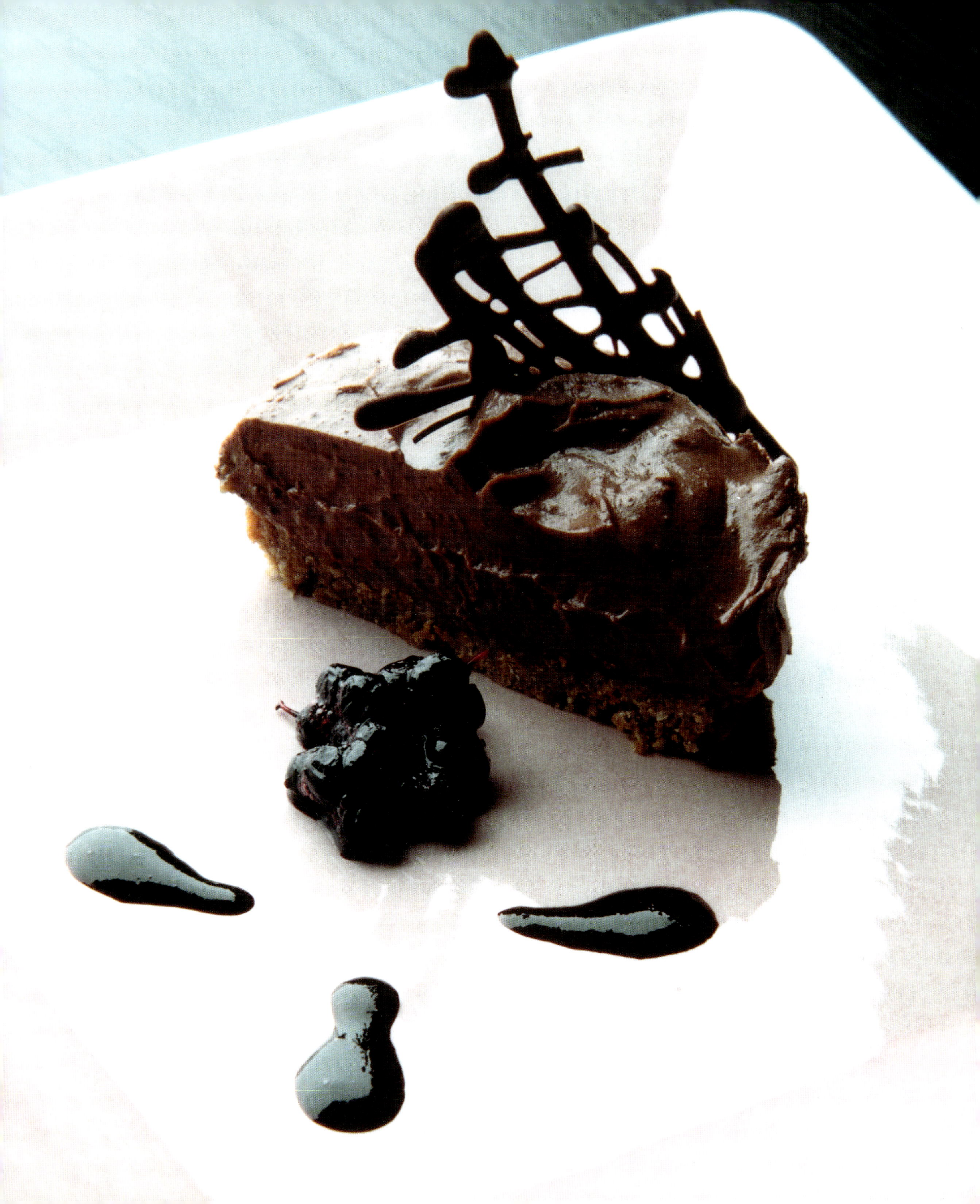

Sashimi made from whiting and alpine char

Fish which are found in cold waters make an excellent basis for sashimi. Raw and thinly sliced, they are served with Japanese soya, wasabi and preserved ginger.
Icehotel lies just a snowball's cast away from the Torne River, one of Europe's cleanest expanses of inland water. Whiting, one of the finest fish in the salmon family, are plentiful here and, if you are really lucky, you may well catch more than one of these fine fish in your net. The alpine char come from the pristine inland lakes that are found all over Lapland.
This time, luck was with us and we came home with 50 whiting, many of which carried the distinctively delicate yellow whiting roe. Our alpine char was purchased from a local fisherman who had even more luck than we on this late autumn morning. Slice the whiting and alpine char fillets into thin slices and clean the roe from skin and blood vessels. Serve in the traditional Japanese way.

INGREDIENTS

Thin slices of whiting and alpine char, whiting roe, preserved ginger, wasabi and Japanese soya.
Many different kinds of fish can be served as sashimi. It is really a case of availability.

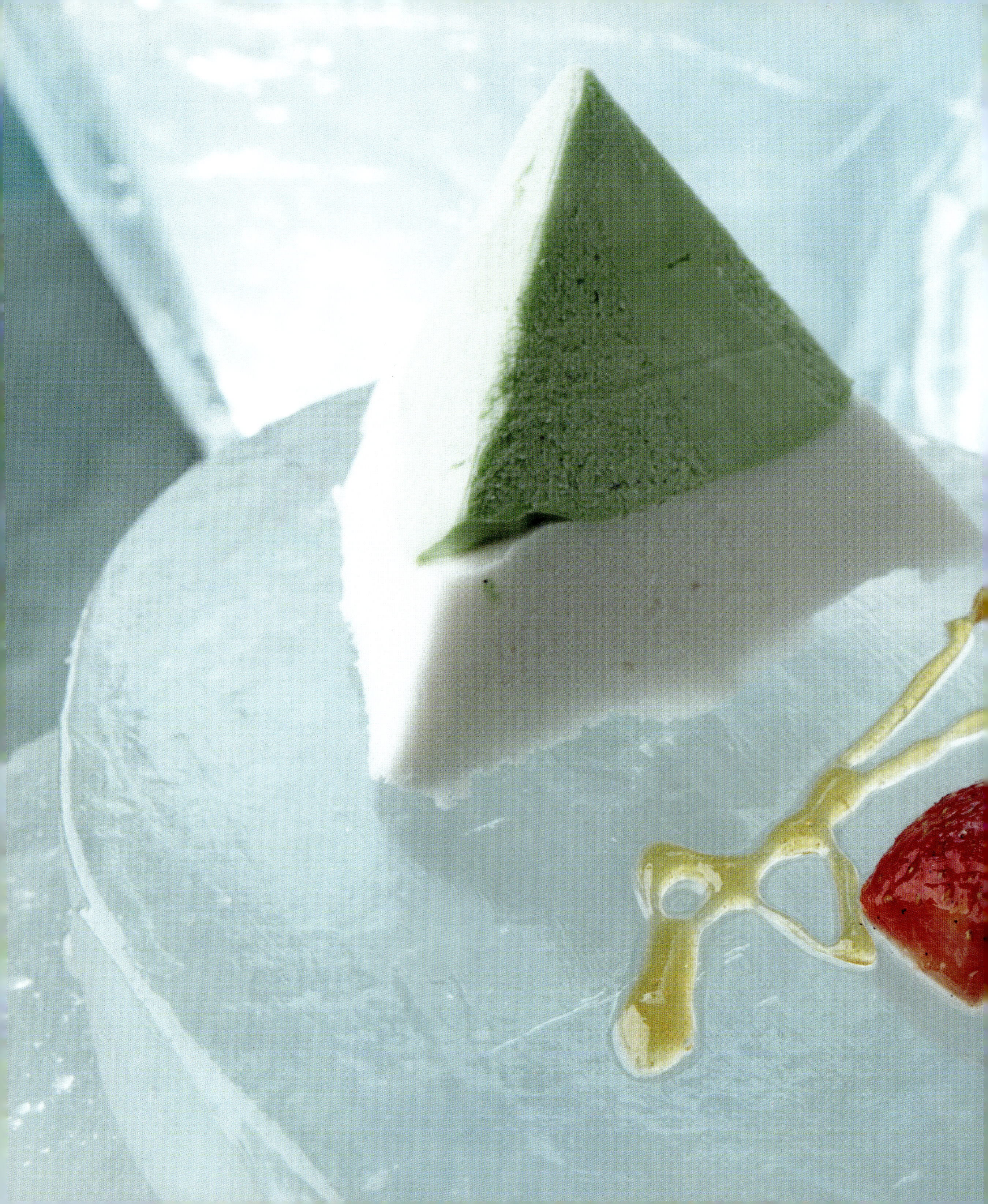

CUISINE

Green tea and coconut parfait

It is not just the many Japanese tourists who visit Icehotel that have influenced its kitchen. The sense of purity and simplicity you experience here never fails to inspire the taste buds of visitors to this, the world's largest igloo. Like in this dessert where green tea is used as the basis for a delicious parfait. Coconut sorbet and chili marinated strawberries also bear witness to the fact that here, an unfettered gastronomic approach abounds.

Fist, boil and reduce a measure of green tea, then flavor a parfait made from egg yolks and sugar. Fold gently into lightly whipped cream. Once the parfait has cooled, turn it into a suitable mould together with the coconut sorbet made from syrup, vanilla and coconut. Allow the strawberries to marinate in a mixture of fresh chili, lime and vanilla which has been boiled to form a syrup that is allowed to cool.

INGREDIENTS

Eggs, sugar, cream, coconut, vanilla stalks, strawberries, fresh chili and lime.

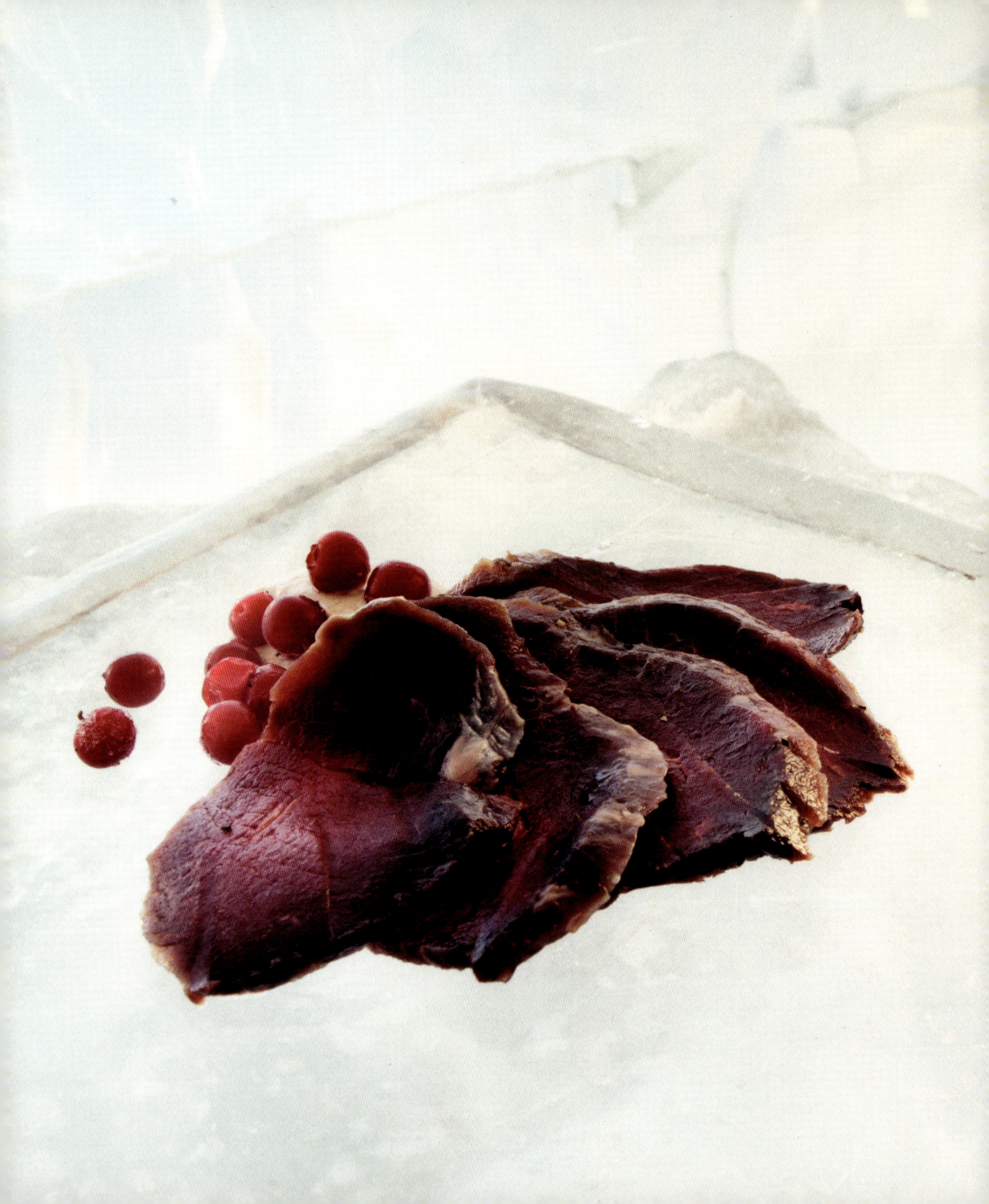

Pickled loin of reindeer venison

Pickling is an old method used to preserve fish and meat. With modern refrigeration, it is no longer needed as a way to keep food fresh, but in the kitchen of the north, the unmistakable flavor of finely pickled fish and meats has lived on.

Meat – game in particular – becomes a delicacy when selected cuts are pickled using traditional methods.

After carefully removing all the fat and sinew from the meat, rub it with a mixture of salt, sugar, white pepper and cognac. Let the meat lay in this mixture inside double plastic bags for two days in the refrigerator. Remove from the bags, slice thinly and serve.

INGREDIENTS

Loin of reindeer venison, salt, sugar, white pepper, parsley and cognac.
Alternatively: Loin of venison from fallow or row deer. Add a little fresh thyme, basil and parsley. Mix together with the liquid in which the meat will be pickled.

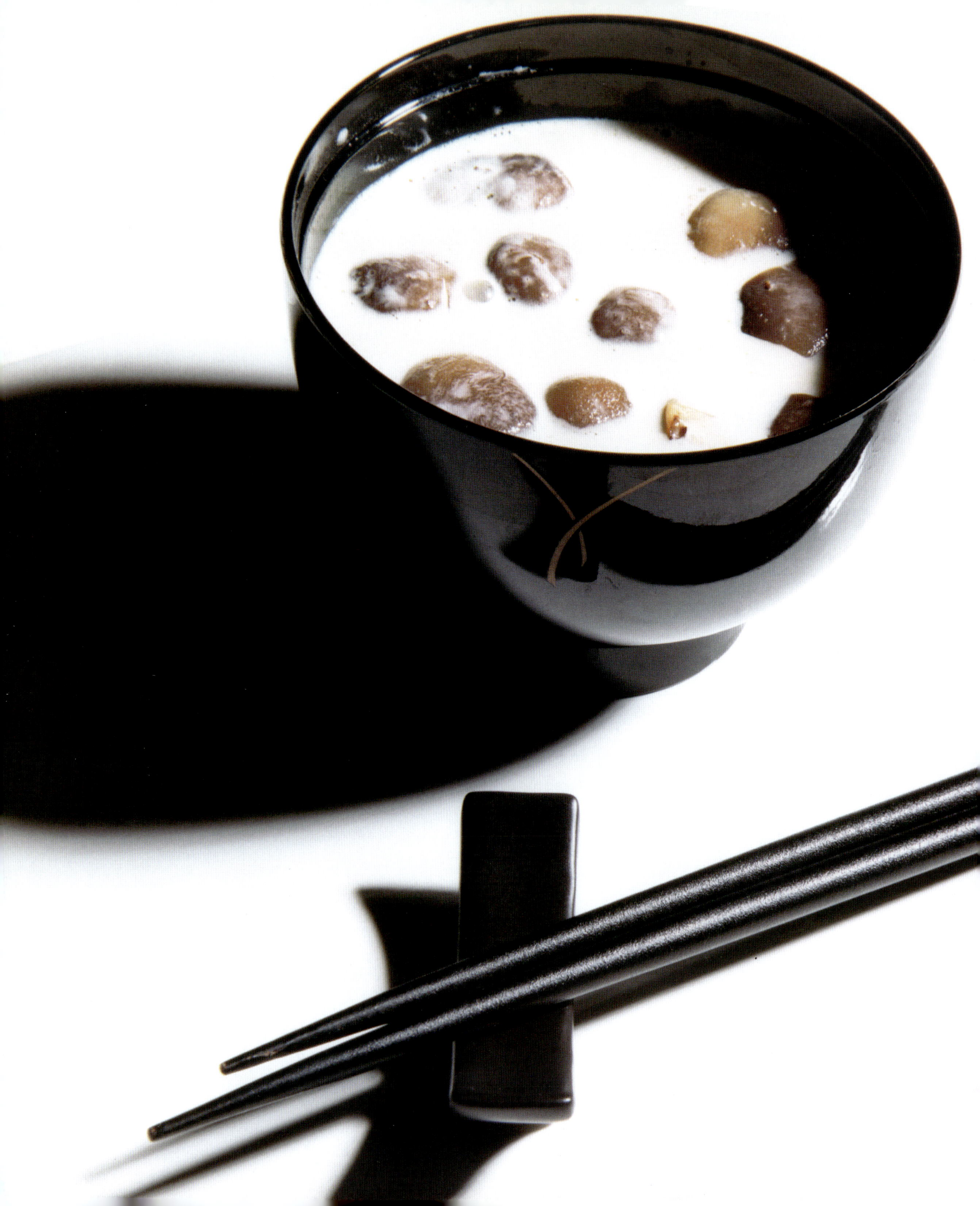

CUISINE

Shii-take soup

The shii-take mushroom is an oriental delicacy much appreciated for its special flavor. It is the largest variety of mushroom used in Asian cuisine, and can also be grown elsewhere on earth if the conditions are right. Like in Kiruna, deep inside in the largest underground mine in the world.
The shii-take mushrooms– also known as the Kiruna mushroom – grow at a depth of 540 meters under the ground in abandoned mine shafts and a former control center. The Kiruna mushroom became famous when it was included as an ingredient in the main course of a dish served at the 1992 Nobel Dinner.
The shii-take mushroom is said to have excellent health-giving properties and is often used in eastern medicine.

We are going to make a soup from the mushroom. First, lightly fry some mushrooms in butter and then add a little water and some cream. Bring the mixture to the boil. Enhance the taste using a little mushroom stock and serve wile still hot.

INGREDIENTS

Shii-take mushrooms from the Kiruna mine, cream, mushroom stock
Alternatively: shii-take mushrooms from Asia can be used.

CUISINE

Seaweed and algae soup

When the mercury falls below -30°C, heat is vital. Dressed properly, and with your energy reserves topped up by a warm dish that's been lovingly prepared in the hotel's kitchen, you're ready for any adventure the day might bring.
Now Sweden is not a country known for its soups, but there is no doubting the fact that soup is the perfect food for cold climates – like this simple, yet delicious seaweed and algae dish.

All you need to do is boil dried seaweed and algae in fresh water, add miso paste, and serve.

INGREDIENTS

Dried seaweed and algae, miso paste (made from soya beans).
Miso originates from the Japanese kitchen and is used to flavor soups, marinades, sauces and glazes.

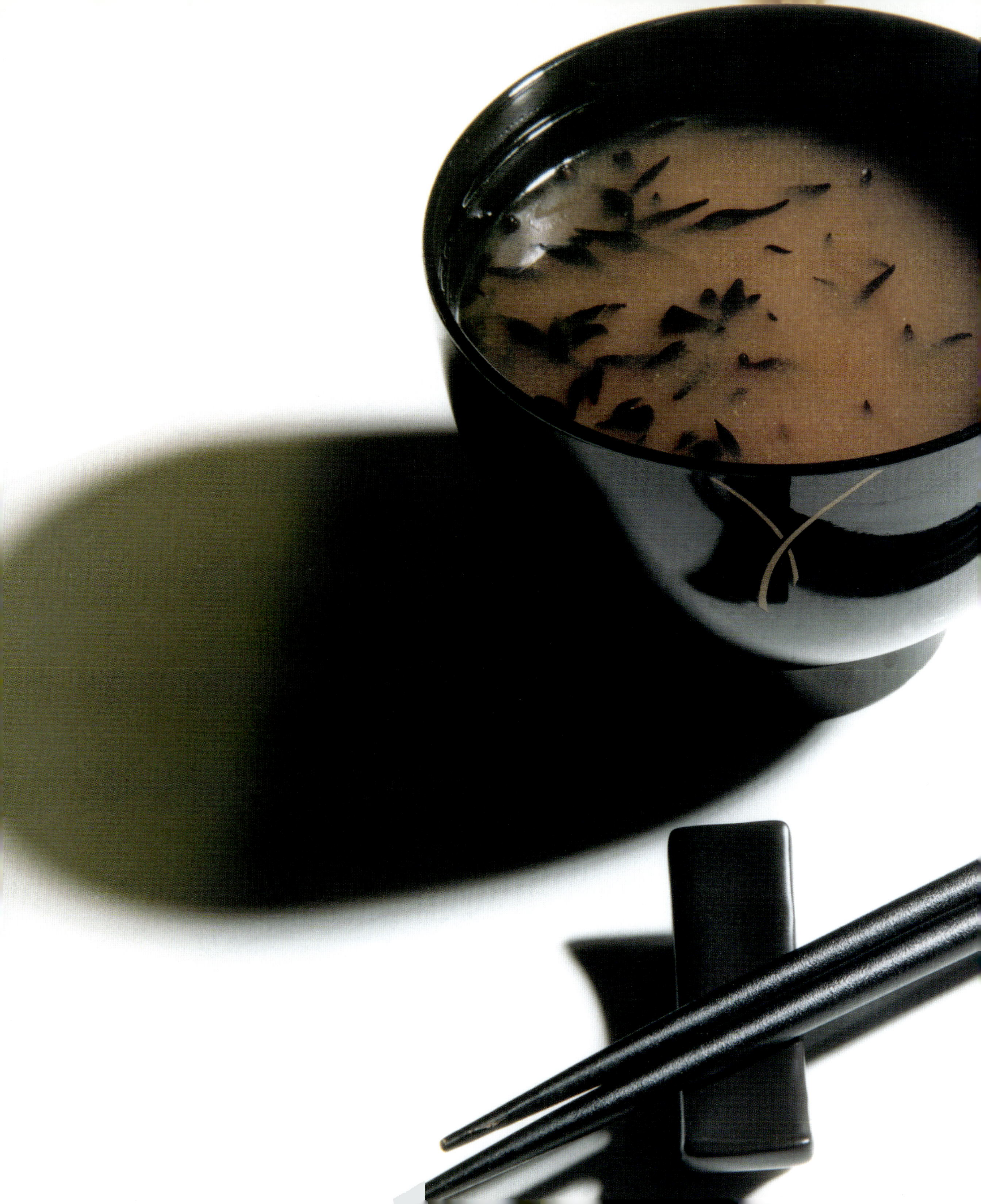

CUISINE

Saltimbocca from the north

Saltimbocca is an Italian dish what is made from thinly sliced veal schnitzel, wafer thin slices of salt-cured ham, and parma ham, all spiced with salvia. We use thin slices of reindeer venison loin in our Sámi-inspired variant of this Italian classic while the hard, mature cheese, famous for its musty flavor, comes from the north Swedish district of Västerbotten.

Cover the thinly sliced venison loin with parma ham and västerbotten cheese. Spice with fresh or dried salvia, then roll the slices together. Fix using toothpicks. Fry in butter until golden brown.

INGREDIENTS

Thin slices of venison loin, västerbotten cheese and fresh or dried salvia.
Alternatively: Other meats and another kind of mature, musty hard cheese can be used.

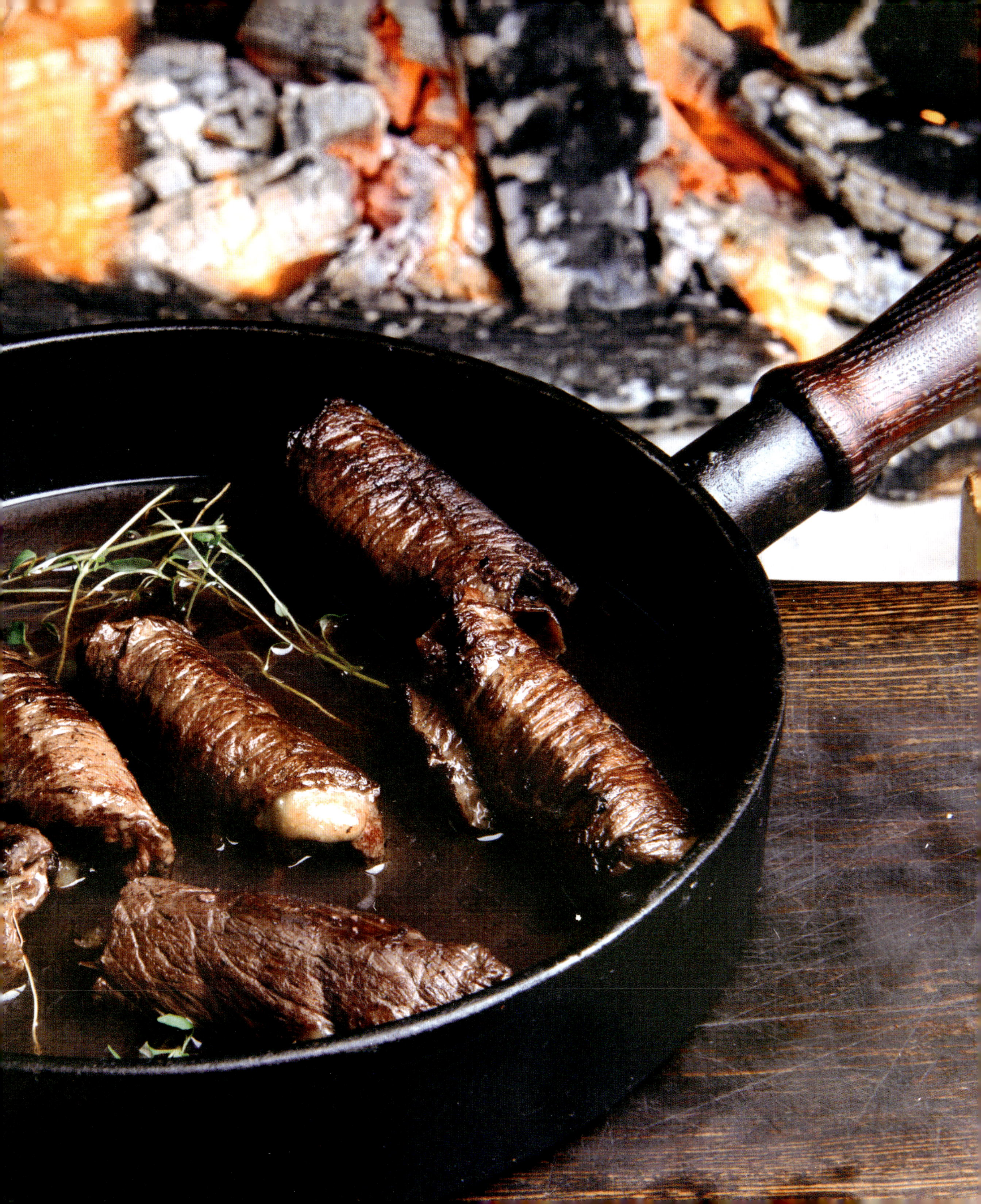

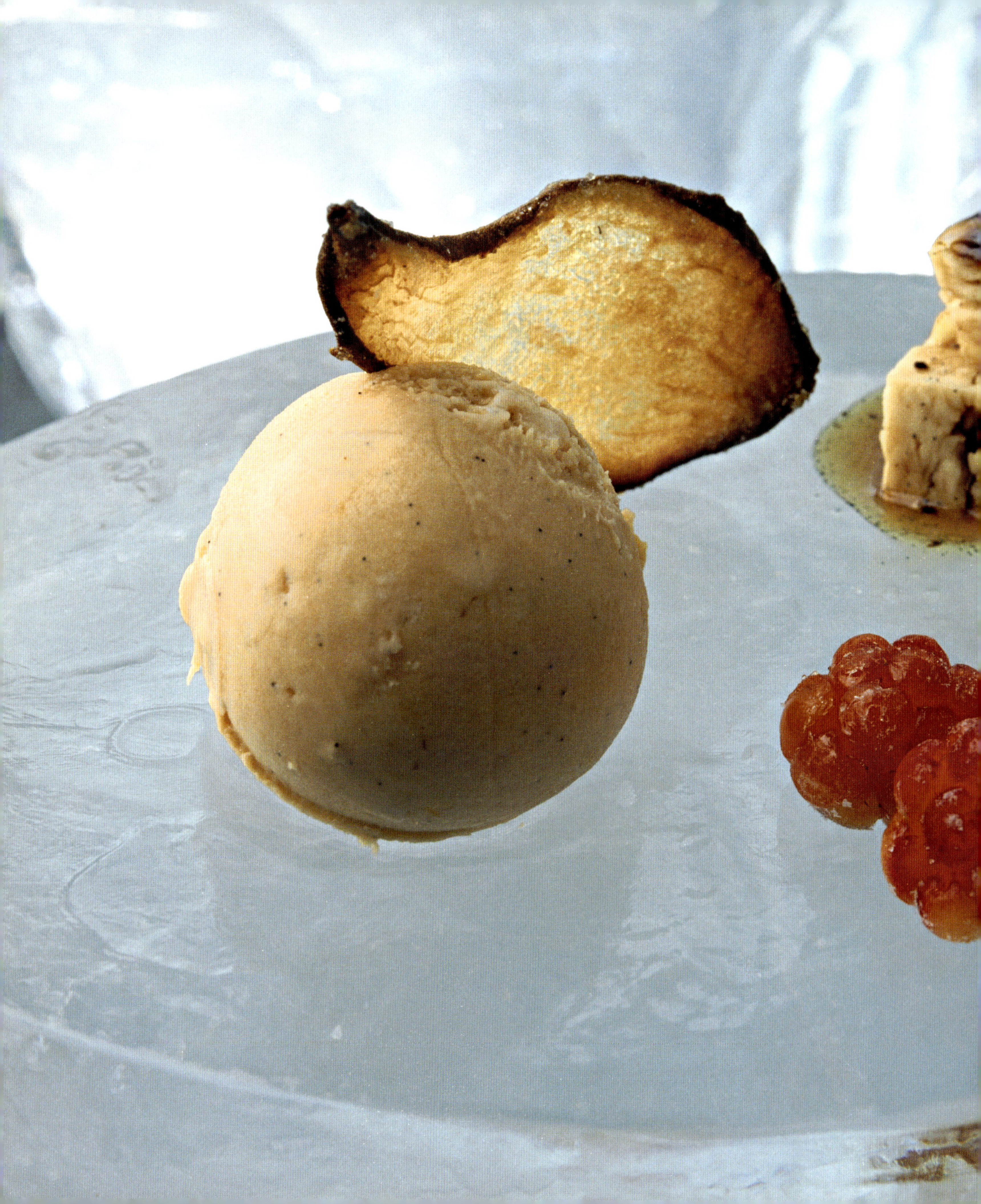

CUISINE

Cloudberry ice cream with Kahlúa-marinated coffee cheese

Out on the marshes and mosses of Lapland grow the wild cloudberry, the choicest of all berries which are often served at large, official dinners such as those held at the Royal Swedish Court. The cloudberry has a white, attractive flower which produces a highly aromatic yellow berry.
Ice cream, flavored with cloudberry, is the delicacy on offer in this dish spiced up with coffee cheese – a special kind of cheese made by the Sámi from reindeer milk. Topping it off, we add a sprinkling of fresh cloudberries and a pear chip.

Using a simple ice cream maker, flavor the mixture with fresh cloudberries. Cut the coffee cheese into cubes and lightly fry. Cover with a syrup made from water, sugar, vanilla stalks, freeze-dried coffee and Kahlúa liqueur. Reduce the mixture. Lightly sprinkle a thin slice of pear with raw sugar, and dry out in an oven.

INGREDIENTS

Cloudberries, eggs, confectioners's sugar, cream, coffee cheese, vanilla stalks, freeze-dried coffee, Kahlúa liqueur, pears and raw sugar.

CUISINE

Grouse served with chanterelles and glazed cabbage

There are two kinds of grouse which are indigenous to Sweden: the Valley Grouse and the Fell Grouse. More than 30,000 Valley Grouse are shot each year while the number of Fell Grouse taken is far less. The Fell Grouse turns a snowy white in winter which makes it hard to detect. It is hardly surprising that it is a prized spoil for hunters looking for a special challenge. This elusive bird is said to have a better flavor than the Valley Grouse.
Grouse meat is dark with a musty, woodland flavor and is best prepared by roasting it until slightly pink. Grouse should never take longer than 15 minutes to roast in a medium temperature oven.
The musty flavor of this game challenges the inventiveness of any chef who prepares it. One way is to use jelly made from cranberries, another is to top off the meat with a garnish of chanterelle.

After removing the bones from the breast, the meat is then browned by frying it in hot butter before roasting it at a temperature of 175°C until it turns pink. Serve with savoy cabbage and brussels sprouts, lightly boiled, then glazed in butter and raw sugar. Finally add whole, fresh lingonberries and boiled potatoes.

INGREDIENTS

Breast of grouse, chanterelles, savoy cabbage, brussels sprouts and raw sugar.
Alternatively: Use another kind of small game bird, and musty tasting mushrooms.

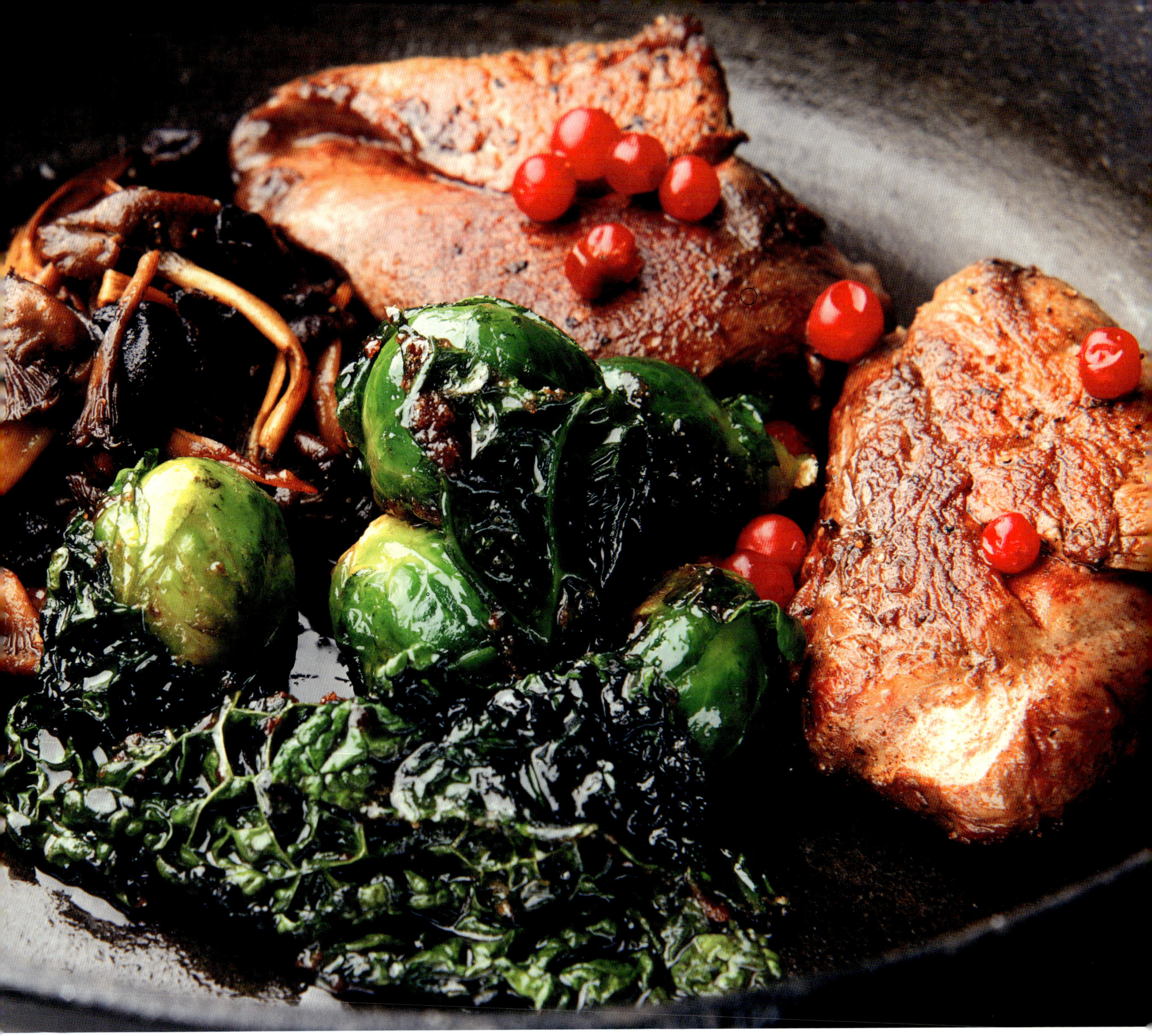

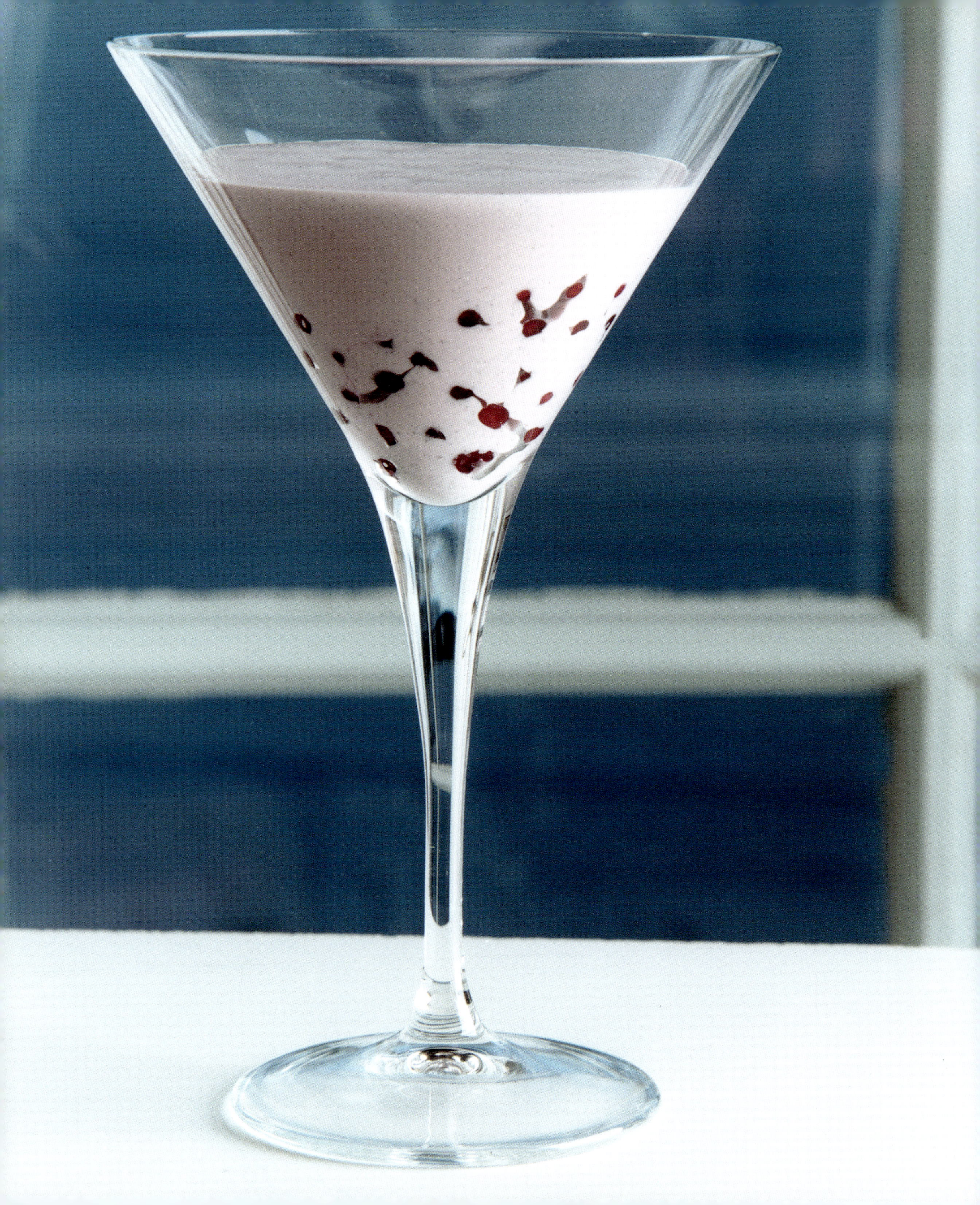

CUISINE

Lingon berry and cinnamon panacotta

The lingon berry is often called the red gold of the forest. It is commonly found growing wild in the alkaline earth of the forests and moors of the northern hemisphere. Lingon preserves have long been a popular ingredient in Swedish traditional food, and many Swedes venture out into the forests in the autumn to pick the ripe berries.
The lingon is common in Sweden. In fact, there is so much of this wild crop that migrant workers flock here to harvest it. But despite this, far from all the berries that grow in Swedish forests are gathered. There are simply too many of them.
This dish uses a panacotta (Italian vanilla cream), that is flavored with cinnamon which provides a perfect match to the pungent flavor of the lingon berries.

First place the lingon in a suitably sized glass or bowl. Mix the panacotta, and then pour it over the fruit. Allow the panacotta to solidify in the refrigerator.

INGREDIENTS

Fresh lingon berries, cream, eggs, sugar, vanilla and cinnamon stalks.

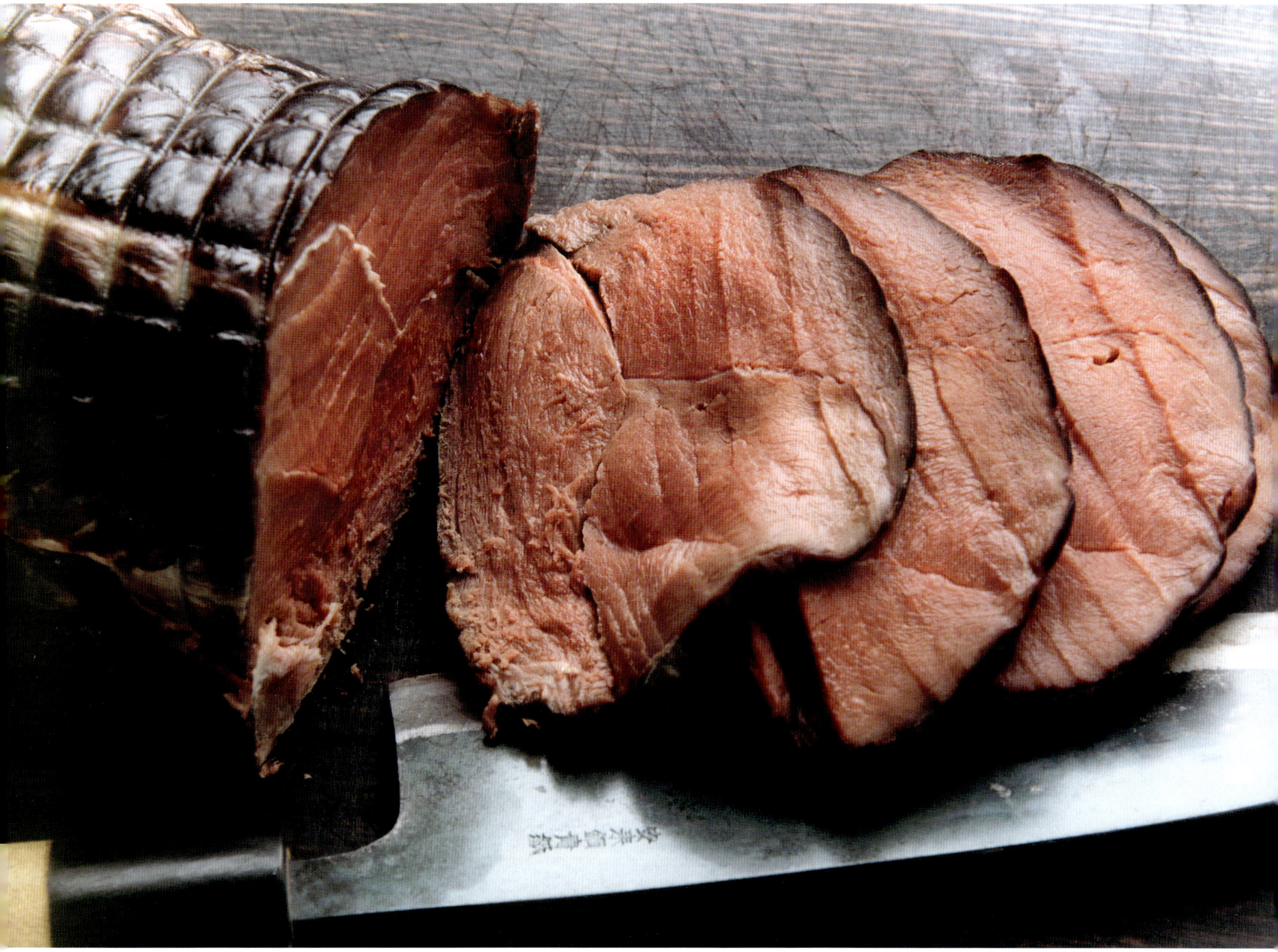

Tjälknöl (Swedish meat delicacy)

Like so much of the culinary art, this genial meat dish came about as the result of pure luck – or rather forgetfulness. The story goes that a woman promised to make dinner for some friends – on the menu, a delicious elk steak. As the meat was frozen, she decided to put it in a warm oven (at 70°C) to defrost. But alas, her guests never arrived and in her disappointment, she forgot to take the joint out before going to bed.
When she awoke the following morning, she remembered the meat and upon opening the oven found that it had shrunk considerably. The meat was warm, and still seemed to be tender, and good for eating.
To keep the joint fresh, she placed it in a salt bath for a few hours, and to her surprise, when she tasted it, it was deliceous.

Place the frozen reindeer steak into an oven set at 70°C. Leave for between 10 and 12 hours before removing. At this time, the temperature inside the meat should be 65°C. Place the joint into a plastic bag and add the salt solution which is made from water, salt, sugar, crushed black pepper and juniper berries. Leave for 4 to 5 hours before serving.

INGREDIENTS

A prime cut of venison and a salt solution.
Alternatively: Beef, pork or boneless venison from fallow or row deer can be used.
The salt solution is not necessary, especially if the joint is to be eaten straight away.

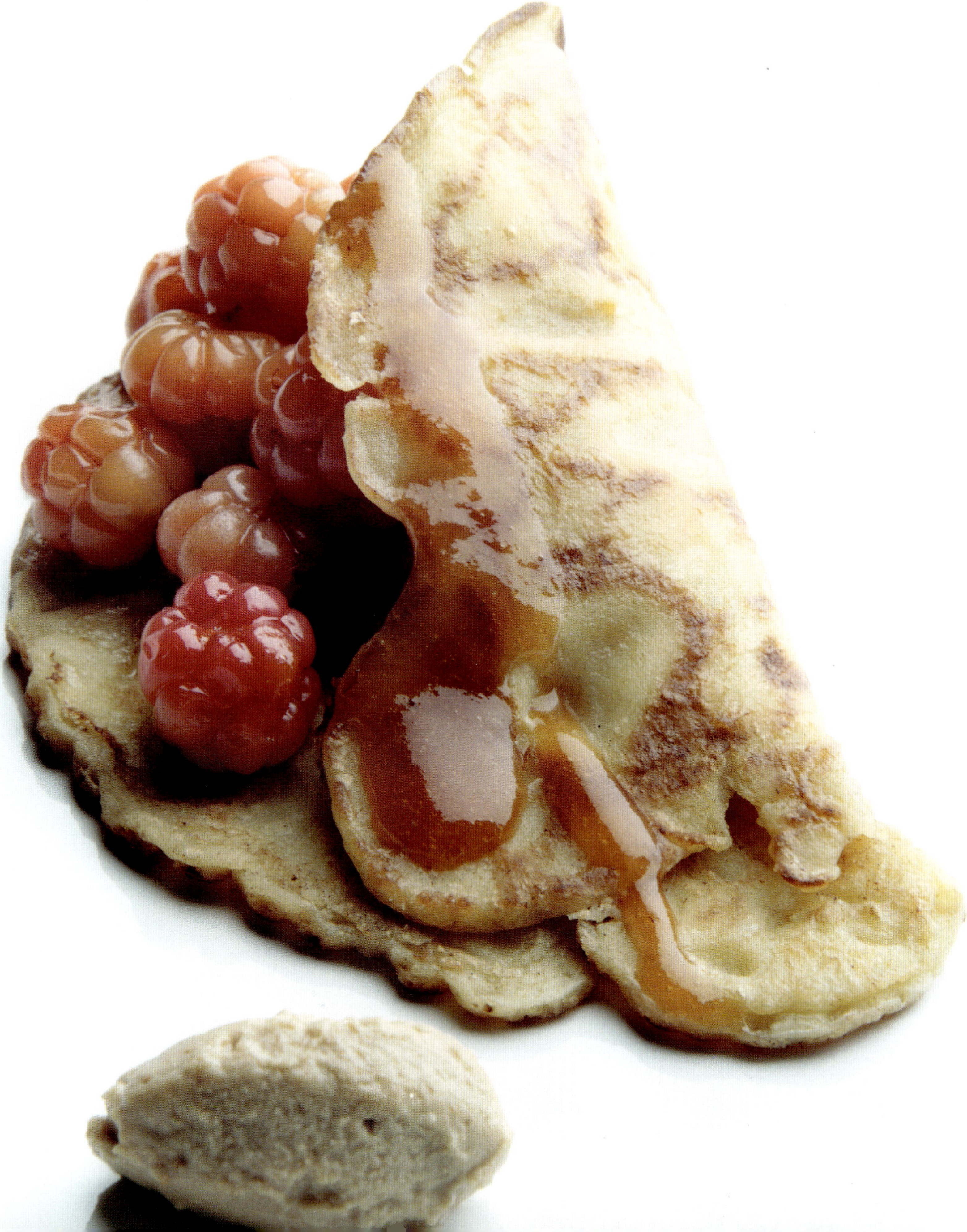

Crêpes with cloudberries, goat's milk cream and cloudberry syrup

Cloudberries are fickle fruits and the cloudberry plant doesn't always produce them. It has to do with the weather. If conditions are not just right, the flowers are not pollinated by the insects of the fells, and the crop is either small or nonexistent. Understandably, when cloudberries are plentiful, it is wise to gather as many as possible and freeze them so that when the crop is poor, you can still make delicious desserts. We've used fresh cloudberries to make this outstanding sweet.

Prepare thin crêpes in a crêpe pan and then fill them with fresh cloudberries. Make a thick sauce out of cheese made from goats milk whey mixed with cream cheese.
Before serving, cover the crêpes with syrup, strained cloudberries and a little cloudberry liqueur.

INGREDIENTS

Eggs, milk, flour, butter, cloudberry, cheese made from goat's milk whey, fresh cheese, syrup and cloudberry liqueur.

CUISINE

Pickled whiting

Pickling fish is a traditional way to preserve this delicate meat, and it is a method that is particularly well suited to salmon and herring. In the old days, when fish were caught in large quantities far from home, they were first lightly salted, then placed in barrels that were buried under ground. When the winter snows made transporting the fish back home easier, the barrels were loaded onto sleds pulled by reindeer.
The art of pickling has been refined over the years, and fish such as pickled salmon have evolved to become true delicacies. Whiting, which also belongs to the salmon family, is also a perfect fish to pickle.

Cut the whiting into fillets, but leave the skin in place. Remove all the bones and then wash thoroughly under cold, running water. Place the whiting fillets into a mixture of equal parts of salt and sugar (iodine free salt should be used) together with coarsely ground white pepper and a few drops of smoky, musty malt whisky – Islay is a good choice. In another part of Lapland, namely Västerbotten, the whisky is left out and the mixture gets its special flavor by adding spiced pepper.
The whiting fillets should be left for 12 hours after which time they are ready to serve, thinly sliced.

INGREDIENTS

Whiting fillets, salt, sugar, white pepper (or perhaps spice pepper) and malt whiskey.
Alternatively: swap the whisky for Absolut Pepper.
Other fish from the salmon family can be used if whiting is not available.

Icehotel **179**

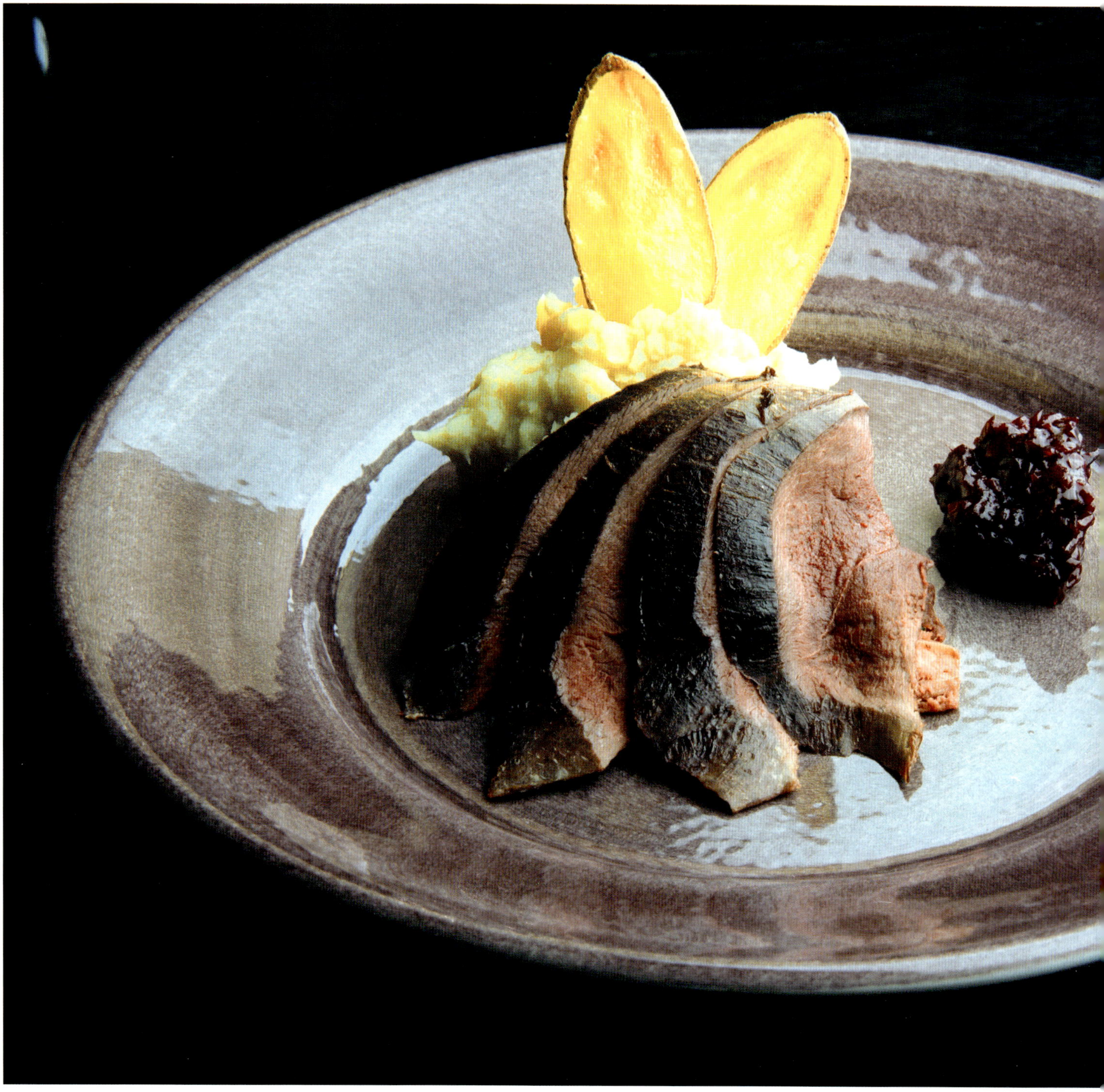

Wood grouse with rosemary cream and cranberry chutney

The Wood Grouse is one of the three most common forest dwelling birds found in Sweden, the others being the Black Grouse and the Hazel Grouse. Some 40,000 wood grouse are shot each year in Sweden – most of these end up in the hunters' freezers. However, some are sold to Icehotel where this tasty meat is served together with local cranberries – a classic garnish. Wood Grouse is also served together with a purée made from almond potatoes and turnips, covered with cream flavored with rosemary.

Slice the grouse breast from the bone, and roast it slowly in an oven until the meat turns pink. Make a purée out of almond potatoes and parsnips using plenty of cream and butter. Cranberries are used to make the chutney. First boil them together with demerara sugar, cinnamon and fresh ginger. Then add the cream, some fresh rosemary and a little honey.

INGREDIENTS

Breast of Wood Grouse, almond potatoes, parsnips, cream, butter, tranberries, demerara sugar, cinnamon stalks, fresh ginger, rosemary and honey.
Alternatively: Other forest dwelling bird meat can be used.

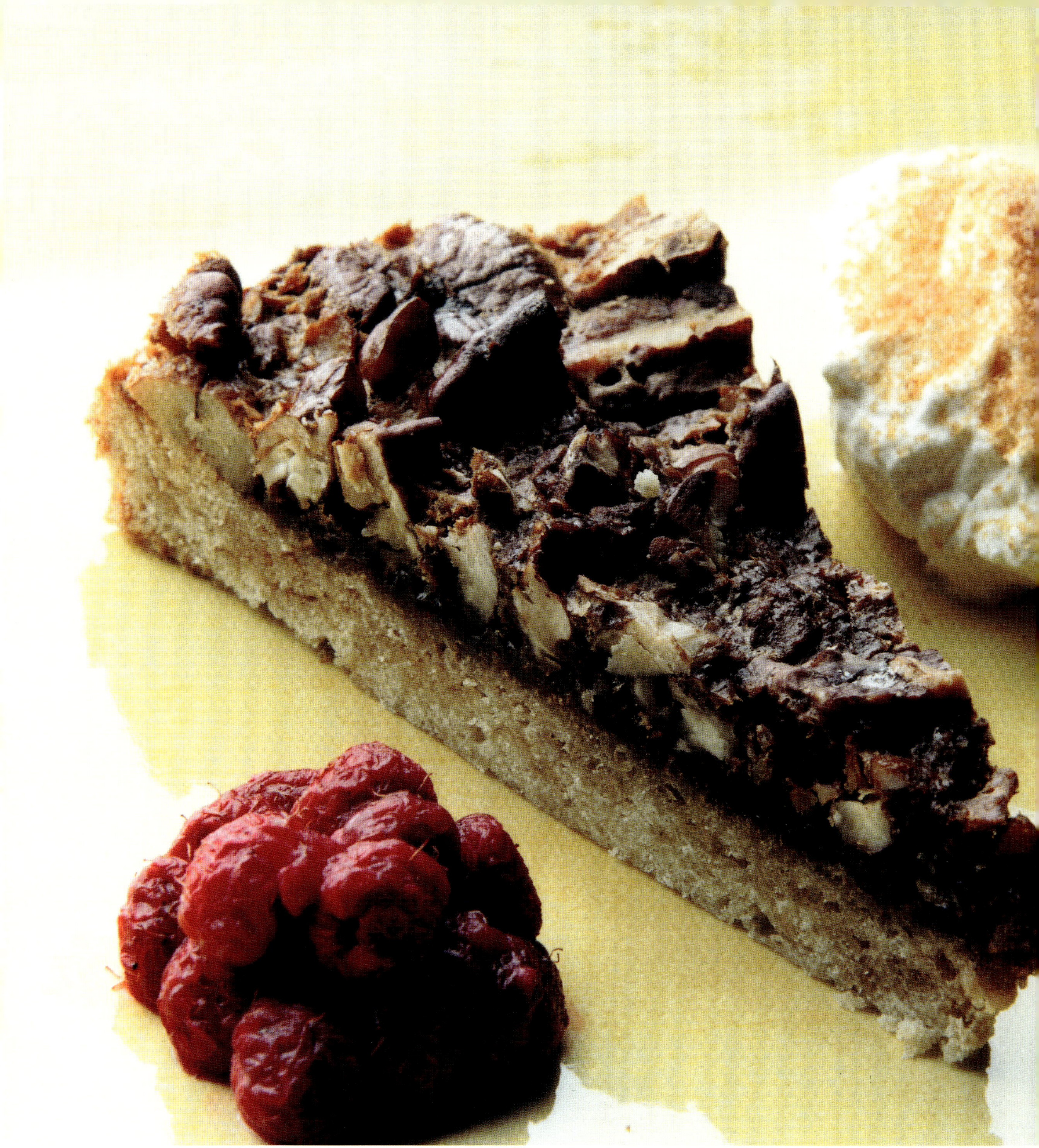

CUISINE

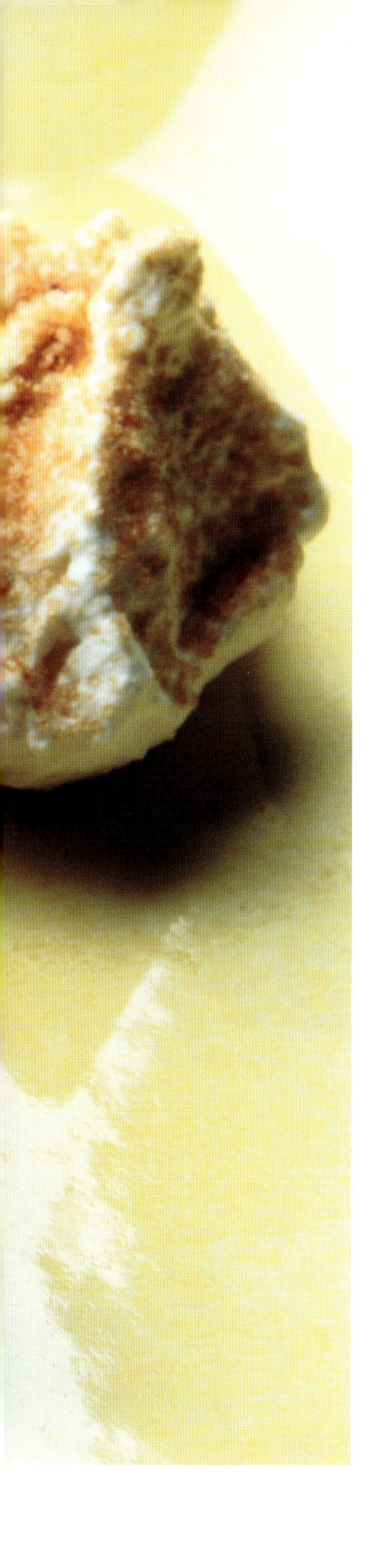

Pecan nut pie with wild raspberries and cream

Wild raspberries are far more superior in taste to those that are commercially grown – something that's true of many of the ingredients we use in our food. The taste of the wild is somehow more intense and real.
To bring out the true flavor of this wonderful berry, Icehotel's chefs have created an exciting dessert – a pecan nut pie which is served together with whipped cream and a little raw sugar.

Make a dessert pastry and put it into a pie tin, pressing it down firmly. Place the pastry into an oven and bake until ready. Fill the pastry with a mixture of chopped pecan nuts, syrup, demerara sugar and melted butter. Place back into the oven until done.
Serve with wild raspberries and whipped cream topped off with a sprinkling of raw sugar.

INGREDIENTS

Flour, butter, sugar, eggs, pecan nuts, syrup, demerara sugar, butter, wild raspberries and cream.
Alternatively: if you have no other choice, you can swap the wild raspberries for commercially grown ones.

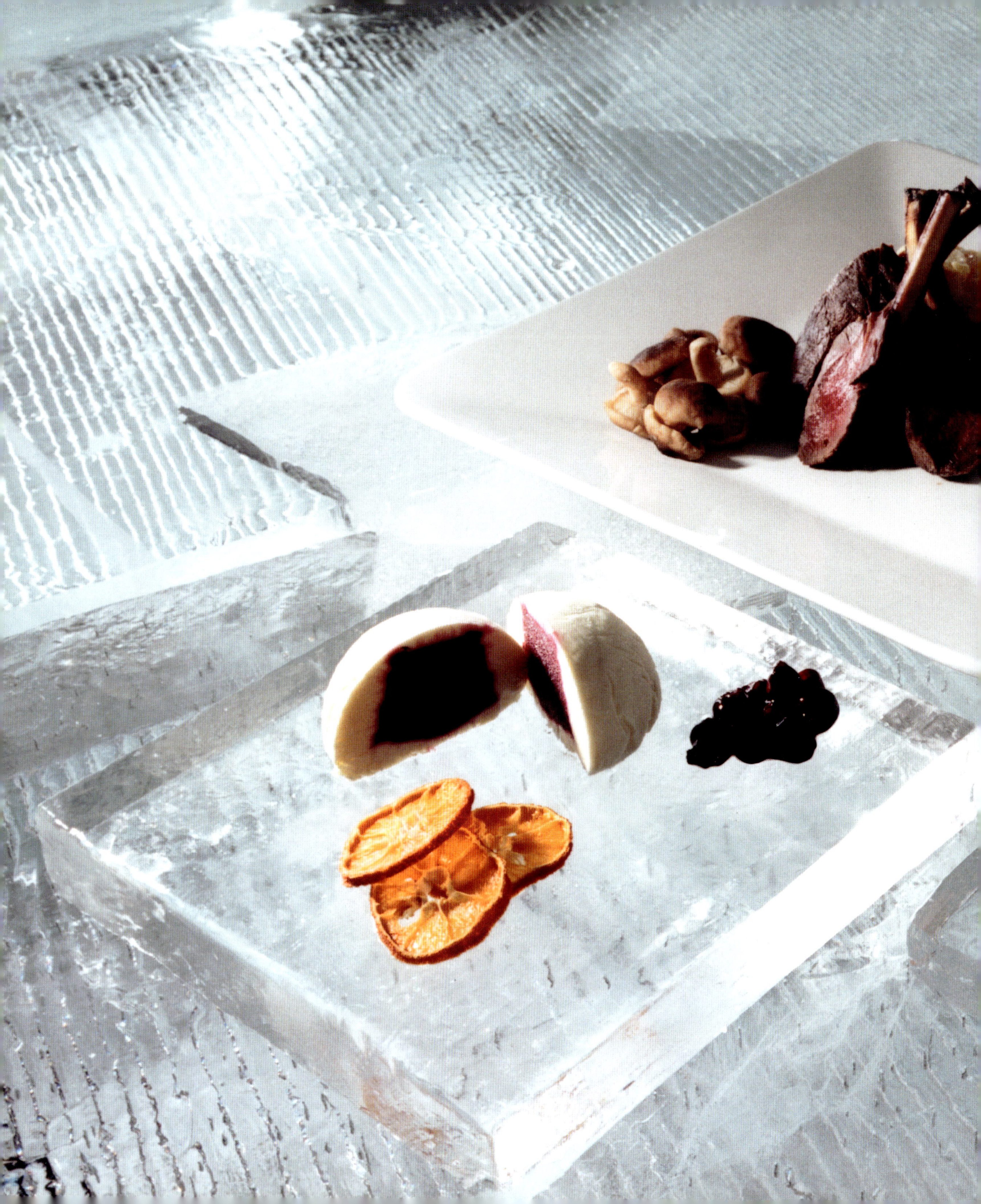

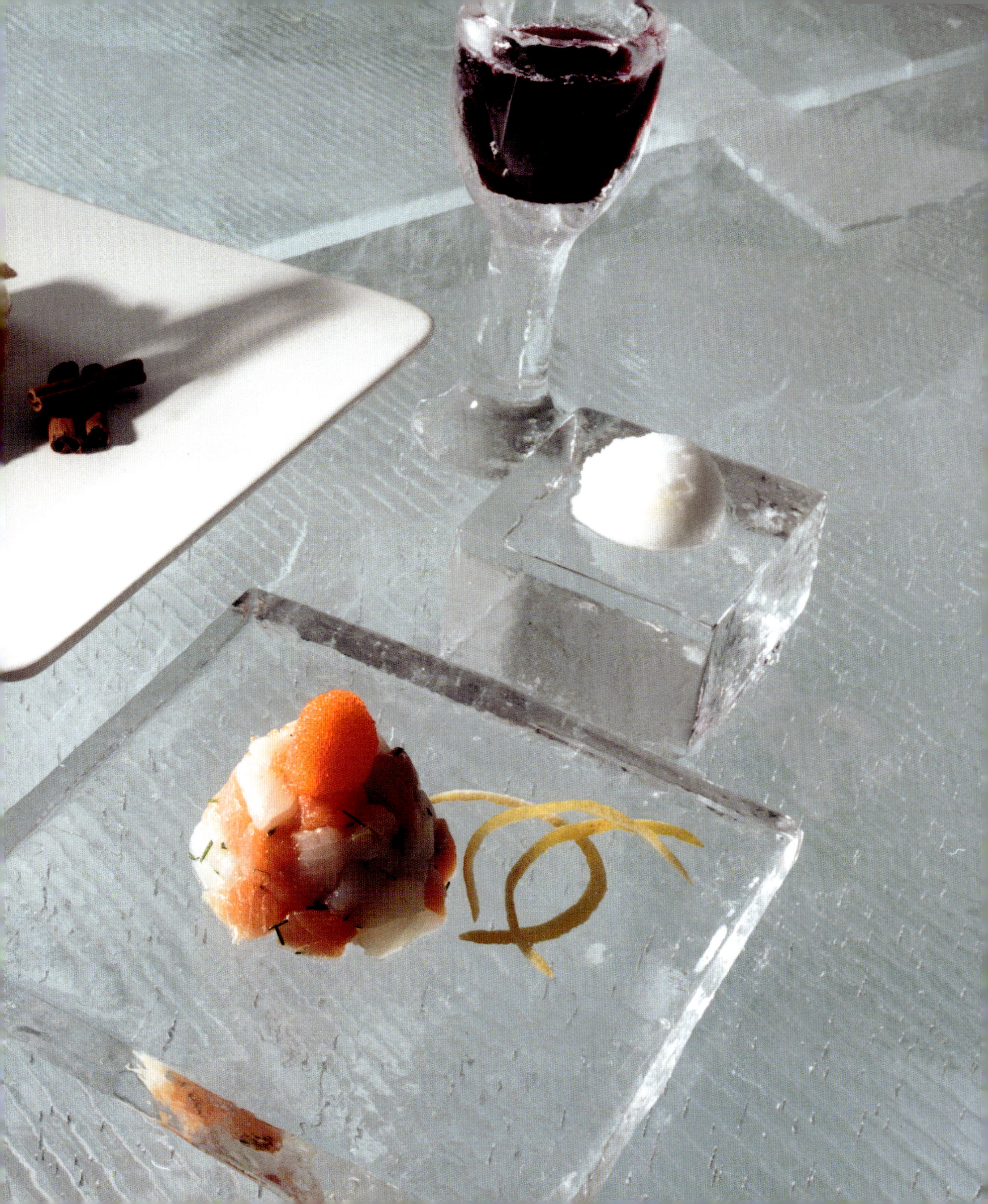

CUISINE

Absolut Meny

Over the years, the restaurant at Icehotel has offered guests all manner of dishes that have originated from the pantry of northern Sweden. A selection of these can be found in the Absolut Meny which features the distinctive flavor of the famous, Swedish ABSOLUT vodka.
Our version of Absolut Meny provides diners with a taste of some of the rare delicacies that are found here in the land of the Sámi. ABSOLUT Citron ceviche uses arctic char which can be caught in the lakes of the fells, and flounder caught off the Norwegian coast some 150 kilometers to the north west of Jukkasjärvi. The whiting roe comes from fish which spawn in the brackish southern half of the Gulf of Bothnia.
ABSOLUT Vodka sorbet lines the stomach like soft cotton. The prefect preparation for the ABSOLUTKurant flambéed, and lightly smoked rack of venison. The whole menu is rounded off with a white chocolate mousse, crowned with a dash of ABSOLUT Mandarin and an arctic bramble sorbet.

Absolut Citronceviche

The white, firm and easily sliced meat of the flounder makes it the ideal fish to use in a ceviche. When it is mixed with fresh artic char, caught from a lake on the fells, and then topped off with a generous helping of whiting roe, the taste is nothing less than pure Nordic gastronomy. Add a little ABSOLUTCitron, and you have the first course of our Absolut Meny.

Cut the flounder and artic char into cubes one centimeter on the side. Marinate them in ABSOLUT Citron mixed with some lemon, oil, white pepper and chives. The fish mixture is then shaped into a dome and topped off with the whiting row.
Serve together with chopped red onion and crème fraiche.

INGREDIENTS

Arctic char and flounder fillets, ABSOLUT Citron, lemon oil, chives, whiting roe, red onion and crème fraiche.
Alternatively: the arctic char can be replaced by similar kinds of fish.

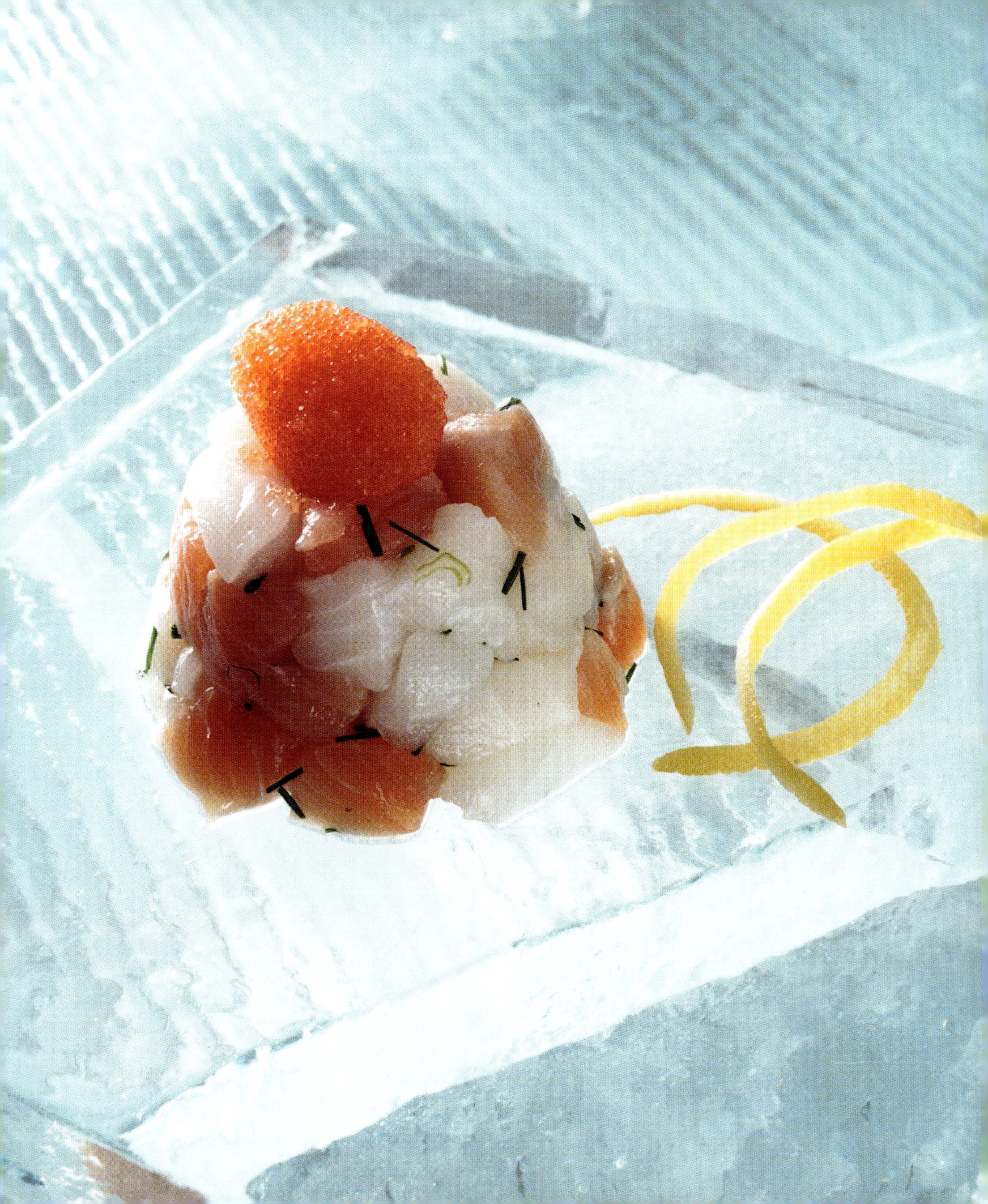

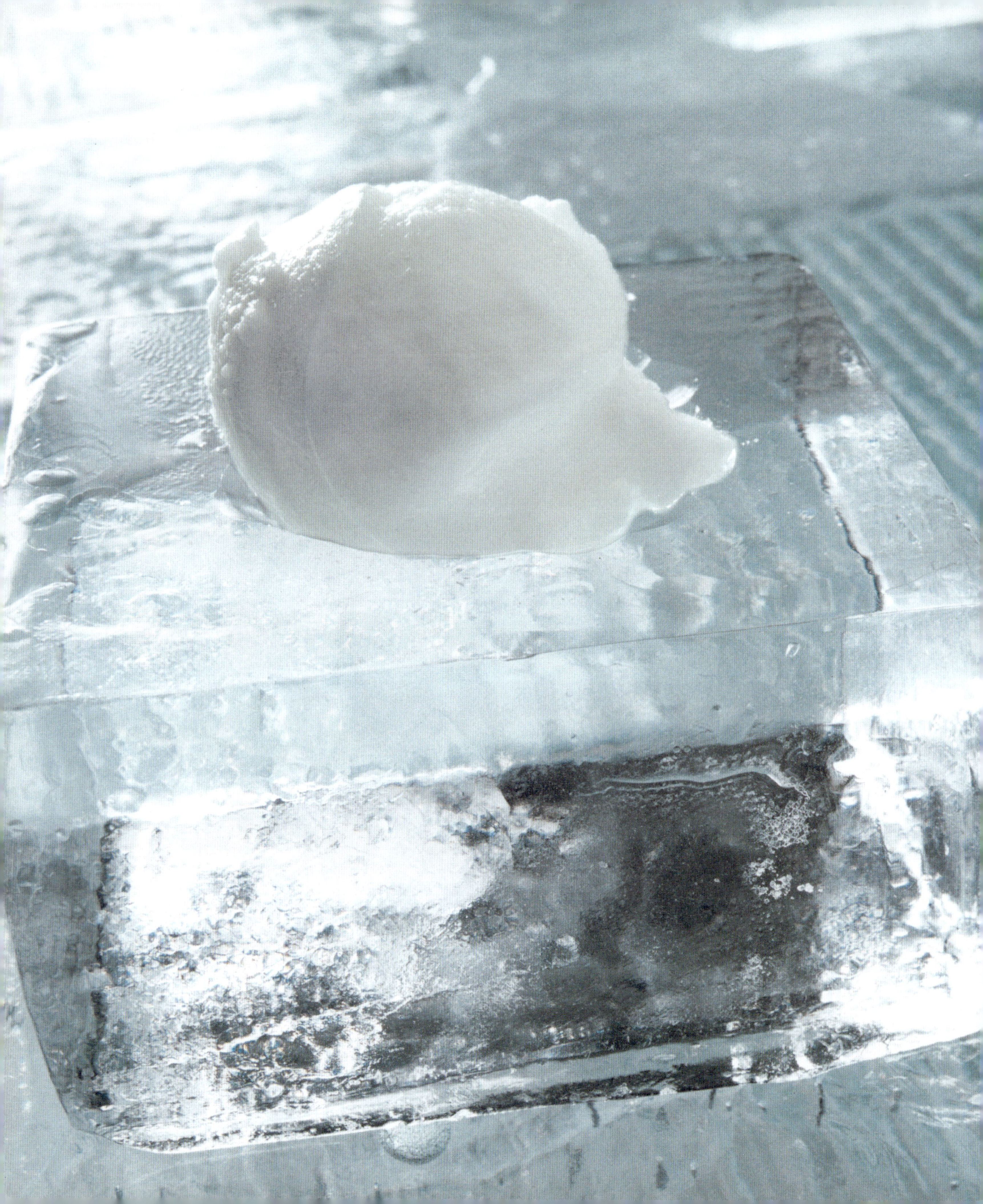

CUISINE

Absolut Vodka sorbet

The best menus always include something mild to rest the pallet between courses, and this one is no exception. We have used a small sorbet that has been flavored with pure vodka.

Make a sorbet from sugar, water and Absolut Vodka in an ice cream maker. Serve over a bowl of clear ice.

INGREDIENTS

Sugar, water, Absolut Vodka.

CUISINE

Absolut Kurant flambéed, souvas smoked rack of venison

Lightly smoked rack of venison cooked in the traditional way of the Sámi requires careful preparation. Brown the racks in a hot frying pan before flambéing them in ABSOLUT Kurant. Once this is done, they only need to be kept warm in an oven while the rest of the dish is prepared.
Absolut Meny uses the rack of venison as the main course, served with meat juice spiced by a little cinnamon, shii-take mushrooms and a cake made from root vegetables.

Brown the venison racks in a hot frying pan and then flambé using ABSOLUT Kurant. The cinnamon flavored meat juice is made from game stock, onions, demerara sugar and cinnamon stalks. Make the vegetable cake by mixing chopped carrots, turnip, swedes and sliced onion together with egg yolks and cream. Allow to bake slowly in the oven.
Lightly fry the shii-take mushrooms in a little butter.

INGREDIENTS

Rack of reindeer venison, ABSOLUT Kurant, game essence, onion, demerara sugar, cinnamon stalks, carrots, turnip, swedes, eggs, cream and shii-take mushrooms.
Alternatively: use racks of venison from fallow or row deer, or even lamb.

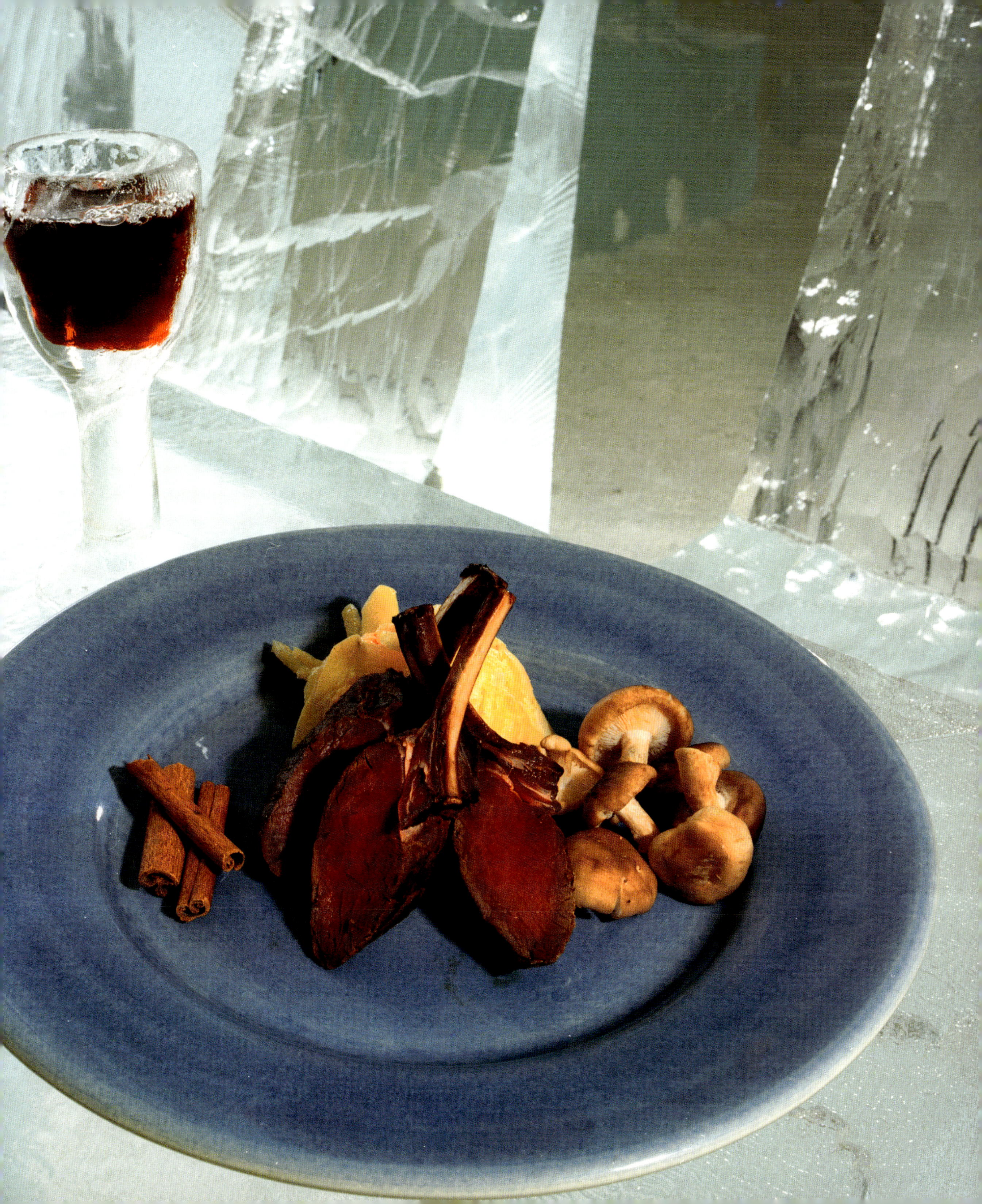

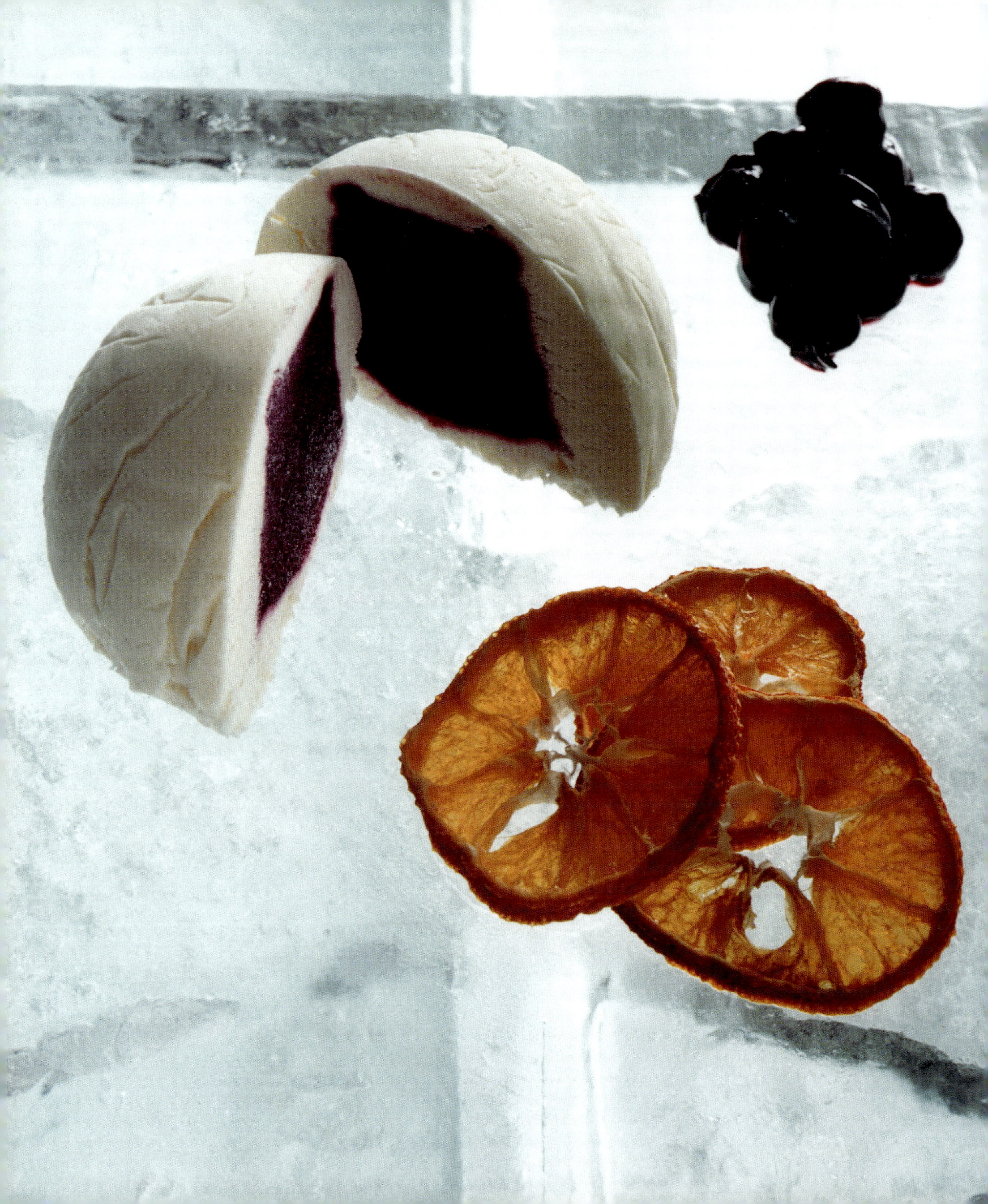

CUISINE

Absolut chocolate mandarin mousse with arctic bramble

To round off the Absolut Meny, serve a white chocolate mousse flavored with ABSOLUT Mandarin together with arctic bramble sorbet.

First make the sorbet using arctic bramble. Cover with the white chocolate mousse flavored with just the right amount of ABSOLUT Mandarin. Decorate a plate with a mandarin flan and sprinkle chopped hazel nuts and arctic cranberries that have been lightly boiled in syrup.

INGREDIENTS

Arctic bramble, sugar, block chocolate, egg yolks, cream, ABSOLUT Mandarin, mandarin, hazel nuts.
Alternatively: the arctic bramble can be replaced with other wild berries.

drinks

DRINKS

The Absolut foundation of the bar

Under a large dome in the center of Icehotel lies Absolut Icebar. Here, guests are served the world famous Swedish vodka, Absolut, which is the main ingredient in a whole range of extraordinary drinks which are, quite understandably, served in crystal clear glasses made entirely from ice. Absolut Icebar is the natural gathering point for the hotel's guests, and many of them end the evening here before retiring for the night to their ice beds and polar sleeping bags.

It is hardly surprising that Absolut has become the mainstay component of the drinks served at the hotel bar. This pure, all-Swedish vodka is one of Sweden's most successful export products which, for many, represents a symbol of Nordic design, the clarity that is ice, and the vast expanse of untamed nature that abounds here. And when it is mixed, as it is at the Icebar, with the essences of berries that have been hand-picked from the forests, fells and mosses of the region, there remains little doubt as to why it has become a central ingredient in the hotel's selection of beverages.

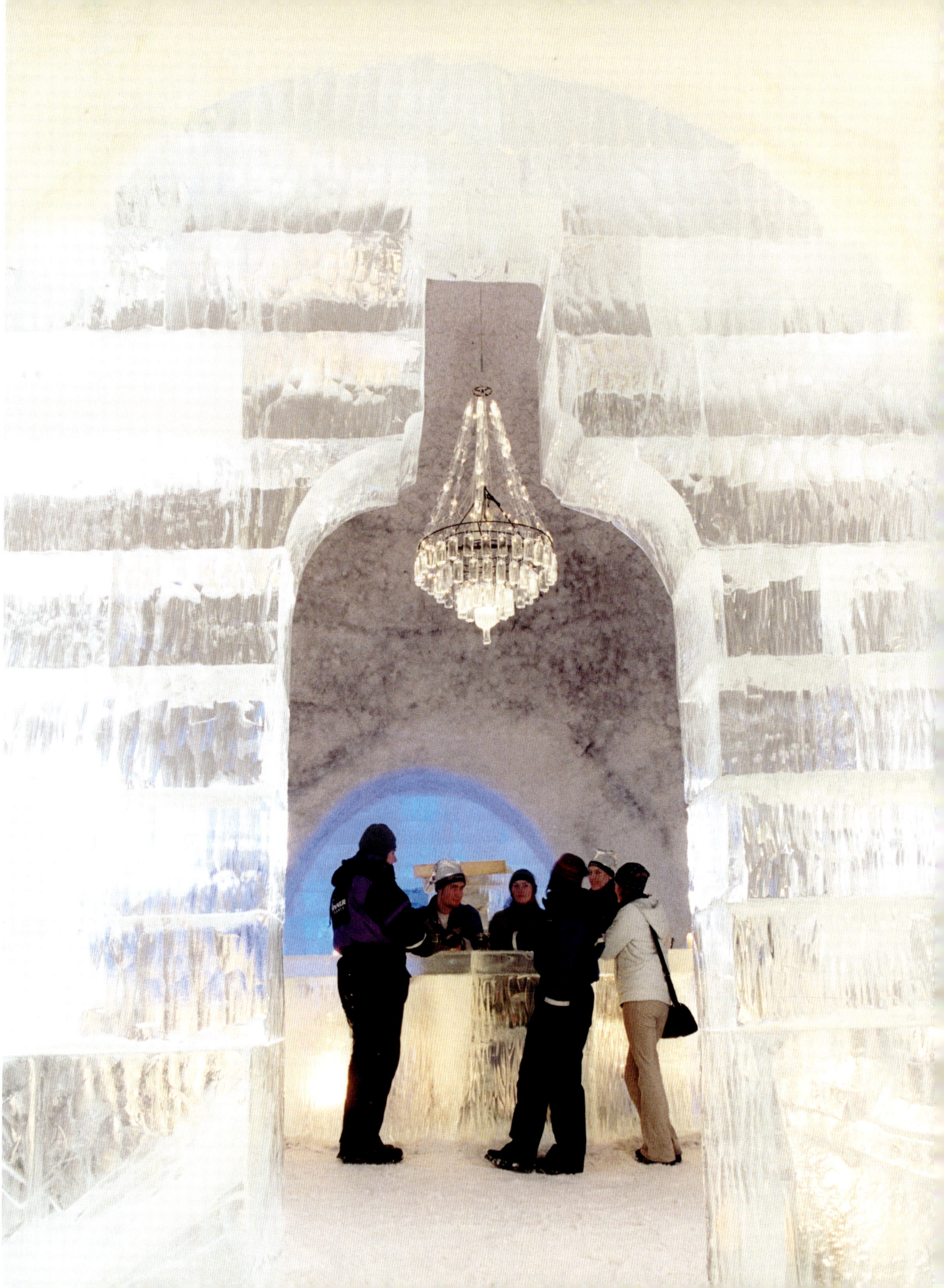

DRINKS

Fish Tail

Pour vodka and lemon juice into a glass that has been milled from ice carved from the frozen waters of the Torne River. Fill the remainder of the glass with apple juice, and decorate with lemon and apple peel.

INGREDIENTS

ABSOLUT Citron (4 cl), lemon juice (2 cl), apple juice, lemon and apple peel.

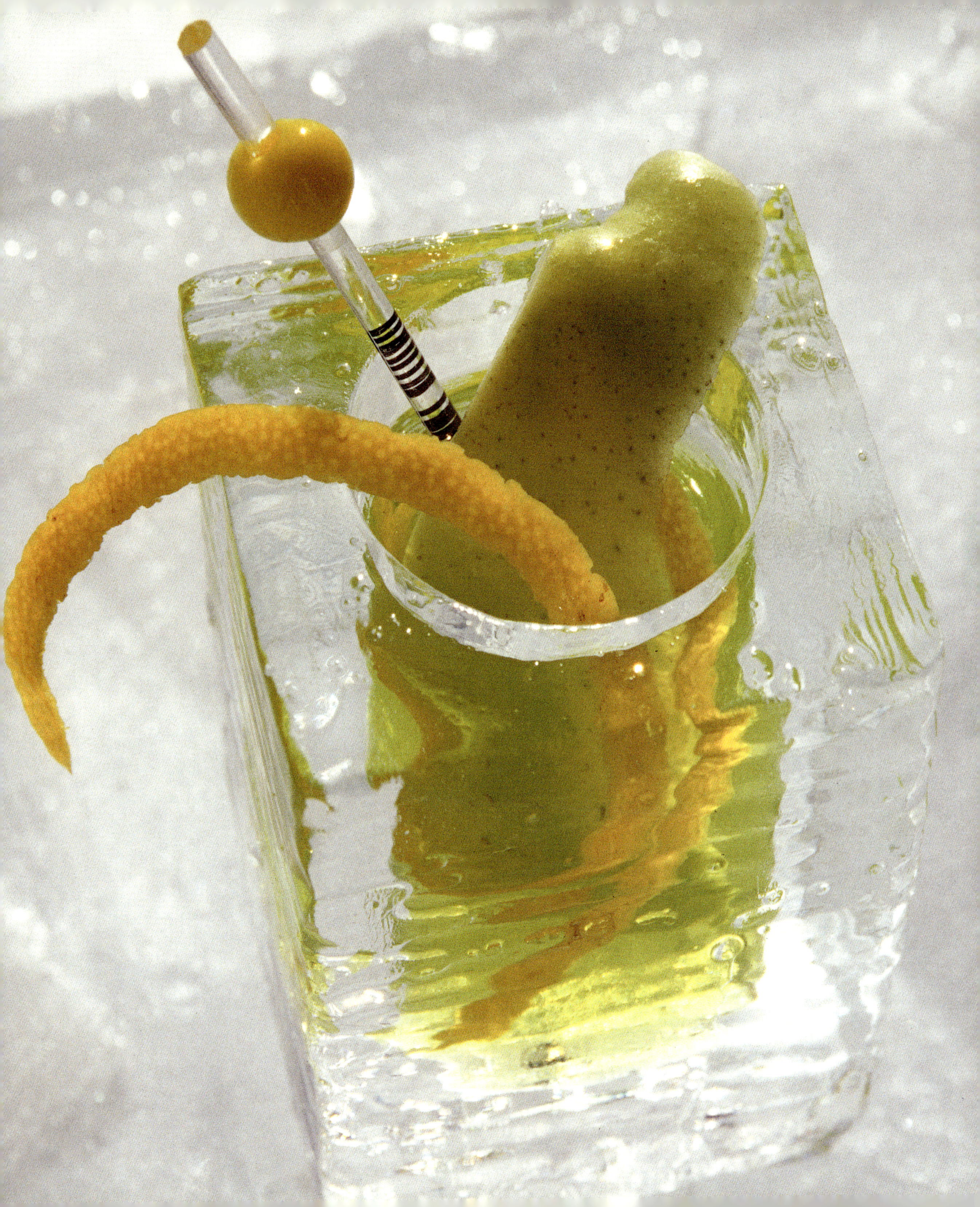

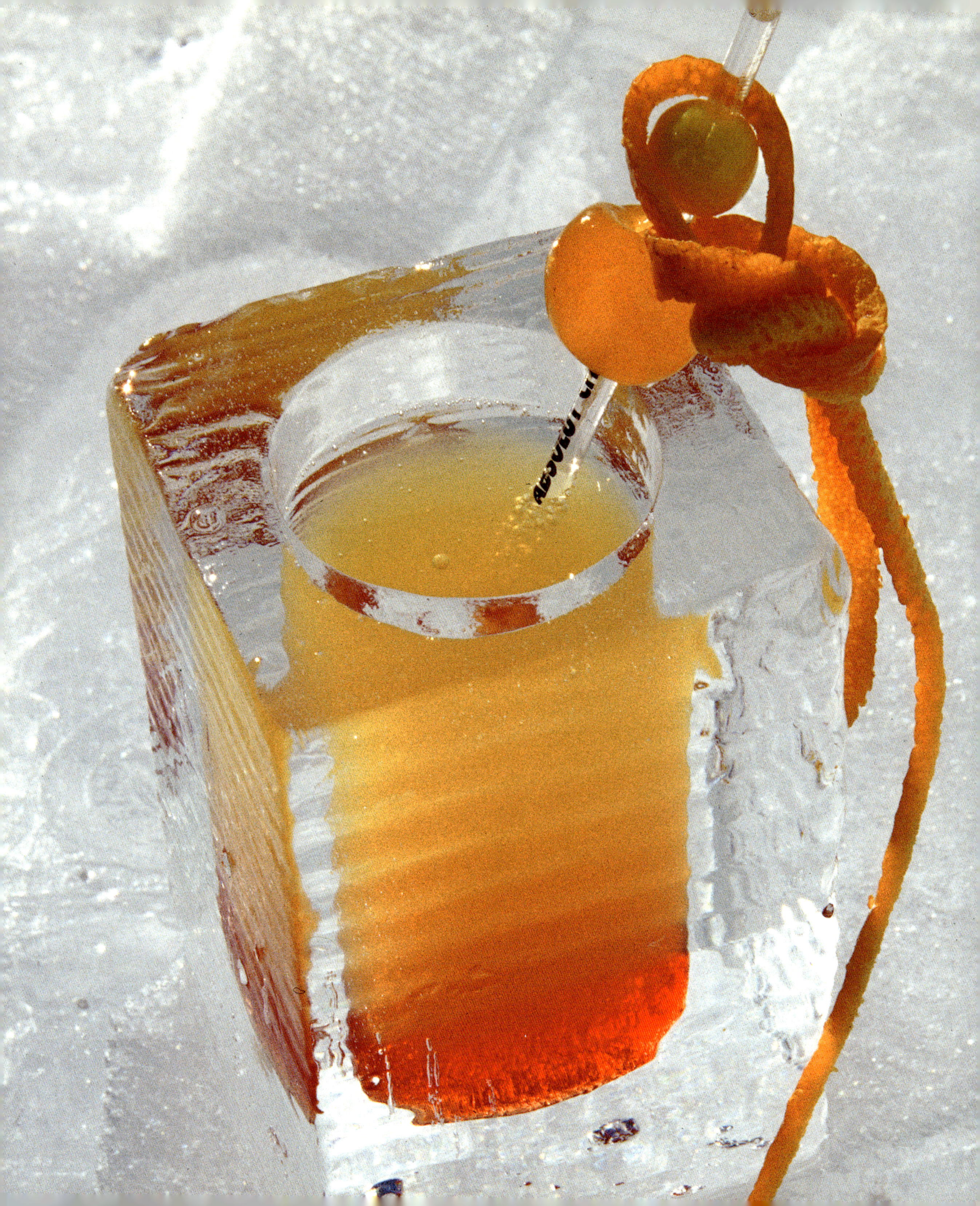

DRINKS

Wolf Paw

Cranberries, which grow wild over the brush lands of the fells, and in patches on the marches and among the moss, are a close relative of lingon and blue berries. If cranberries are left unpicked until the snow begins to melt, they loose much of their characteristic bitterness and become mildly aromatic. This drink uses cranberry juice, a brew that is more common in Finland, Russia and the Baltic countries than it is in Sweden, mixed with a measure of ABSOLUT Kurant, and garnished with a large piece of orange peel, all topped off with a red berry on a cocktail stick.

INGREDIENTS

ABSOLUT Kurant (4 cl), cranberry juice, orange peel and red berries.

Fox on the run

This drink uses two different kinds of vodka – one flavored with lemon, and the other with mandarin. Equal measures of each are added and then topped off with orange juice. The drink is then completed with a couple of splashes of Grenadine Syrup, and garnished with a yellow berry on a cocktail stick and a piece of knotted orange peel.

INGREDIENTS

ABSOLUT Citron (2 cl), ABSOLUT Mandarin (2 cl), orange juice, Grenadine Syrup (2 splashes), yellow berries and orange peel.

DRINKS

Icy Hat

Strawberries and pepper are a tried and tested taste combination. This drink uses pepper flavored vodka, strawberry liqueur and strawberry juice. Begin by mixing the vodka and liqueur, then fill the remainder of the glass with the juice. Garnish with lemon peel and blueberries on a cocktail stick.

INGREDIENTS
ABSOLUT Pepper (4 cl), strawberry liqueur (2 cl) and strawberry juice

Cloudberry Sunset

Cloudberries are often called "the Yellow gold of the forest". Highly dependent upon the weather, this fickle fruit is found in the marshes and mosses of the fells. Sometimes, they simply don't grow, but when they do, they are worth their weight in gold. When we make a Cloudberry Sunset, we mix lemon-flavored vodka with lemon juice and cloudberry liqueur – the latter comes from Finland and is readily available in Sweden. To finish, the drink is garnished with a fresh cloudberry on a cocktail stick.

INGREDIENTS
ABSOLUT Citron (2 cl), cloudberry liqueur (2 cl), lemon juice (2 cl) and fresh cloudberries.

Lingonberry Bear

If cloudberries are the "yellow gold" of the forest, then the lingon has to be its "red gold". This common berry grows is such large quantities that they can never all be picked at the same time.
Lingon are strongly associated with the Swedish palette with its penchant for sweet/sour ingredients. Pure vodka, mandarin vodka and lingon squash is an exciting combination. The drink is topped off with fresh lingon berries.

INGREDIENTS
ABSOLUT Vodka (2 cl), ABSOLUT Mandarin (2 cl), lingon squash and fresh lingon berries.

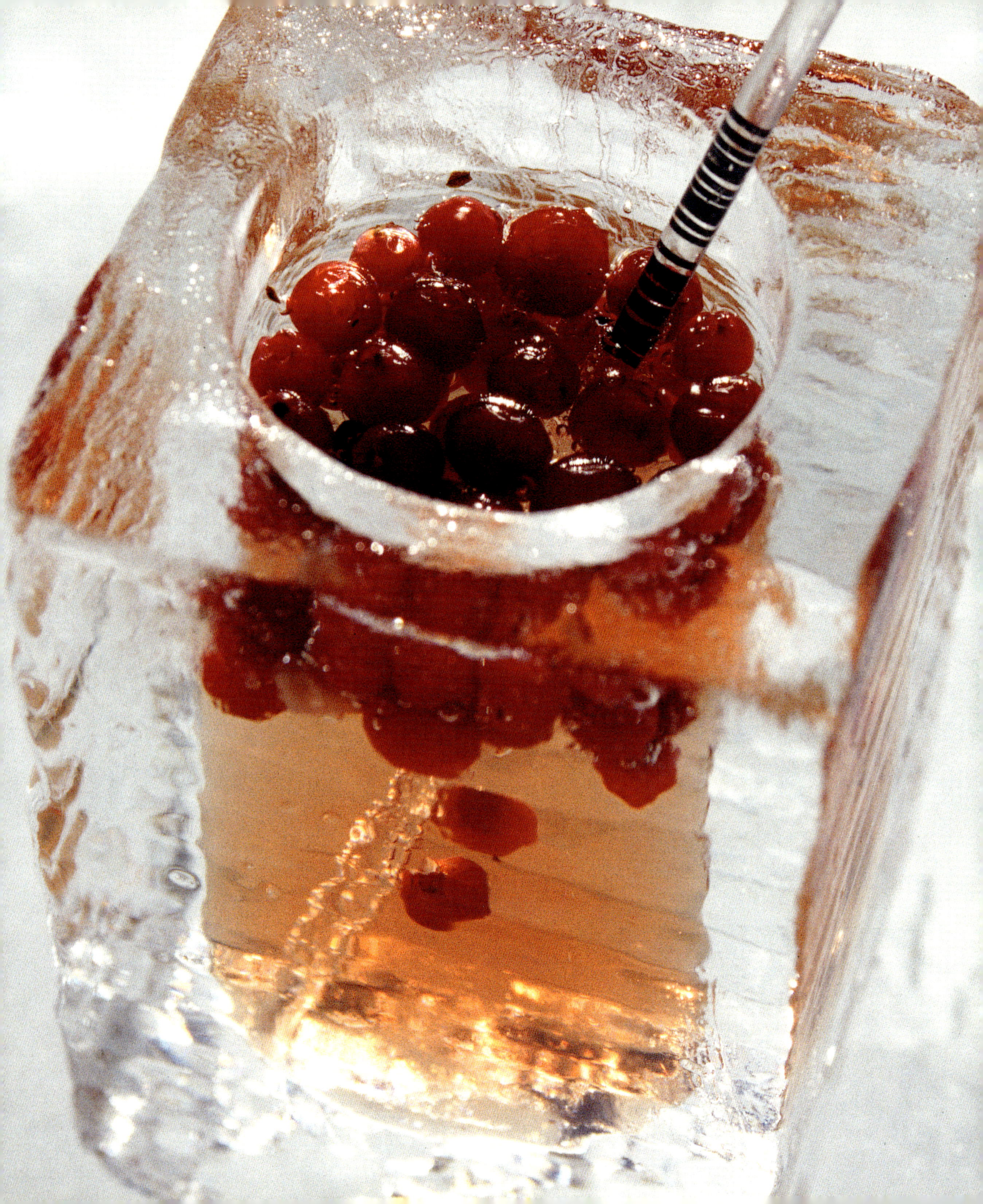

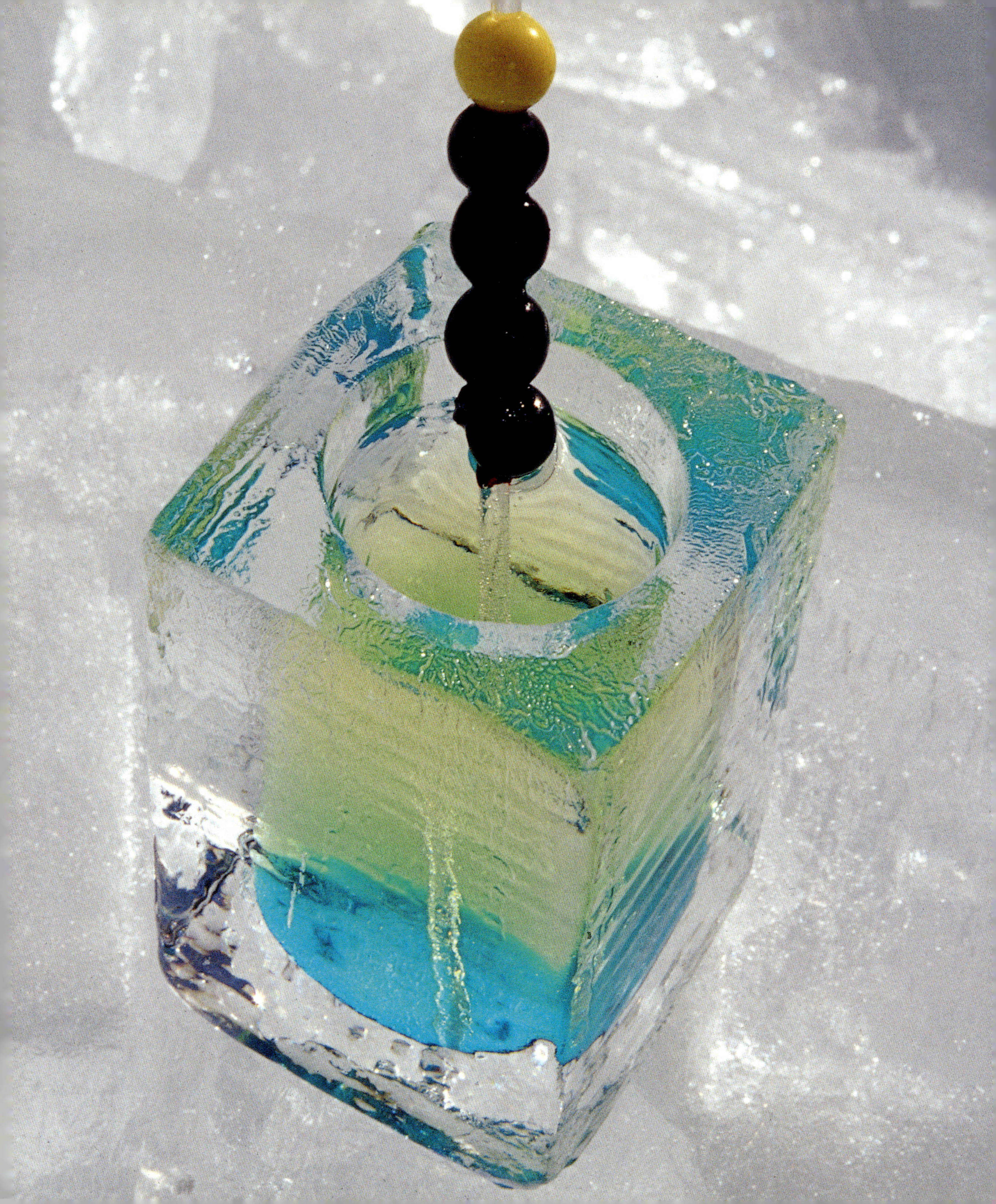

Northern Light

Elder can be found in two different forms – true and false. True elder forms black berries, while false elder develops a red berry. The latter should be avoided as these are slightly poisonous.
The fruit which comes from true elder is used to make elder squash which is said to protect against colds, evil sprits, witches and trolls. If this actually works in our drink – Northern Light – remains to be seen, but we'll begin by mixing elder squash with some lemon vodka and a couple of splashes of Blue Quracao. The whole creation is then garnished with blueberries on a cocktail stick.

INGREDIENTS

ABSOLUT Citron (4 cl), elder squash and Blue Quracao (2 splashes)

Nordic Sky

Just like the drink, Northern Light, Nordic Sky is a celebration of the exhilarating, troll-like and unpredictable Nordic heavens. It is made by mixing ABSOLUT Kurant, Blue Quracao and Rose's Lime Cordial, and is garnished with some richly dark blueberries on a cocktail stick.

INGREDIENTS

ABSOLUT Kurant (3 cl), Blue Quracao (3 cl), Rose's Lime Cordial (2 cl) and fresh blueberries.

THE BAR

High up in the ceiling of the 10 meter high and 14 meter wide dome which lies at the heart of Icehotel, hangs a chandelier that has been painstakingly carved from ice. Under its magnificent glow the hotel's guests gather to enjoy one of the delicious drinks that have made Absolut Icebar one of the world's most exotic watering holes.

Swedish bartender, Per Holmberg concocted the drinks that are described on the preceding pages. All of these are include various kinds of Absolut Vodka, mixed with berries found naturally in Swedish forests, marshes and fells, and combined with fruits from warmer clines.

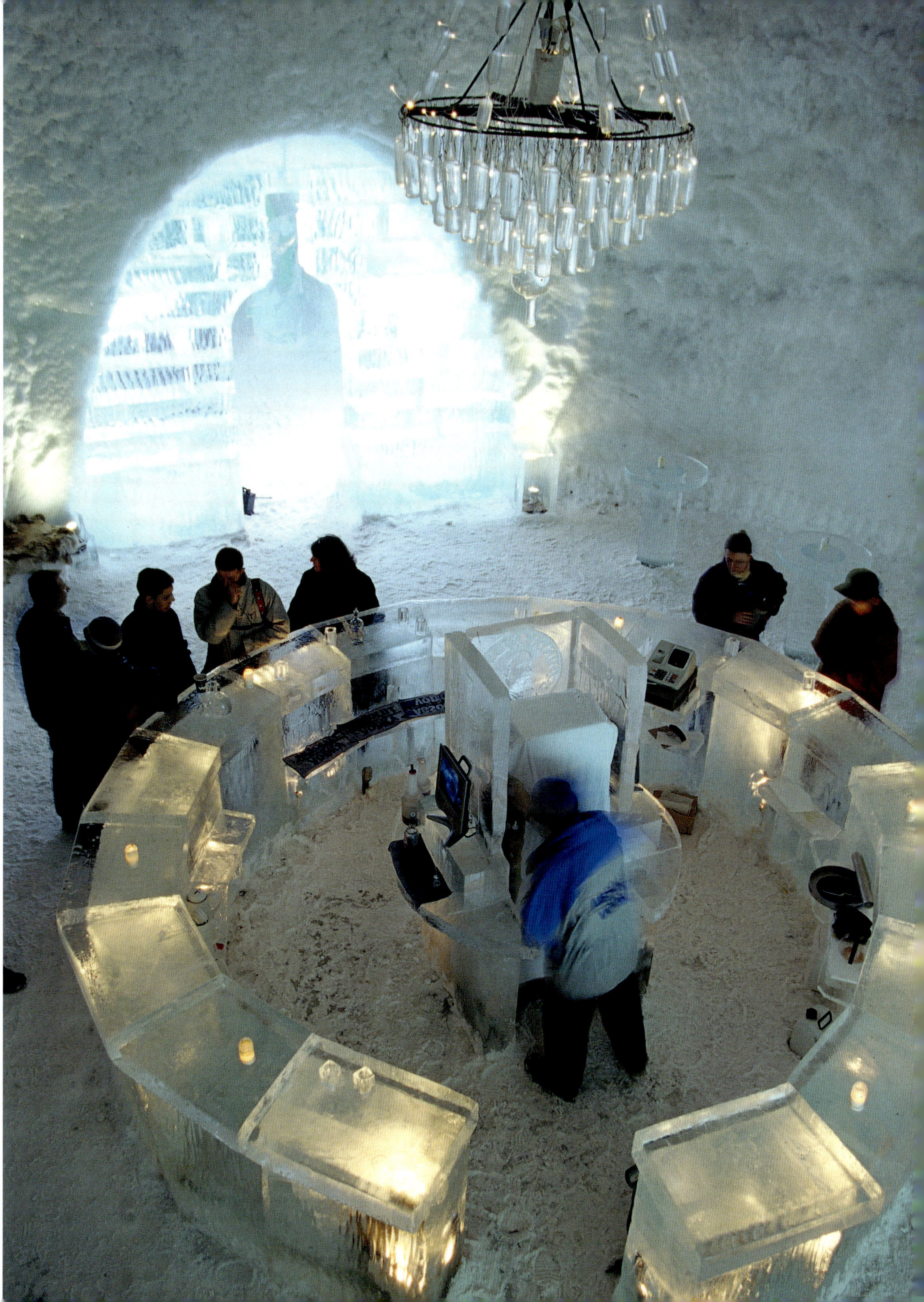

portraits

PORTRAITS

Driving forces

Åke Larsson

Åke Larsson, a native of Kiruna, and the man responsible for the construction of Icehotel, first saw the building in 1993. It was a dark afternoon in Jukkasjärvi with the mercury stubbornly hovering around -35°C and the hotel was no more than a large dormitory. On the river, workers cut blocks of ice. Åke was fascinated by the sound. Then someone told him of the idea to build a whole town made out of ice and snow. And he was hooked.

Åke had been away from Lapland for more than 20 years, living in Uppsala where he had carved out a reputation as a master carpenter, skilled in wood crafts. Each year, he sought to chase away the gloomy dejection which always set in during the winter months by traveling to the ski slopes of Sweden and Europe, spending a month up at Riksgränsen in northern Sweden, and a second in the Alps.

A year later, and Åke Larsson is on an ice sculpture course in Kiruna together with Arne Bergh. It's not long before the two practically take over. In 1995, Åke is once again in Jukkasjärvi, this time carving sculptures and by 1996, he is hard at work creating the interiors for Icehotel's guest rooms. Together with Arne Berg, he constructs a 50 meter long, 37 meter wide, and 8 meter high glacier cave for Billie Augusts film "Smilla's Sense of Snow". Åke is convinced that he has returned home as he gradually takes over responsibility for construction of Icehotel. Together with Arne Bergh, he creates one Icehotel after the other until today, when he is the uncrowned master in the art of constructing buildings made from snow and ice.

Arne Bergh

When Arne Bergh, the creative director of Icehotel project, attended the Konstfack Art School in Stockholm, a friend told him about Åke Larsson from Kiruna, master carpenter and handcrafts expert who was then residing and working in Uppsala.

The two men met, and together with an instrument maker, formed a company that was to be called Trätrojkan AB. They learn from each other. Arne Bergh reaps success as a sculptor with wood as his preferred material, and following a successful exhibition at Sweden's most famous tourist attraction, the Wasa Museum, his work is displayed at the World Exhibition in Seville in 1992. In 1993, Arne attends the annual Snow Festival in Kiruna where he hears about the Jukkasjärvi Ice Hotel for the first time. One year later, he calls Åke Larsson who, as tradition has it, is spending his annual vacation in the Alps, dulling his winter depression. So convincing was the content of the call, that Åke took the first available plane up to Kiruna to join a course in snow sculpting. Not long after, the two men met Yngve Bergqvist, who easily convinced them to spend time working on his Ice Hotel. Today, Arne Bergh lives in Poikkijärvi on the opposite bank of the Torne River from Icehotel – just a snowball's cast away from Åke Larsson. Arne Bergh is now the creative director for Icehotel and, together with Åke Larsson, plans each new version. It is Arne who proposes and selects the sculptors who are then invited to create and decorate the hotel.

Yngve Bergqvist

Yngve Bergqvist, the man who originally conceived Icehotel, left the merchant navy after traveling around the world many a time. He missed skiing. And he wanted to buy a house in Jukkasjärvi. Once there, he began organizing white-water rafting expeditions and built overnight cottages for tourists. Despite the fact that Jukkasjärvi lies in one of the coldest and most remote parts of Sweden, he had an idea that he believed would turn the cold, dark winter into something special — something that could be sold. But before he settled, Yngve decided to travel the world one last time looking for ideas that might attract winter tourism to Jukkasjärvi. Then in 1991, journalist Pär Granlund, put forward an idea for an art gallery, made entirely out of snow. Immediately, Yngve Bergqvist saw the possibilities and the "ARTic Hall" quickly became the first component in a concept that was to ultimately evolve into Icehotel. One year later, and the first true Ice Hotel stood completed in a building that covered an area of 600 m^2. Ten years on, it had grown ten-fold and was the most written about Swedish phenomenon in the world. More than 600 journalists from all over the globe visit Jukkasjärvi every year to write about a place which attracts some 50,000 tourists annually. Yngve Bergqvist has been awarded a number of prestigious prizes for his efforts. He was even declared an honorary Doctor at the Technical University of Luleå (Humanistic Philosophy Faculty) and named "Swede of the year abroad" in 2002.

THE STAFF

An international team

Icehotel is open all year round – even during the summer months when the midnight sun never sets, night becomes day and the frozen materials that were borrowed to construct that winter's building have long since melted back into the Torne River.
In a large, refrigerated warehouse where the ice blocks that were cut from the frozen river in March and April are stored, there is an ice sculpture gallery. Guests can even stay overnight in their own igloos.
It is a business which requires the year-round efforts of a dedicated team, and some 30 full-time employees make up the mainstay of the workforce. During the construction period, this number doubles. The people who work at Icehotel come from all over the globe. Rumor of the world's largest igloo has spread far and wide, attracting numerous adventurers who curiously seek their way to the small village of Jukkasjärvi. Some come to build the hotel and the Ice Theatre which stands adjacent to it. Others welcome guests at Kiruna Airport making sure that they safely find their way to Jukkasjärvi. And for most of them, it's an experience far beyond what they have ever done before.

There are lots of different things which need taking care of at Icehotel. From cleaning to maintenance, blacksmithing, sawing ice blocks and preparing for the arrival of the guests.

Icehotel 213

THE STAFF

A day in November. The team who were working on the construction of the 2001/2002 Ice Hotel, gather before the camera. From the left: Arne Bergh, Lasse Torneus, Ari Kymäläinen, Tjåsa Gusfors, Katarina Engman. Second group at the front: Dave Ruane, Jessica Svonni, Åke Larsson, Jörgen Wallmark.

Small group in the middle: Artur Tornéus, Gaddo Larsson, Inko Åström, Danne Åkerström.
Sitting in front of them: Mark Armstrong.
On his own to the left: Gunnar Lindström.
The group at the back: Hasse Abrahamsson, Kendo Hamaguchi, Janne Haglöf, Ander Porter.

EXPORT

Exporting ice

Shipping ice that was originally cut from a frozen river which runs through some of the most breathtaking scenery in northern-most Sweden to destinations all over the world may seem at best, rather strange, and at worst a complete waste of time and money. After all, water can be turned into ice wherever you may be.
But there is no other ice like that which comes from the Torne River. Its purity, lack of air bubbles, and the absence of cracks makes it singularly unique. And demand is feeding a thriving export industry.
Ice bars can now be found all over the world. Built in sections at the ice warehouse, which lies adjacent to Icehotel, they are shipped in large, insulated containers to all manner of customers. Torne River ice was even flown to last year's EU summits where it was turned into fantastic ice sculptures – striking reminders for the other member nations of who was Chairing the EU at the time.
It was the Nordic Sea hotel in Stockholm which fist created the phenomenon that was to become the ice bar. A concept which is likely to be found in all the major metropolis in the not too distant future. The bar comes from Jukkasjärvi. So too do the carefully milled glasses for the drinks.

Many creative minds and famous brands have come to Jukkasjärvi, inspired by the unique environment of Icehotel. The Absolut Company shot the images here for what turned out to be one of it's most successful advertising campaigns to date. The adverts featured super models like Naomi Campbell, Kate Moss and Marcus Schenkenberg and were lovingly photographed by Herb Ritts. The campaign was seen by almost one billion people. Volvo too has made spectacular commercials with Icehotel as a dramatic backdrop.

Åke Larsson and Arne Bergh, who together plan, design and oversee the construction of each and every Ice Hotel, also built the world's first ice bar which is housed in a cold storage room at the Nordic Sea Hotel in Stockholm. Ultimately, the concept is destined for export all over the world. Look out for Ice Bars in some of the world's hottest metropolis in the foreseeable future, all built from ice that has been carved from the frozen Torne River, just a snowball's cast away from Jukkasjärvi.

The ice warehouse, which lies adjacent to Icehotel, is where the ice glasses used at Icehotel's Absolut Icebar, and the Ice Bar in Stockholm, are milled and cut each day. Also produced here are other products, made from ice, which are destined for export. On the far left, stands an ice bar that is almost ready to be shipped to a customer in London.

Icehotel **217**

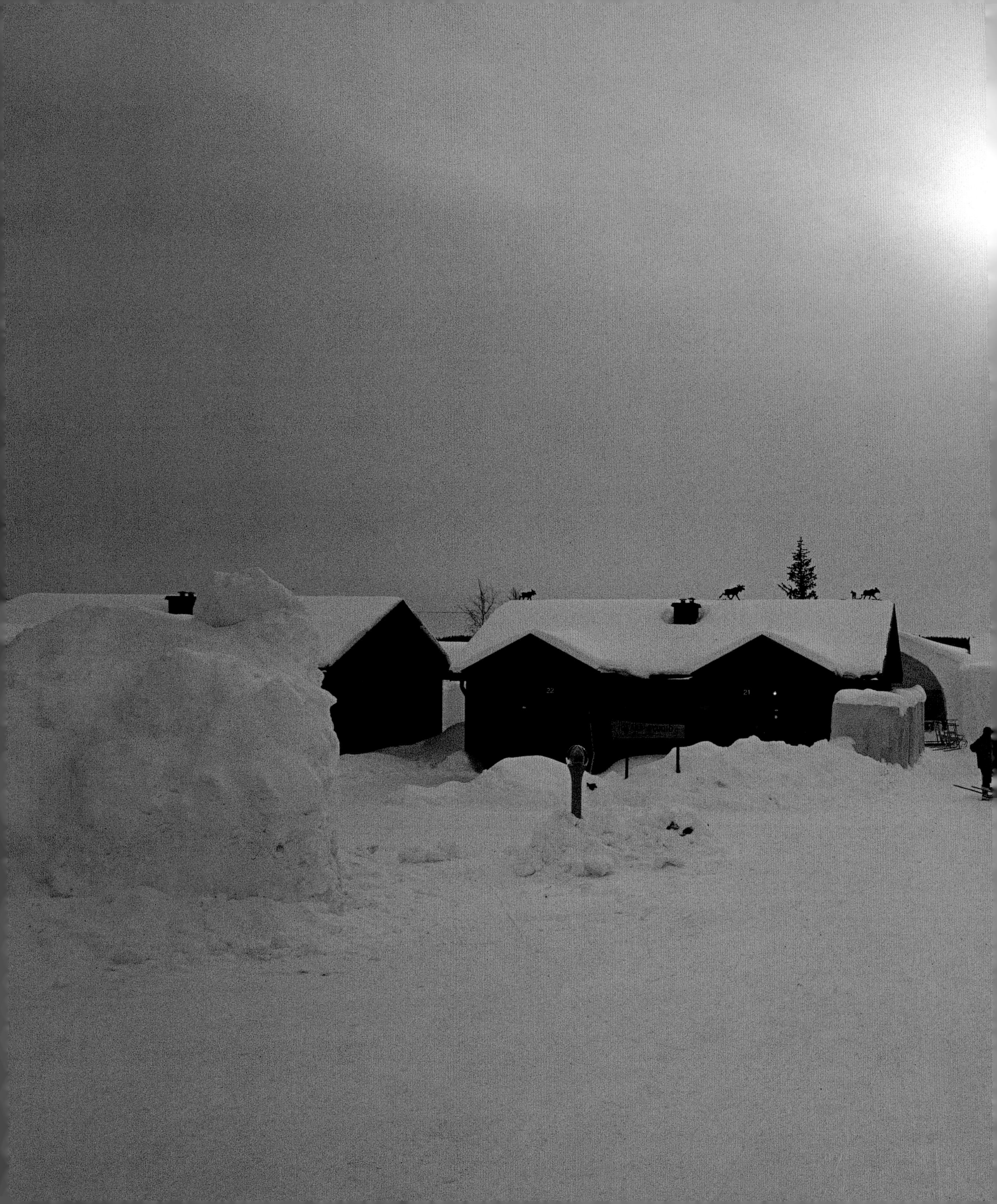

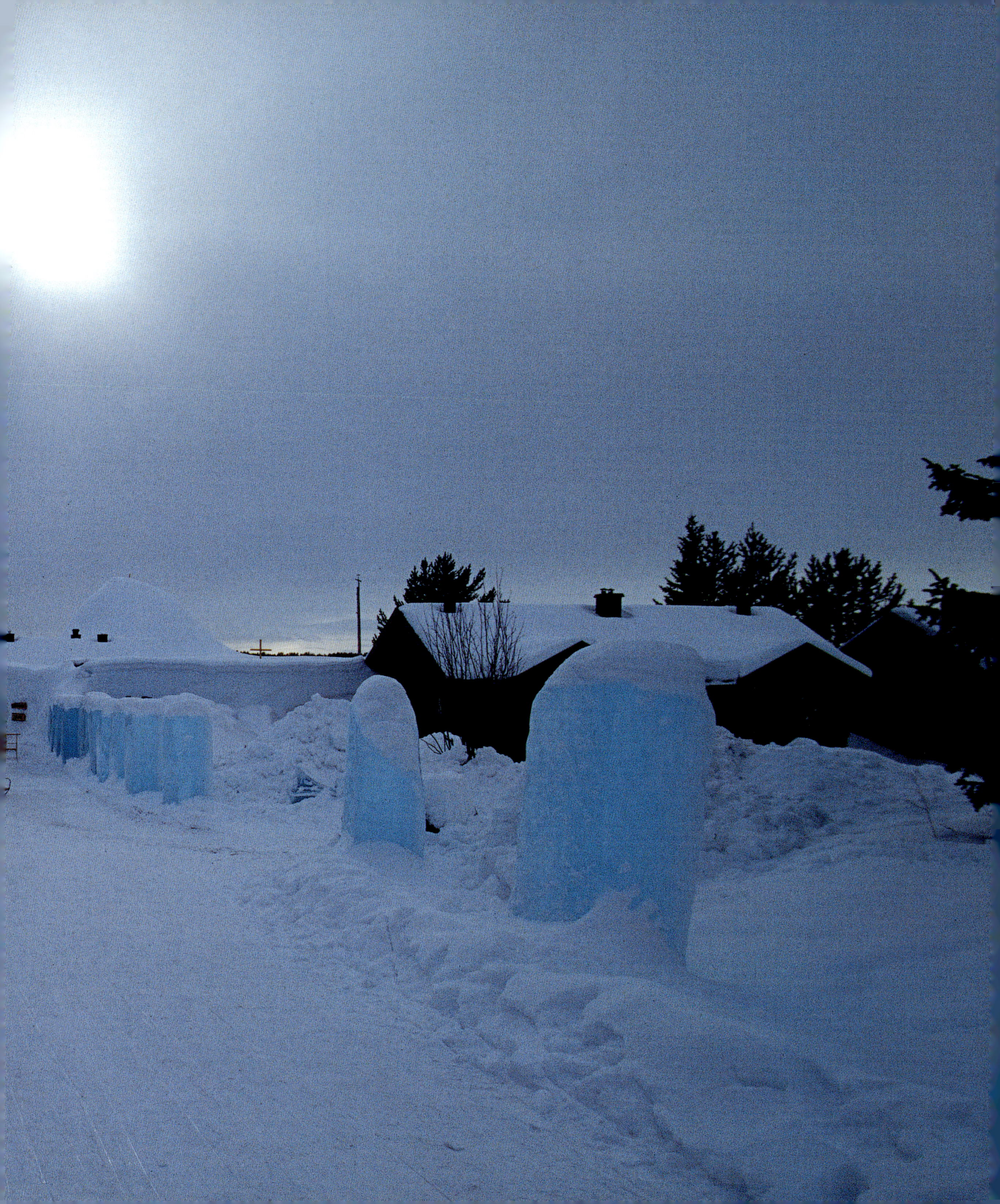

index

Index cuisine

Absolut Meny	186
Absolut Citronceviche	186
Absolut chocolate mandarin mousse with arctic bramble	193
Absolut Kurant flambéed, souvas smoked rack of venison	190
Absolut Vodka sorbet	189
Carpaccio made from filleted elk meat	149
Chocolate cheesecake with port wine marinated blueberries	154
Crêpes with cloudberries, goat's milk cream and cloudberry syrup	177
Pickled loin of reindeer venison	161
Pickled whiting	178
Cloudberry ice cream with Kahlúa-marinated coffee cheese	169
Lobster filled flounder nori	150
Lingon berry and cinnamon panacotta	173
Green tea and coconut parfait	159
Pecan nut pie with wild raspberries and cream	183
Fillet of young reindeer venison with shii-take mushrooms	153
Grouse served with chanterelles and glazed cabbage	170
Salad garnished with reindeer heart	143
Saltimbocca from the north	166
Shii-take soup	163
Sashimi made from whiting and alpine char	156
Sushinori with a thin omelet and cognac marinated whiting	144
Wood Grouse with rosemary cream and cranberry chutney	181
Tjälknöl (Swedish meat delicacy)	175
Seaweed and algae soup	164
Arctic bramble and cloudberry sorbet	147

Index drinks

Cloudberry Sunset	202
Fish Tail	198
Fox on the run	201
Icy Hat	202
Lingonberry Bear	202
Northern Light	205
Nordic Sky	205
Wolf Paw	201

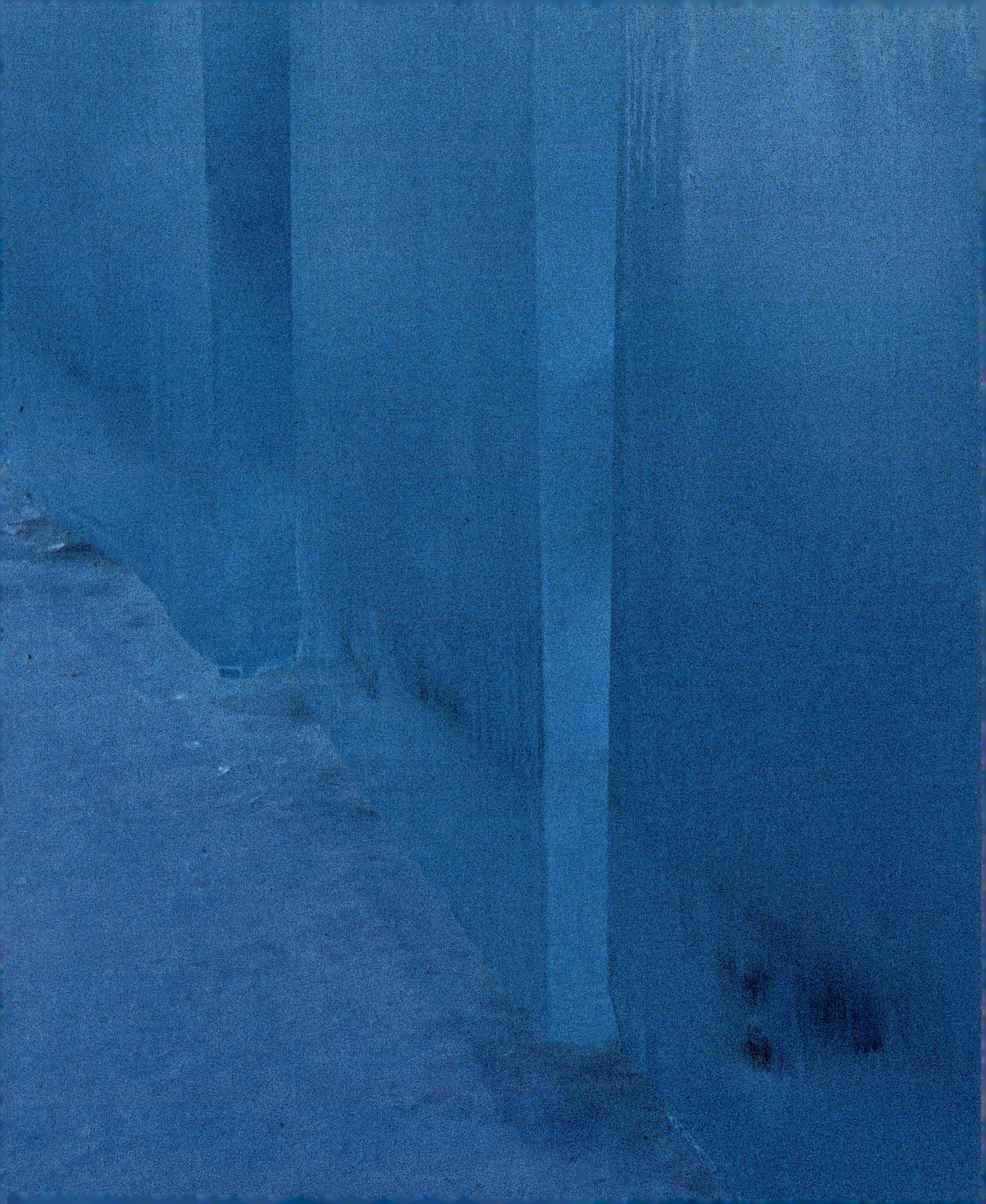

We made this book

All the background material used to create this book was gathered during the winter of 2001/2002.

The texts were written by Lars Magnus Jansson and Lars Petterson, Bokförlaget Goda Sidor, who managed the project. Also part of the project team: Arne Bergh, of Icehotel.

The recipes were compiled by Åke Larsson, of Icehotel and Birgitta Ståål, Kiruna.

The drinks were created by Per Holmberg, Tasteful Trade, Stockholm.

Puck Petterson, Bokförlaget Goda Sidor, gave the book its graphic form.

Most of the images used in this book were photographed by Erik Svensson.

Translated by Daniel Cooper.

Thanks also to

Jonas at Sjöbergs Classic

OTHER PHOTOGRAPHERS

Arne Eriksson/Hörnell-Riksgränsen *p 76, 84, 120, 136, 226*
IBL *p 132, 136, 137*
Harry Johansen *p 72*
Naturfotograferna *p 12*
Norrlandia *p 114, 121, 126, 130, 135*
Hans-Olof Utsi *p 72*
Pix Gallery *p 82,*
Pressens Bild *p 11, 32, 36, 68, 69, 215*
Scanpix *p 128, 134,*
Sjöbergs Classic *p 46, 78, 79, 86, 87, 98, 108, 111, 112, 115, 116, 117, 208*

MAP

Karl Åstrand *p 10*

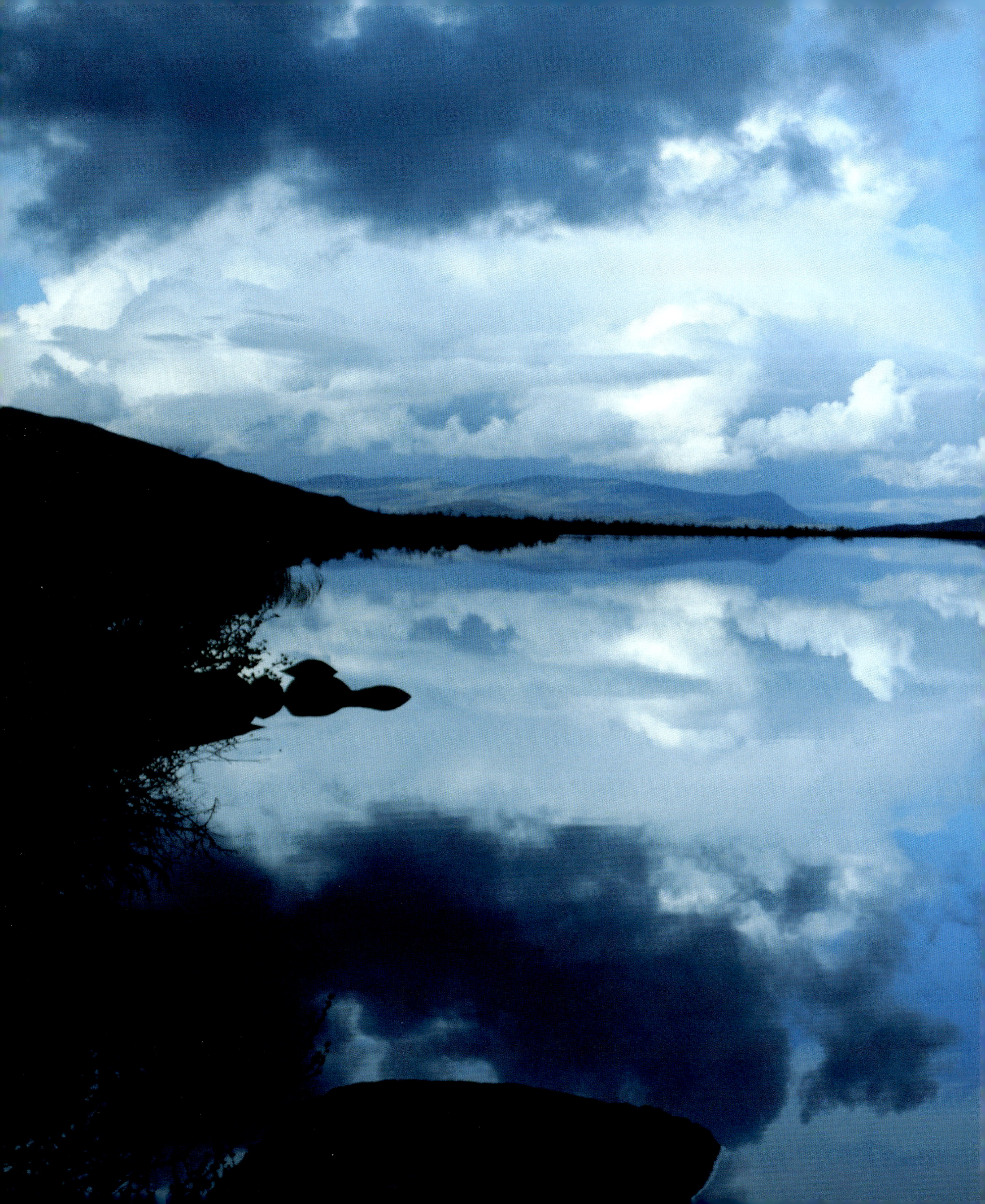

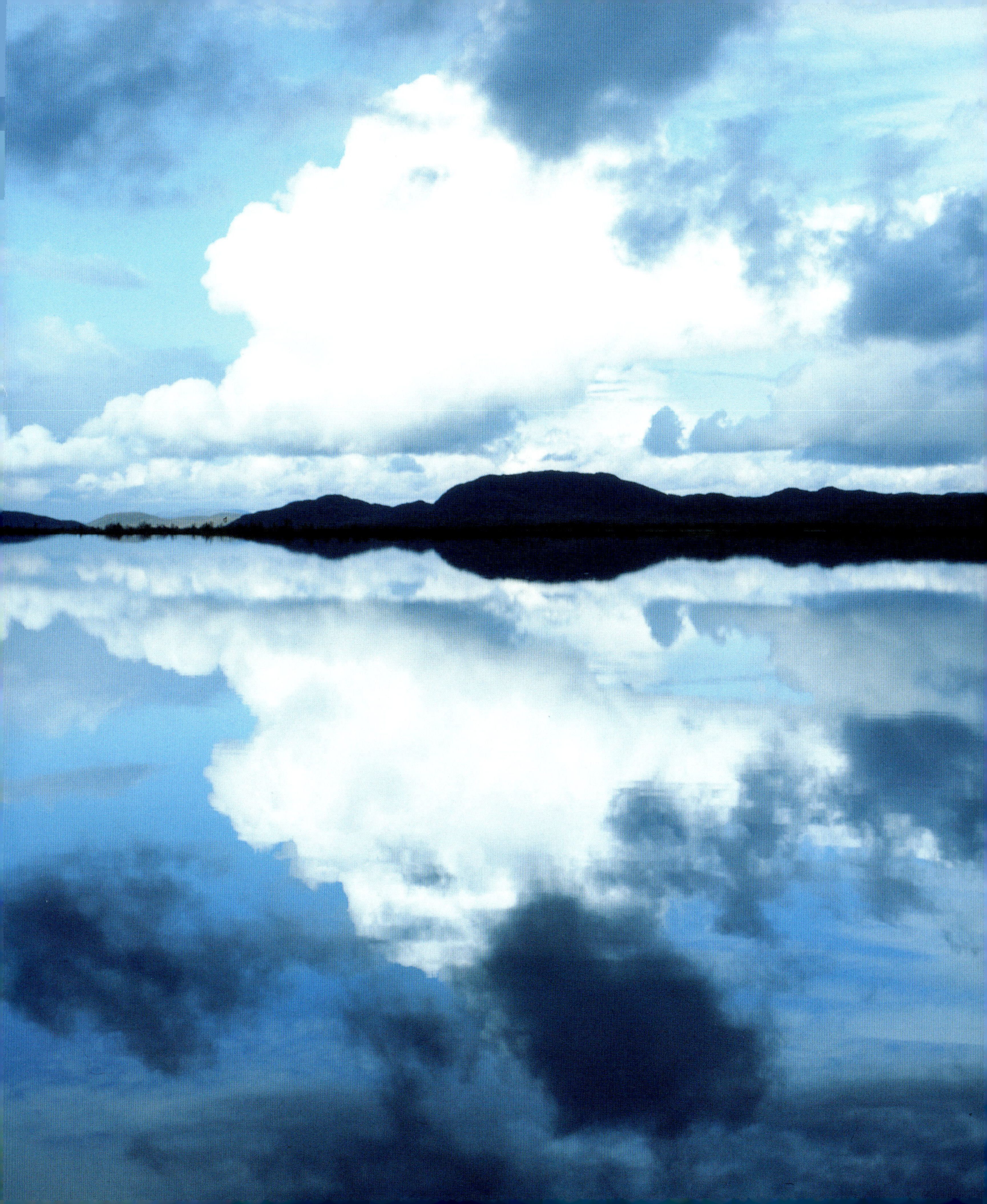